StOryeller

StOry Teacher

Discovering the Power of Storytelling for Teaching and Living

Marni Gillard

STENHOUSE PUBLISHERS
York, Maine

Stenhouse Publishers, 226 York Street, York, Maine 03909

Library of Congress Cataloging-in-Publication Data

Gillard, Marni, 1951–
Storyteller, storyteacher : discovering the power of storytelling
for teaching and living / Marni Gillard.
p.   cm.
Includes bibliographical references (p.   ).
ISBN 1-57110-014-8 (alk. paper)
1. Storytelling.   2. Teaching.   I. Title.
LB1042.G52   1995
372.64′2—dc20
95-30399
CIP

Credits
Page 2: "I Remember It Well" From *Gigi*. Words by Alan Jay Lerner. Music by Frederick Loewe. Copyright © 1957, 1958 by Chappell & Co. Copyright Renewed. International Copyright Secured. All Rights reserved.

Page 9: "The Mountain Whippoorwill" by Stephen Vincent Benet. Copyright 1925 by Stephen Vincent Benet. Copyright renewed © 1953 by Rosemary Carr Benet. Reprinted by permission of Brandt & Brandt Literary Agents, Inc.

Page 58: "The Poem as a Reservoir of Grief" by Tess Gallagher. From *A concert of tenses*. Published by the University of Michigan Press.

Page 105: "Etelephony" from *Tirra Lirra: Rhymes old and new* by Laura E. Richards. Copyright 1931, 1932 by Laura E. Richards. Copyright © 1960 by Hamilton Richards. Reprinted by permission of Little, Brown and Company.

Back cover photo courtesy of Susan Wilson
Cover and interior design by Darci Mehall
Typeset by TNT

Manufactured in the United States of America on acid-free paper
99 98 97 96 8 7 6 5 4 3 2 1

For the Gillards, Walshes, McGoverns, and Mehegans
who touched my life
and for a boy named Brian Schwartz

Kathryn,

Every teacher is a storyteller.

Hope you enjoy these tales of

my family and students.

— Marni Gillard

Contents

🍂 *v* 🍂

FOUR

Choosing a Tale to Tell and Learning to Listen Well 37

FIVE

From Performing to Telling 51

SIX

Personal Stories—One Place to Begin 63

SEVEN

Triumph and Trauma Tales 74

EIGHT

The Personal Tale as Teacher 88

NINE

Poems and Songs for Telling 104

TEN

Looking Within for the Story in History 119

ELEVEN

Honoring the Interior 133

TWELVE

Trust the Story 144

THIRTEEN

Critics, Coaches, and Storyteachers 164

FOURTEEN

Relinquishing Old Beliefs in Order to Grow 180

Acknowledgments

Grandma Gillard taught me the art of the thank-you note. She helped me name the sweetness of gifts and honor the friendship they represent. A writer's voice is a gift of many. I hope this thank-you note will touch all who have shone the light of love and wisdom into my life.

My first thanks go to my siblings, friends all. Special thanks go to Pat Cordeiro who introduced me to Philippa Stratton and to all at Stenhouse, so patient and helpful. I want to thank Adrian and Johanna Peetoom, whose early support helped me believe in the book, and Lil Brannon, Peter Johnston, Kathy Oboyski-Butler, and David Dillon, who for many years have gently but firmly reminded me to tell my truth.

Five women read the book in early or later stages and their responses meant so much: Nancy Farhart (and Ivy), Ellen Sadowski, Leanne Grace, Gerry Hart, and Martha "Rabbit" Merson.

Linda Welles and David Bagley delightedly listened the night the book was born, and Bonnie Ivener "oohed" and "aahed" from Albuquerque at the birth details until sunset brought the Sabbath.

I feel such gratitude when I think of how the passionate writings and speeches of Lucy Calkins, Shelley Harwayne, Georgia Heard, JoAnn Portalupi, Ralph Fletcher, and so many more in the writing/whole language movements brought rain to my parched teaching soul.

I thank all of the children, principals, and PTA arts committee people who have believed in my work, and offer sincerest gratitude to Ruth Gilbert, Carol Reynolds, Chalmers and Barbara Means, Mary Kitagawa, and Av Green, who gave me opportunities when my work was first developing.

I so respect and thank those who parent the professional organizations that mean so much to struggling teachers and artists: the National Council of Teachers of English, the Whole Language Umbrella, New York State English Council and Reading Association, Artists with Class, Albany League of Arts, NYS BOCES systems, Teachers and Writers Collaborative, and the International Women's Writing Guild. Without them this would be truly lonely work.

The voices of many daring women writers and storytellers gave mine strength, especially Susan Ohanian, Linda Rief, Judith Black, and Abigail Adams.

My thanks to those at the Center for Body and Mind Awareness who danced into my life just as I needed them, midwives all: Casey Bernstein, Ellen Sadowski, and Shelley Glick, and dearest Barbara Cheney, who built my book cradles.

I thank all who graced my studio with stories, especially Evelyn Kent, Leah Reukberg, M. E. Anderson, Alan McClintock, Dee Ellen Lee, Joni Goldberg, and my many friends from the Story Circle of the Capital District where I first told "The Mountain Whippoorwill." I send thanks to Becky Holder, Lois Foight Hodges, and Tom Weakley, who gave important nurturing at key times.

My gratitude goes to: the Niskayuna colleagues who touched my life and helped me find my way in and out of a middle school classroom—Dorothy Meyer and Jane Soule Karp, Debbie Wein, Ron Beauchemin, Risa Gregory, Kathy Cotugno Surin, Donna Cavallaro, John O'Connor, and Owen South; all the city teachers in Albany, Troy, Schenectady, and New York who helped me make my flight from the suburbs, most especially Lib Burger and Dewey Hill; my many teachers and friends over the years at the National Storytelling Association and the League for the Advancement of New England Storytelling, especially Barbara Lipke, Linda Palmström, Jay Stailey, and Priscilla Howe; Doug Lipman, who gently yet masterfully coaches my spirit as well as my tales; and Bill Wheeler, who teaches me about silence and faithfulness.

Introduction: A Learner's Journey vs. a "How-to" Book

When I skim professional books looking for one to buy or ask colleagues to recommend titles to me, I look for those with a *story*. I want to see a teacher perhaps at first failing but in the end experiencing the delight of discovery. This makes the teacher's advice about methodology real to me and therefore accessible. I see the process, the journey, that led to the insights the teacher writes about in the book, and my own journey as a teacher-learner seems less out of the ordinary, less scary. I feel able to face my own failings and trust my own discoveries. Reading someone else's story gives me the courage to tell mine—to myself and to the world.

I realize that not everyone delights in hearing or reading about the journey to new understanding. "Just tell me how to do it," I hear some colleagues say. They want the shortcut, the pamphlet version of discovery with numbered steps. As their words reveal, the dark side of innovation, which involves uncertainty and the risk of failure, terrifies them. Change, like a roller coaster, can be terrifying, but it can be exciting too. Shortcuts tend to produce only surface changes.

Why do we resist so mightily the hard work of change in education? I think that as teachers, for too long we have been led to believe that we're supposed to be certain all the time, sure of our learning, sure of our teaching. I believed that once. As a young teacher I wanted so much to be sure. "If only I can survive three years," I thought, as if three years would earn me the badge of certainty and teaching would no longer be hard. Ha! The magic number three, right out of the fairytales.

We in education (and perhaps in other social services?) keep secrets, even from ourselves. We know there is little certainty in our work. Sometimes, tired of the *un*certainty, we grasp for "the ten easy steps . . ." or say, "Skip the theory, just tell me how." But our hows need to match our whys. Children's bodies, minds, and souls are in our care, and that enormous responsibility requires us to be utterly conscious of our work, not just to seek the "how-tos." We need to wrestle with our unspoken truths and with our confusion and never stop looking at the beliefs (the whys) on which our practices (the hows) are based. We do this by talking and writing together. Other-wise, all that uncertainty, all that false certainty, stays locked in our hearts or sits like concrete in our necks and shoulders. If we are to focus on what children really need to grow up safe and strong and smart, we need to risk being less certain.

Encouraged by the Stories of Others

The stories of others encouraged me to begin to tell my truths and expose my uncertainties in my first articles written under the name Schwartz during the mid-eighties (Schwartz 1985[a,b], 1987). The tales that inspired me included those told by researchers and workshop presenters, but they also included those told by colleagues and, espe-cially, by children. I began to look long and hard at the images—the stories—of my own learning history, the joyful as well as the painful moments. I began to examine my teaching by writing about it. I wrote in story form and trusted my readers to give storytelling a try in their own ways.

Some readers of an earlier draft of this book cautioned me, "It's too much your story. Teachers want the 'how-to.'" At first, I resisted the changes these remarks suggested. I have never had much use for manuals that tell me "Do this . . . Say this . . ." or list *the* steps to success. Yet, I knew my stories of learning and of rediscovering story-telling would not be valuable unless I told them in a way that made them practical for teachers. This book is very different from that early draft, and I value the advice of those who said it wasn't ready yet. My hope is that what follows—still very much the story of a learner's journey—will trigger the memories of other storyteachers and encourage them to set off on their own journey.

As I wrote, I realized how many others before me have written about children telling and writing stories, and I knew I could not begin to credit them all. I did not set out to survey the literature about children's narratives, but I gratefully acknowledge that the work of many others has paved the way for my teaching and my writing.

Storytelling—A Radical Idea?

What I suggest in this book—that we allow children to *tell* their stories—doesn't seem so very radical. But I think we still aren't listening to children very well (Newkirk and McClure 1992). When I visit schools now, as a full-time storyteller, I see that many classroom teachers do consider it quite radical. "Let them tell their stories? They won't ever stop!" "They'll go on and on and we'll never accomplish anything!" "There is too much curriculum already. There's no time for storytelling." Linda Wason-Ellam (1993), a professor and storyteller who has done research in the classrooms of Native Canadian children, believes that the practice of hurrying children away from talk and into work with paper and pencil—of discounting their oracy—has grave effects on their literacy.

Worst of all I hear, "What if they tell the *truth?*" In one middle school I met up with a former college friend, whose idealism and fervor for teaching I had once admired. Shocked to think that I "let" students tell their stories aloud, uncensored, she asked, her cynicism obvious in her voice, "Do they talk about anything besides sex and drugs?" I wondered what could have so damaged her once strong commitment to children's language.

Allowing our children's lives—their knowledge and their questions—to be not just a distraction or some sideline to give a bit of time to, but the *center* of the work is still a pretty radical idea. Research on the teaching of reading and writing has encouraged us for two decades (and further back if we look) to put children's words at the center of our teaching, but my experiences in teaching and visiting schools across this country and Canada tell me we've barely begun. We are still so busy filling children with our knowledge that we don't begin to tap into what they know and wonder about.

One problem, which my friend's cynical remark undoubtedly alludes to, is that more than a few children today come to school hungry, abused, angry, on drugs, with far more "grown-up" experiences to tell about. Their lives contain hard stories. Should those stories be told publicly in school? That's a question teachers justifiably ask. Other children come to school well fed, even overfed, or purposely starving themselves on diets. They are "bright" but, frankly, bored because their lives outside of school are overfilled with travel, lessons, clubs, and adultlike experience. Yet school isn't tapping into what they know or encouraging them to build on it, let alone helping them sort out their confusion. We're still sitting children down before too many worksheets and teacher-planned art projects that don't elicit the life-knowledge and creativity children bring to school with them each day.

In my travels I also hear teachers complain about what they *have* to do. They see that the lessons they offer from approved texts bore some children and overwhelm others, but rather than challenge the status quo, they separate children by "ability groups" as a way of dealing with the diversity of learners. Still other children come to school almost too eager to please the teacher and comply with the school's demands. Because these children create no disturbances, they give teachers the illusion that they are the ideal—that easy, quiet children represent what students "should" be like. We are still a long way from honoring our students' unique stories and devising curriculum that stretches their knowledge, encourages their questions, and engages their imaginations.

I do not fault teachers for their uncertainty, their questions, and even their hesitation in the face of change. Teaching full-time presented me with many, many questions. Initially, I was reluctant to deal with the incredible diversity in my classroom. But what I soon learned as a teacher, and continue to believe and profess through my work as a storyteller, is that *diversity is a gift*. But it demands new kinds of understanding and new strategies if we are to break through children's pain, disillusionment, boredom, and anxiety in order to spark genuine, joyful learning.

I believe we are up to the task. We simply need allies. We cannot do it alone. Most of the teachers I meet show me they have the heart for honoring the gifts of every child. Many just need support: a gentle hand of encouragement and specific ideas about how to begin to make changes. Mentors would make a difference—new teachers aren't alone in needing them—and *respect* for all that teachers have already accomplished. A little of that would go a long way to support change. A teacher in one of my summer workshops, when asked what had brought her, said, "Last year all my friends retired. I am the senior teacher in my building, one year from my own retirement, but the young ones have no use for what I know. They want to tell me *their* newfangled ideas, but they don't want to listen to what *I* have learned after all these years." She sighed and smiled. "So I came to get some new ideas."

Her "oh-all-right" resignation made me laugh. I was reminded of my mother the summer I brought home one of Frank Smith's books, which I'd bought for a reading course. My mother, a highly respected first-grade teacher, had only sampled Smith when she started getting her back up. His writing criticized aspects of her practice and, in essence, threatened her very belief in herself near the end of a long career. Yet she had had questions and long-unattended-to misgivings about the way schools worked. It took till well beyond that summer, but in time, *by telling our stories to each other*, my mother and I became true colleagues who could speak the truths of what we saw in children, and in classrooms, and in ourselves because of our histories. We didn't have to agree; we mostly needed to talk and to listen to each other with courtesy and attention.

Listening to that senior teacher and recollecting how my mother and I had reconciled our different perspectives on reading instruction, I thought, what we all need is to have our stories honored. In "Autobiographical Understanding: Writing the Past into the Future," JoAnn Portalupi (1995) talks about how, by telling and writing about their teaching, teachers become not only highly conscious of their work, but they begin to imagine their future teaching selves. Our practices and beliefs—our learning, just like children's—grow out of our stories. With new information we can construct new understanding on the foundations of what we have already experienced and what we have fantasized. As Brian Cambourne (1988) recognized, we can only engage in learning if we believe we are "potential doers." Too many teachers are threatened by the new; having our stories honored might open us up to our potential for growth.

A few open-minded administrators listened to my stories about my changing classroom. They rolled their eyes now and then, but they trusted me because I told them stories like the ones in this book. I wish now that I had asked my old college friend to tell me about her years of teaching. Perhaps it was only a handful of experiences, what I would call her "trauma tales," that had turned her cynical and made her afraid of children's truths. By listening to her stories, I am sure I would have found the idealist alive in her still.

Stories—the ones children bring from their lives and from listening to elders, earlier teachers, librarians, friends, and "big kids"—took center stage in my middle school classroom (see Schwartz in the index to Hamilton and Weiss 1988). Our stories became the place to begin and a source from which to draw throughout the year. Through stories my students told me who they were, what they believed as a result of their life experiences and their listening and reading, what opinions they held, and what they were curious about. Although boredom, anxiety, and the troubles of life knocked at our classroom door, as every teacher knows they do, we either shooed them away or let them in and learned despite their presence.

Teachers, administrators, parents, and even government bureaucrats say the future calls for thinkers, imaginers, reasoners, and arguers. If we hope to do our part in helping children assume these roles, we must model our own thinking, imagining, reasoning, and arguing by honoring our questions and laying claim to what our stories have taught us. Then we must listen to children's stories with rapt attention. If we do, we will glimpse the future and we will not be afraid.

Telling How

In this book I will tell "how": how I discovered (or rediscovered) storytelling, how I lured my middle school students into it, and what they taught me about trusting their judgement. I also share what I am currently learning about the how of it all by visiting schools and by inviting adults to my Story Studio, where we explore the layers of meaning within the tales we dig out of our attics and our psyches. But is this a "how-to" or "step-by-step" book? No. It is a collection of stories that I hope will invite you to recollect or seek out your own tales of teaching and living.

ONE

Acknowledging an Old Friend

hen I was writing under the name of Schwartz, I drafted one of my earliest articles (Schwartz 1985a) to explain to teachers that I had just discovered storytelling and to invite them to consider it. Storytelling seemed to be an interesting offshoot of process writing. I also saw it as a way to help children develop performance skills without having to put on class plays. However, I couldn't seem to finish the article. An uneasiness came over me, as if I weren't writing the whole truth. An inner voice seemed to scoff, "You didn't *just* find storytelling!"

I remember resting my fingertips on the keys and my wrists on the edge of the shallow desk drawer that held my keyboard and trying to let go of the need to finish the article (thoughts of the deadline). I let my mind drift off the way I do when a passage I am reading reminds me of a long-ago event. If I hadn't *just* found storytelling, when did I find it? I started to freewrite, traveling back in time. First, I saw myself at about age fifteen, standing alone on the apron of my high school's stage and dramatically reciting the poem "Patterns" by Amy Lowell in a citywide recitation contest. I watched my younger self become the proper but bitter young woman Lowell writes of who walks "the garden path in my stiff brocaded gown," enraged at the message I had just received: my fiancé has died in battle.

Yes, I realized, that was storytelling. So I traveled further back until I saw myself at about age eight, sitting on my father's left knee as we sang the duet "I Remember It Well" from *Gigi*. We had performed the song a number of times at family gatherings, but in this memory I saw us performing for my father's friends at a faculty picnic. As a sometimes tough assistant principal in a large middle school, he loved showing off his family to his staff, revealing a side of him they didn't often see. In our little song-skit, I played the part of the somewhat miffed but still smitten elderly woman who reminds her former lover, old now himself, of the details of their courtship. He recalls it, singing, "We met at nine," and she corrects, "We met at eight." My father would counter in his best Maurice Chevalier accent, "I was on time?" I would roll my eyes to the delight of the audience and sigh dramatically, "No, you were late." Pretending to be the great lost love of my father and scolding him for remembering less than I about the past—surely that was storytelling too.

I wondered, could I travel back even further? I saw a blur of backyard and classroom dramatizations performed for parents, and I observed from afar the small girl whispering tender fantasies to a Tiny Tears doll before sleep. Then my mind landed, somehow, on the image of a four-year-old in a blue crepe-paper teapot costume performing for a summer park Parents' Night. Clearly I was telling my "story" to the world: "I'm a little teapot short and stout." I beamed like moonlight to the charmed adult crowd and begged, "When I get all steamed up hear me shout / 'Tip me over and pour me out.'"

At four I already knew a great deal about the world and was taking in new knowledge faster than I could make sense of it. I lived in a large Irish-American family where, as a child, you didn't always get listened to (unless, of course, you were performing). That summer I had spent hours at the neighborhood park trying to slide and swing and play "Red Rover" as skillfully as kids more than twice my age, including two older brothers. I wanted to be noticed and valued. I was "all steamed up." But I needed the adult world's permission, and its help, to "tip over" and "pour out."

As I sat at the keyboard seeing each image of my younger self telling stories, I cried, the kind of quiet tears that rise up with no warning when you tell someone of a powerful dream or when a song on the radio invades some pocket of sorrow tucked tightly away. The article I was trying to finish suddenly had a whole new meaning. I had not *just* discovered storytelling, I had *rediscovered* it. In the article— and in my teaching—I needed to acknowledge that storytelling was an old friend, one that had introduced me to the wonderfully safe, though perhaps at times dark, world where humans express feelings of great intensity through symbol and metaphor. All my life, storytelling had carried me through the fear of speaking my true feelings.

At four, in the guise of a teapot singing a "cute" children's song, I had begged those around me to help me express all that was bubbling up inside me. At eight, behind the mask of a show tune, I had played at romantic love and been allowed to voice, publicly, how I adored (and struggled for power with) my father. In essence, his invitation had answered my call and shown me a way to pour out at least some of what bubbled within.

However, a month after I turned thirteen, on a foggy drive home from a similar faculty gathering, my father drove his Volkswagon into a tree. None of us had gone with him that night to show off, and we never saw him again. It wasn't until I was fifteen, having struggled to "be brave" for two years after his death, that I found a way to voice my rage and sadness by reciting "Patterns." Through the metaphor of the grief-stricken young woman furious at being locked within society's patterns, I poured myself out. I told my story.

My tears as I recollected all of this were more than just belated grieving. They released a joy and an awareness of something my intuition or unconscious had been trying to tell me for a while. I only thought I had just found storytelling by following my adult academic questions. In fact, I had returned to something I had been unconsciously involved in since early childhood. You might say that the parent in me was crying in recognition of the resourceful child I had been all along: a four-year-old able to find a metaphor through which to speak, an eight-year-old who could sing out her love, and a grief-stricken teenager with the courage to face her grief publicly, if only through another character.

The tears also expressed my relief at making an important discovery through writing. Although this book is about storytelling, the speaking of tales, I would not have been able to synthesize what I've learned, let alone share it with others, without writing. As much as I hope to encourage teachers to tell stories, I also hope to move them to make time to write. Writing-to-discover-what-I-know still makes me cry, but I won't stop doing it. Breaking through confusion by writing has helped me to teach writing more honestly and to ask others the questions that free up their truths.

My recollected "stories" included two songs and a poem. As I have changed in my understanding of how children learn, I have realized that students include storytelling in their lives in many ways: delivering research reports, debating, displaying artwork, playing in a band or an orchestra, preparing a dance for gym class, playing chess, or participating joyfully in a sport. Through such activities students symbolically tell me about their lives.

Yet, even when my view of "storytelling" shifted, I still watched students with a critic's or an evaluator's eyes, looking only for skill. Why? Because my early stories, elicited by adults, were almost always a performance. I was applauded or corrected as adults saw fit. Now, I am coming to a new perspective on storytelling, watching it in all its forms: I see it as self-expression before I measure it as performance. This perspective allows me to watch a student-choreographed dance or look at a child's artwork with the eyes of a fellow-artist, rather than a critic. I listen to a student's guitar-playing or to my son's singing, noting the expression as well as the skill. I realize now that children don't have to be in a show to tell their most heartfelt stories. But they do need listeners and observers who honor what they have to say.

For most of this book I limit my examples to students' efforts at telling stories in my language arts classes and my storytelling courses. However, having watched students of all ages tell the stories of their lives in many ways, I am convinced that what we need to encourage more often in school is not just language expression but *self*-expression in many forms. Most children are able to express themselves through the spoken and written word with our support, but some express themselves more comfortably through programming computers, designing toothpick bridges, playing kickball, or leaping a high jump. During language arts time they are simply reframing those stories in language.

In my first year of teaching, I watched Stephanie struggle with her reading and writing. Even her friends thought of her as slow. A tall, lanky girl, she seemed more shy and awkward than the usual eleven-year-old. Then, the last week of school, I saw her in her element. At field day she took first in the long jump, the hurdles, and the high jump. Like a deer, she leapt into the air with a natural confidence. She had never brought such confidence into my room, and I knew that had as much to do with what I hadn't seen in her or asked of her.

As Paulo Freire (1987) has noted, long before we come to books and school we *read the world,* and such reading prepares us to read texts of all kinds. Likewise, children prepare for the many tasks ahead of them in school and beyond by being encouraged to explore through their own "stories" from the moment they enter school (Paley 1990). If Stephanie's achievements had accompanied her into my room, she might have had a very different experience there.

When our children are beyond the days of show-and-tell, oral storytelling, the focus of this book, is one way to bring their stories into school. Some teachers and curriculum makers think of it as merely a fun diversion from work. That is a false notion. Storytelling is rehearsal for many other kinds of composing. Not least of all, it embraces the study of design, practice in mental imaging, and the development of oral competency.

Everyone tells stories—to friends and family through simple conversation, or to audiences through dramatization, debate, recitation, stand-up comedy, song, and a variety of nonverbal communication arts. Since I have reexperienced the power of storytelling to provide self-knowledge and offer self-expression, I see it as the very core of my teaching. My students try on different faces and voices through story; they find the courage to free their own voices; they see each other and perhaps the world differently because of the stories they listen to and the ones they tell. In the process, they learn an enormous amount about the way language works. My experience with adult storytellers continues to inform me about how, at every age, we heal and teach ourselves and each other by telling stories. Perhaps you, too, have known this old friend all along.

TWO

A Leap of Faith Away From Reading Aloud

y adult connection to storytelling came through my love of reading aloud. In college my favorite course was Oral Interpretation. We could pick *anything* and read aloud for up to eight minutes. For a lonely freshman, oral interp became a place to meet people, unlike my other lectures where only the teacher and a few "talkers" spoke. I remember the entertainment aspect of the course. Students would try on the voices and gestures of characters. After all, our work was to interpret as we read aloud. In a few cases it was like watching a stage play. In others it was like watching a college kid play dress up or "cops and robbers." For me, the "work" of that course was the chance to gather all the pieces of literature that expressed the true and sometimes secret parts of myself.

Our teacher, Linda Sternberg, who had a very cultured ("cul-tyahd") speaking voice, read one day from a play that included a shouting match between a husband and wife from Brooklyn. More than the words themselves, the *speed* and nasal Brooklynese with which she read had us all laughing. She admitted later that somewhere within those voices was her own girlhood voice, one she had disowned during her study of speech and theater. I remember being amazed and saddened at the thought of that. I had never heard of someone disowning her own voice, though the idea of being silenced struck a chord deep within me. More significantly, I had rarely heard a teacher share any aspect of her childhood, any story of younger days, and certainly never before this place of higher learning called college.

I include this recollection because, along with the literature we interpreted for Sternberg's class, the course itself is something I've reflected upon many times since, finding in it layers of meaning for my own teaching and interpretation of stories. Sternberg created a community in which we could take the risk of exploring ourselves and sharing that exploration publicly. She taught us how to listen respectfully to each other's voices, even if it was our turn to speak next and we were preoccupied with performance anxiety. She gave us instant feedback in an efficient and private way, although later, as a group, we discussed her feedback and shared the processes of choosing a work and developing an interpretation. Using a carbon between two small pieces of paper, she took notes on our readings, keeping one copy and offering us the other, each a valentine. I learned from her how to watch a student intently and jot responsive notes at the same time, a practice I've honed over the years. She instilled in me a respect for preparing an oral reading, for thinking deeply about a text, its rhythms and multiple meanings.

Just Tell Us the Story

So how is story*telling* different from reading aloud? One can find lots of opinions on this in children's literature textbooks and in treatises on the art of storytelling in the 398.2 section of the library. My own sense of the distinction comes from three personal experiences rather than from books.

The first was when I watched and listened to Jeannine Laverty, a storyteller from Saratoga Springs, New York, tell stories at my first two weekend workshops on storytelling. Her tales came at me like great ocean waves, nearly drowning me and certainly taking my breath away. All I knew was that the experience was markedly different from hearing the most masterful reader or from watching a play or hearing a speech. At those moments I didn't try to name how it was different; all I knew was that I wanted to tell stories and offer my students the chance to tell them.

I had been teaching an oral interpretation unit for years, simply giving students time to prepare an eight-minute oral reading much the way I had learned to in Linda Sternberg's class. I would demonstrate how to hold a book and not lose the place while looking up, how to make eye contact that engaged rather than distracted the audience, how to vary the pace, pitch, and volume of the voice, and how to use body language to enhance the expression of the words. I sensed that a storytelling unit would be similar, yet somehow distinctly different. I don't know why I had the confidence to jump in with both feet—I guess my teapot days had taught me well—I just knew that the kids and the art of storytelling would show me how to proceed.

The second step toward understanding how storytelling differs from reading aloud came the night I attended a storytellers' circle at the local public library. Such guilds or circles exist in small towns and big cities all over the United States and Canada. It is easy to start one: most libraries have a free meeting room, and local newspapers will print a notice free of charge. Our group, which meets every month, celebrates its eleventh anniversary this year. We pay annual dues of five dollars to print a newsletter. Some guilds hold huge festivals or Tellebrations (see National Storytelling Association in Resources for Storyteachers) to promote storytelling. But even after all these years, our local group is low-key and casual about storytelling, the kind of just-go-for-it gathering that helped me believe I could call myself a "storyteller."

The first time I attended the circle, there were fewer than ten people in the small upstairs room of the library. The person leading the group first asked us to introduce ourselves. Only three or four people had come with a "prepared" story, and after hearing those I asked, "How do you pick a story? Where do you find these stories?" The group's response was a collective chuckle. Someone said something about "just loving a story"; another said to read hundreds of stories until one says, "Tell me." One teller turned the question back to me: "What's a story you really like, maybe something you just enjoy reading each year to your class?"

I went blank. Every year I would read different things, depending on what I was interested in at the time or what the class was like. Then something came to the surface and I laughed to myself. "Well, I do direct a choral reading of Stephen Vincent Benét's 'The Mountain Whippoorwill' every year. I sometimes read it aloud first and tell the kids about learning it for my high school drama club. I tell them how, at the time, I thought it was a pretty dumb poem." Everyone laughed and I relaxed a little.

"Well, tell us that," my questioner said, grinning at my reminiscence.

I suspect most teachers know the momentary panic of suddenly realizing that you are once again in the role of the student, being asked to produce and feeling quite resistant.

I laughed again, nervously. "But I can't. It's a poem, a three-page poem."

"Then just tell us the story," my self-appointed mentor said again. "*Is* it a story?"

"Well, yes, it's a narrative poem. But it's a poem. I might know some of it by heart, but just bits and pieces."

"Then say the lines you know, and when you draw a blank just tell us the *story*."

I thought *I* was a stubborn teacher! Kids didn't get away with "I can't" in my classes, but now, in the kid position, I was squirming. This teacher wasn't taking no for an answer.

I hesitated and scowled. I did want to try this thing called storytelling. But tell Benét's story in my own words? It seemed sacrilegious. I felt my resistance slip just enough to crack a nervous smile. My confronter smiled back. I think she must have known the idea intrigued me as much as it frightened me.

What happened then changed my life.

I did start off with Benét's words. I knew the opening by heart. I had learned the poem in ninth grade, used it for a lesson demonstration in my college methods course, and for almost ten years, read it aloud with each class I taught. It was a work I loved. But I soon drew a blank on the words. I could picture the blue ditto paper on which the poem was typed. I could actually see the stanza shape in my mind with the line numbers sprinkled down the right side of the paper. But I couldn't remember the words. I must have looked panicky.

My stubborn but gentle mentor nodded encouragement and whispered, "Just tell the *story*."

And I did. I finally released Benét like the ghost of a loved one and stepped into the world his words had brought me to so often. In walked the cocky but inexperienced young fiddler who "plunked" a silver dollar down, so sure he was the best at the Essex County Fair. There stood little Jimmy Wheezer who laughed and called it a "dead dollar." Big Tom Sargeant just offered his "yeller toothy grin." I saw the young fiddler's confidence ever so slowly shrink. Then out stepped Old Dan Wheeling. I felt the great pause, heard the crowd's silence. The awesome "kingpin fiddler" was everything Benét had described and more, only now he was alive to me. Playing *big* and small, playing salvation in the deep South, playing "the heart right out of yore mouth." The words meant new things to me now. I *became* the kingpin fiddler, oblivious in that moment to the newcomer. Yet at the same time I watched the great Dan Wheeling from inside the young fiddler's skin. In storytelling you play all the parts simultaneously. You are inside a painting. It has come to life. You are painter and brushstrokes in one.

Most delightful was seeing and being the narrator, the boy from up in the mountains who, as the poem progresses, loses his cocky confidence watching the well-known fiddlers and hearing the audience's applause. I saw him almost quit; I felt him want to. Then together we reached within for the courage, for the mountain images and the sweet side of "lonesome," to step forward and play the "whippoorwill." When I materialized back in the upstairs room of that library, I knew I had found out the difference between reading aloud and storytelling.

Almost a year later, a third experience—hearing George Shannon speak at a National Council of Teachers of English convention—gave a name to what I had experienced that night. What follows is a combination of my memory of his talk and the insights I've come to since he spoke. An oral reader holds a text, an artifact, which proves by its very existence that the story resides in the book or the script. It is evidence to reader and listeners that the story has been created at some other moment by an author separate from them.

With the help of listeners, Shannon said, a storyteller composes the story anew in the moment of telling. It is original work, borrowed from the original author, but newly formed to fit this occasion, this teller, these listeners. What happens is more experiential than when someone reads aloud. What the teller offers is a recreation of the tale. The listeners, leaning in close or hanging back as they do, making faces that say "I'm scared" or "Huh?" and joining in through participation—or refusing to—contribute to the storyteller's telling. As listeners become aware that they are influencing the telling, they may influence it even more. The teller, in turn, allows herself to be dependent on the participants to the degree that she is comfortable in doing so, and dependent on the story to show her how to tell it this time. Different tellers move an audience in different ways.

I couldn't name this phenomenon until I heard Shannon's talk. Then I realized that, with the help of the intense faces around me that night in the library, I had created a telling uniquely mine and theirs, and certainly one I would never replicate. At some point, I went back to my old dittoed copy of Benét's text and made myself learn his words by heart, but even today, ten years later, it is the *story* of "The Mountain Whippoorwill" that I tell. It never emerges the same way twice, despite my recitation of Benét's musically rhythmic words. I see the images in my mind differently. I speak the words of the young fiddler in different voices. Some days he's fourteen, others more like twenty. Sometimes he's almost devastated when he believes he hasn't earned even one person's applause. In other tellings he shrugs like Gomer Pyle and shakes his head a bit, perplexed by such a fickle audience when he says to his fiddle, "Whippoorwill, you been bossed."

In the first lines of the poem the boy describes the mountains as "lonesome." In some tellings I feel the sadness of that word, and in others the gift of solitude the boy has brought with him. For it is that lonesome quality, the mountains' silence, that helps the fiddler play masterfully in the end. In some tellings I see the other fiddlers and the images of their music in brighter or duller colors, depending on my mood or on my audience's willingness to enter the tale. If I tell the story standing up it feels significantly different than if I tell it seated close to a group of children.

When my son was in first grade, I visited his class and told a few participatory stories. I sensed that the audience could sit for about one more, and I paused, deciding how to close the session. My son, Brian, who had accompanied me to many tellings with older children and adults said, "Mommy, you *have* to tell the fiddler!"

"Oh, I think that's kind of long for first graders." I glanced at the teacher for corroboration, but she and the other children looked to Brian. If he wanted the fiddler, they wanted it too. Since then I've learned again and again that the audience will provide evidence of what they can and cannot appreciate through their body language. That little group of listeners came right into the Georgia mountains with me. They loved that young, naive boy who "never had a pappy" "ner" "a mammy to teach me pritty please." They loved and believed in him and knew exactly what it meant when the fairgoers didn't make a sound after he stopped fiddling.

Give Up Reading Aloud? No Way!

Many teachers and librarians love to read aloud. I do too! Yet being enamored of oral reading can make it harder to let go of the text, of the beautiful, carefully crafted words in a book. My most resistant storytelling students, young and old, are those who read aloud brilliantly. They love to caress the words of a tale and find comfort and strength in the book they hold in their hands. They feel a respect for and perhaps a kinship with the writer. They believe in the author as wordsmith (Denman 1988).

I understand that feeling of kinship and I share that love of wonderful writing. I still struggle to tell certain stories and sometimes abandon a tale if I cannot find a way to honor the words while letting them go at the same time. In Chapter 12 I will talk more about abandoning stories and this struggle with words, since it is a necessary one in getting to the heart of storytelling.

I stumbled on an image that has helped me accept my own resistance to telling certain tales: storytelling is a first cousin to oral reading but a sibling of talk. Among my students, the ones most often at ease and most imaginative as tellers are those who have not had an easy time with reading and writing. Talk, on the other hand, has been their ally. Talk is easy. It comes naturally. They talk a good story about why their work isn't done. They talk their way into a visit to the school nurse or the bathroom and then talk in the hall with other wandering talkers until a roaming teacher says, "Where are you supposed to be?" They talk to avoid working on the tasks of reading and writing assigned during class. When it dawns on them that they can get class credit for telling a story, something at which they sense their natural competence, they are elated. Again and again I've seen struggling students excel at storytelling and later walk into reading and writing a little less reluctantly because telling honored their ability to talk.

Storytelling, a Sibling of Talk

My most memorable example is John. He was mainstreamed into English for the first time in sixth grade. In elementary school he had traveled from his resource room only for homeroom, art and music, gym, and a few other activities that schools for some reason call "nonacademic."

"He's an imaginative boy," his earlier teacher told me when she requested that he be placed in English. "If someone gave him a chance . . . " John clearly was imaginative, but he needed more than one chance. He gave up quickly on most writing or reading tasks, wrote illegibly on the ones he attempted, acted out his frustration in a variety of negative attention-getting ways, and alienated other students most of the time. He was also absent a great deal, so when he began to make progress, the interruption would set him back.

During the storytelling unit John was frequently absent. On the days he came to class he tried various rehearsal exercises, but I had a hunch he hadn't really settled on a story. I asked his middle school resource room teacher to work with him on it and suggested ways they might explore the story. Later, she reported that he wanted to do a personal story about a time he got into trouble, but in her eyes it was silly, and it wasn't very developed. Because "trouble" was John's strong suit, that sounded about right to me. I stopped worrying. The day he was scheduled to perform I had yet to see him rehearse the entire story, but he came to class and said, "I'm ready."

I think John's instinct told him that this was just "showing off," his area of expertise. And that is exactly what it was. He told the story of a playground incident from elementary school that had caused him to be "sent to the office." The kids were grinning already. His impression of the playground aide and his own self-mimicking cry, "I didn't do it!" brought down the house. Then, in another great impression of the principal, a large man whom most of the children loved but who could be stern with troublemakers, my young storyteller boomed, "*John*, I might have known it was you." Again, the class roared. That was the end of the story John had rehearsed, according to his resource room teacher. However, with his imagination, his wits, and a knowledge of narrative that had been developing in him for years despite his lack of success in reading, he launched into episodes two and three. At the end of the second, a run-in with a well-known teacher, he scolded himself once again in a facsimile of her voice, "*John*, I might have known it was you." The third time, of course, he paused just long enough for the class to take a breath and join in the chorus, "*John . . .*"

John had created a participatory tale with a predictable structure. The praise he received from his other teacher and me didn't begin to match the appreciation of his peers. Did John's academic skills take a major leap forward after that? No, but he didn't quit so easily on tasks and his attendance improved. Both his resource teacher and I saw another side of him that day. His tale, funny as it was, also told us what John's elders, perhaps unconsciously, had conveyed to him about their expectations, and we took a hard look at what we said to students. We also vowed to find ways for John to succeed in front of his peers more often. We knew we couldn't give him success, but we could watch for opportunities where he could stumble upon it.

Similarly, many students who have tamed reading and writing feel suddenly unsure without notecards, a typed report, or a book to read from when they stand before the class. They have discovered comfort and safety in their solitary work with the written word. Back in the early grades or, in some cases, even before they attended school, they traded lots of oral talk for silent inner talk, the kind necessary for competence in reading and writing. For them, coming back to a kinship with orality isn't easy. The students who, for various reasons, never befriended silent or oral reading or tamed inner talk to help them write, however, have been sharpening their talking skills since before kindergarten. For at least some of them, as John showed us, stepping into storytelling seems delightfully familiar.

Because I came to storytelling by way of a love of reading aloud, I sympathize with readers who do not want to relinquish the book in their hands. I certainly haven't given up reading aloud. But as my father used to say to reluctant divers kneeling at the edge of the pool or crouching over the end of the diving board, "Come on in, the water's warm." If you treat yourself to stepping inside just one tale you know so well you can hold its images in your mind, you will see what I mean.

I remember the first time I memorized a piece for the piano. I was seven or eight. The thought of learning every note and keeping each one in my head terrified me. But I loved to watch my teacher's face when she went inside the music as she played by heart. It was as if she left the room and she and the music became one. I never did master very many pieces or come to think of myself as a pianist, but a few times I knew the feeling of music coming out my hands. I wasn't playing the notes; I was playing the music. If you let go of the words of a story in order to step inside it and tell it in a way that feels natural, something new will happen to you. You may not believe you can call yourself "storyteller" after that one time, but just as I haven't lost the feeling of that music in my fingers, you will remember what the story looks like from within.

You don't have to tell it fancy. You don't have to be an actor. You just have to dare to go inside. The story's rhythms and images will support you. If you love a story, you will be true to it. Doug Lipman (1994), who coaches tellers and supports their unique interpretations of tales, advises them to simply ask themselves, "What's the most important thing in this story?" In other words, what do *you* particularly love about the tale? Then focus completely on whatever that answer is and on sharing that sense of the tale with the audience, and the right words will come.

JoAnn Portalupi first introduced me to Taro Yashima's beautiful *Crow Boy* by tentatively trying a first telling of it during a workshop attended by leaders of the Writing Project at Teachers College. She said it was a book she had often read aloud to students, calling their attention to Yashima's use of words. JoAnn clearly had a deep respect for the tale and its author-illustrator. I remember watching her discover the images beyond the words as she rather nervously opened the door to the story. All of us listening that day smiled and nodded encouragement to her, believing she could do it. She smiled back and then got serious as she experienced this touching picture story about "Chibi," a child set apart from other children. JoAnn let herself talk the story in a natural way. There was very little drama in her telling; it was more a remembering. Yet I recall vividly how she characterized the lonely boy's ability to concentrate. She saw him touch the scratch marks on his desk, stare at the droplets of water on the windowpane, and study the designs on a nearby boy's shirt and on the schoolroom ceiling. JoAnn had no trouble conveying these details even though the words were from her own understanding of the tale and its essence. I suspect Taro Yashima would have been most honored by her telling.

In like fashion, I write this book to encourage others. I sincerely believe that every teacher and librarian, every parent and grandparent, every child and elder is, by nature of his or her humanity, a storyteller. We all have stories to tell, our own and the ones given to us by the authors and the storytellers in our lives. If we accept the gift of that first telling the way JoAnn did, the experience just may lure us into retelling, which allows the tale to deepen within us even more. For it is in *returning* to a tale, as Gregory Denman (1988) writes, that you "make it your own."

After learning one tale, others stories come more easily. My students have shown me that once they experience the process of telling a tale, the next one is a "piece of cake." Once they see what it feels like to go way inside a story, they want that sensation again: pretty exciting stuff for "school work"! New divers at the pool's edge may initially be afraid to plunge in headfirst, and some never let go of their fear. But my father never gave up teaching diving because of the look on kids' faces when they pushed through the fear and found the thrill—"Hey, I did it, Mr. Gillard!" they would shout, running for the ladder to do it again. My students at every age say "Whew!" after their first telling before an audience, but next thing I know they're looking for a second story to tell and a third . . .

Returning to Benét's "The Mountain Whippoorwill" not as a choral reading or recitation but as a *telling* has taught me so much about story—its shape, its dependence on clear characters, its need for rising action, its ability to mean different things in each retelling. Of course, rereading a tale can bring that experience of story to the reader and to listeners, but telling alone allows teller and audience to create the world of the tale anew. The teller is narrator and characters, giver and recipient, offering the story to listeners and pulling it from them simultaneously. In this way, the story belongs to the teller and the listeners in that moment. It will never exist in the exact same form again.

Storytelling is contagious at every age. I hear refrains from stories echo in the corridors days after a tale has been told. Parents report, "My child told me every detail at bedtime." When I revisit schools, children tell me back the stories I told them a year or more before. Teachers and other adults say, "You've got me telling stories I'd forgotten I knew." As they found out, the water is warm. You will too.

THREE

Looking for Tales to Tell

elling Stephen Vincent Benét's story that night in the library gave me the sense of what it means to let go of words. It also taught me—and other experiences along this journey have confirmed—that the place to begin looking for stories to tell is one's own childhood bookshelf of favorites or, lacking the actual books, the story memories deep within the heart.

Everyone has a collection of story fragments, or even whole and undamaged heirloom tales, within them. The stories may not be from books, but book memories were where my students and I began to look for tales when I introduced them to story-telling. Just by talking about the stories and rhymes we could remember, we unearthed whole fairytales (or parts of them), legends, fables, poems, songs, proverbs, prayers, and an unlimited supply of personal memory images connected to the places and people who had brought us stories. These inner resources offered us many surprises, and once we had explored the lore we already possessed, those "stories" led us to new ones.

Visualizing

When I help children or adults look for story treasures, I sometimes begin with a visualization exercise. I talk at a normal pace and in a normal voice—not like a hypnotist—but I do pause between images so listeners can form pictures in their mind and have time to look at them. I always preface my remarks by saying that they can trust whatever their mind's eye brings them. They don't have to see anything if they don't want to, but I ask them to be quiet so everyone will be able to form their own mental pictures. I am gentle but firm about this requirement and have found that a quiet, serious tone helps children take the activity seriously.

During the visualization exercise, I alternate between offering direction and suggesting examples (shown in italics below). I make up what I say as I go along and do not read from a text, although some teachers might prefer to do so. I might say something like the following:

"Close your eyes or just look off into space so you don't get distracted by anyone around you. Take a deep breath. Let your mind wander back in time to a place where you heard, read, or saw a 'story.' Maybe you were sitting on a couch or in a big chair with a grownup or a big brother or sister who read to you. *My nana's prickly sofa scratched my legs but I loved curling up next to her in my pj's and hearing a story.* Maybe you had your very own book and looked at the pictures and said the words. Sometimes babysitters or neighbors are good storyreaders or storytellers. You can find stories at libraries and even on television. *I used to ask for* Madeline *at every library story hour. I first heard* Stone Soup *on the television show, 'Captain Kangaroo.'* You may have been read to or told a story as you were lying in bed getting ready to fall asleep. *My mom would read to me at night, and I could 'see' the picture of the little pine tree in my mind.* Maybe at the dinner table you heard relatives talking about the olden days, the way things used to be. Or maybe you sat up on the workbench while your dad talked about what he used to do with his dad or his friends when he was a boy. *My sisters and I perched on a stool as our mom trimmed our hair in the back yard. She would tell us about her hair when she was a girl. Then we would take a bath in the deep kitchen sink or in the tub and sing songs, tell stories, and pretend to be queens or Indian maidens as we smoothed our soapy hair into different shapes.* Maybe you had a teacher who used puppets or a felt board when she told stories? Did you ever sing any story-songs as you stood in a circle at summer camp or on the school playground?"

I lead the visualizing journey slowly because it takes time to formulate images in the mind. I have listened to others imaging journeys and felt frustrated because my mental-imaging couldn't keep up with their rate of talk. I adapt my words, tone, and tempo to the age of the listeners. I realize they may recall only fragments of a story or song or nothing at all. I tell them, "That's fine. There are no right or wrong answers in a visualization. What you see is what you see." I let students know that sometimes visualizations work for me and sometimes they don't. If my mind wanders because of a noise from the playground or I'm distracted by other thoughts, it is perfectly natural. I do try to breathe and let the distraction go, but I don't worry about not following the directions. Visualization simply exercises the memory and the imagination the way riding a bike exercises the stomach and leg muscles.

The kind of visualizing activity I am suggesting draws listeners to *their* own stories. My memories, offered sporadically, simply give examples. My concrete images help to trigger theirs. I know some listeners will recollect or "see" more easily if I mention sounds, smells, textures, or even movements, so I use as many sensory words as possible. Students later comment, "When you said 'curling up on your nana's scratchy sofa' that reminded me of the scratchy chair at my aunt's house."

The teacher's job is to find a balance between directing listeners toward places or people they associate with story memory and *leaving enough quiet, empty space* for them to see their own thoughts and realize that they direct their own imaginations. With practice they get better at visualizing just as they do at other skills.

Many teachers ask me how I remember so much about my past. The more I think back on childhood, the more memories I "see." I can do this kind of activity alone at my desk and freewrite or draw the images that surface. I might meet an old friend for the express purpose of reminiscing about events from the past. Talking and writing about memories makes them accessible to me. June Gould's (1989) *The Writer in All of Us* as well as Natalie Goldberg's (1990) *Wild Mind* and Donald Murray's (1982) *Learning by Teaching*, and other books have helped me search my memory.

Exercising the Imagination

Recently I have heard that more and more people feel uncomfortable asking children to visualize. Perhaps this fear comes from associating visualizing with hypnosis or mind control—something teachers certainly do not want to be accused of. What I am advocating is just the opposite of mind control. I'm teaching children to *exercise* their memory and their imagination, which is an important part of a teacher's job. When children close their eyes or look off into space and "go inside," they practice thinking creatively. This is the same kind of thinking they need to design bridges, create computer programs, grasp the importance of political and historical events, determine solutions to mathematical problems, or prepare for a job interview. Teachers must champion creative visualization not fear it. The fitness of the "muscles" of our children's brains must be as important to us as those in their arms and legs.

Today's children have not developed their imaginations fully because images are given to them on TV, in videogames, and at the movies. Having grown up on TV myself and watched my son learn about his world from TV, I don't fear its effects as much as some. However, I do know that because communication media provide children with so many images, they get little chance to practice bringing any to mind on their own.

Many adults who grew up before the days of television have told me about the joy of listening to radio stories. One woman loved "Let's Pretend" so much, her mother made it an incentive for her to be "good" all week. Radio shows tapped children's need for fantasy, as do today's action hero cartoons, only the radio allowed children to create their own mental pictures. One reason radio stories and audiotapes are making a comeback is that adults have seen how much children hunger to use their imaginations (see Resources for Storyteachers). Visualization is a "looking within." Writers use it to create scenes and to see imaginary characters come to life. Sports enthusiasts use it to envision the perfect golf or tennis swing. Storytellers use it for everything from memory scanning to scene development.

My sixth graders wrote about traveling back to the books they first loved or about their memories of learning to read. The following excerpts are from some of the longer written narratives that grew out of their original visualization and freewriting.

> When I was about two years old, my mom would call me over and I would sit on her lap. She would get out a book called *Whose Mouse Are You?* [Kraus]. I would be the mouse and she would be the question-asker.
> "Whose mouse are you?"
> I would say, "Nobody's mouse."
> Then she would ask me where my family was, and when she asked me where my brother was, I would say, "I don't have a brother." Then she would ask me what am I going to do about it, and I would tell her, "Free my mother . . . ," etc.
> When she asked me, "Whose mouse are you now?" I would say, "My brother's mouse."
> "Your brother's mouse?" she would ask.
> "He's brand new," I would reply.
> I always loved that part. I really don't know why, but then again, why does my four-year-old brother like the ending too?
>
> *Jim*

> There are a few things that I remember about reading when I was young. Story hour for one. Sitting in the big room (to a nursery schooler that is). With the paintings and pictures up and the displays behind the glass windows. Then listening to the stories as you sat on the little pillows. The librarian had a soft voice which really drew you into what the characters were thinking.
>
> *Joanna*

> One afternoon out of boredom I made a tape of two stories: *Cloudy with a Chance of Meatballs* [Barrett] about a town far, far away that rains food for the people to eat, and *Cinderella* about an unhappy girl who becomes a princess. I taped them and

then I took the tape to school for my friends to listen to. They all told me they liked it.

Carrie

When I was little I read (or my mother read to me) a lot of books *Cat in the Hat* [Seuss], the *Babar* [Brunhoff] books, *Too Much Noise* [McGovern], and *Did I Ever Tell You How Lucky You Are?* by Dr. Seuss. I liked them because they took me to different imaginary places.

Chris

I first learned how to read when I was four. My father used to read me a story called *Little Red Riding Hood* [Grimm]. I used to love that book so much that I memorized it. And to tell my father how much I loved it, I used to read it all the time to *him*. Very soon he got bored of it and bought me all these books leveled 1–10. Level one was really easy because it had ten pages and most of them had drawings on them. Level ten was really hard because they had no drawings and a hundred pages of hard words. Most of the books were about kids' problems.

Erin

Students not only dip into their story memories, they become reflective about how parents, teachers, librarians, and other adults interacted with their younger selves. These reflections will enrich their development as people who will one day have children of their own or work with them in community organizations and schools.

After we find our stories we realize that we don't have to learn them. We may have to spend a little time brushing off the moss and dirt and roots that have attached themselves to our memories over the years, but their essence already belongs to us. We see their images and recall their sounds; we don't think of them in words so much as in scenes. Even if obscured or less than entire, what is within us we have already learned "by heart" as Jeannine Laverty says.

In my own work with stories, I have found it invaluable to continue to trace these bits of lore—all containing knowledge of narrative structure—stored within me. Some were given to me by family members who read or sang or talked to me, and some came from the "daytime dramas" I watched with my grandmother. I can still feel the sadness of Mike Carr's wife Sarah's death on "The Edge of Night." For weeks I pretended to be the doctor who saved her. Saturday morning cartoons and drama series such as "Sky King," "Flicka," and "Zorro" also filled me with story, and, of course, Disney movies and the Sunday funnies. I wasn't much of a comic book reader but adult students testify to how much they learned about stories from those.

Digging up my buried stories has taught me that I choose to treasure and remember certain ones, or sometimes just a specific image from a story, for important reasons. Images stuck with me as a child because in some way they were *about me*. I longed to hear the fairy in "The Pine Tree and Its Needles," say, in the rhythm of my mother's voice, "You shall have your wish" (Piper 1952). I yearned for certain "Flicka" and "Hardy Boys" episodes to be rerun because they made my heart pound. I played "The Sound of Music" and "Climb Every Mountain" a hundred times on our old record player and then sang them as I flew back and forth on the swings. To some extent I was conscious of the flame those songs lit inside me. Yet I am sure each touched something deep in me, something I didn't begin to understand back when I sang unselfconsciously at the top of my lungs.

I can still picture Heidi running into the arms of her beloved Grandfather just as I did when Mrs. Stocks, my second-grade teacher, read about the little girl returning home from Frankfurt to the snowy Alps. I played that scene in my little-girl fantasies all that year and have found solace in returning to it in the decades since. Exploring these interior images has offered me so much insight that I now urge students at every age to begin their storytelling search by looking at what they loved in the past.

I don't mean to suggest that young students in a school setting, or even adults trying on storytelling, must look closely at *why* they liked certain stories. In the schools I visit the students or teachers sometimes talk about the reasons certain images reverberate with meaning, but most often they just go about digging for what is there. I believe that when we review what touched us at an earlier time—what made us giggle or feel sad or experience a sense of wonder—our current story work has a solid foundation.

When my sixth graders looked back at the stories they liked (it took some convincing to get some of them to admit that they once read "children's stories"), they felt wise and wonderfully nostalgic. They laughed at and cherished their younger selves. They had fun remembering times that otherwise, at age eleven, twelve, and thirteen, they were happy to forget ever existed. Young adolescents long to be people of the world. They know they are not yet adult, but they are certain that they are no longer children. They resist looking back initially, I would guess, because doing so might turn them young again, a fate few would desire despite the angst that accompanies their current age. On the contrary, a trip down memory lane helps them to feel older and wiser, to see the distance they have traveled.

Adult Story Treasures

Adult students, many of whom I meet at teacher conferences, have also traveled with me into story memories.

> A memory I have of a story was *The Adventures of Tom Sawyer* [Twain]. I remember being sick for a few days, being in bed, and my mother reading me a chapter a day. She made the characters seem so real. Her expression was wonderfully theatrical. I begged her to keep on reading . . . just one more page.

> My mother says I wore out a Golden Book of *The Little Red Hen* [Piper] when I was very little, she had to read it so often.

> *Caps for Sale* [Slobodkina]—this book will always stick out in my mind because I saw the filmstrip of the story at the library story hour. This was my first time experiencing a book I knew come to life on screen. I will always remember it. *Winnie the Pooh* [Milne]—I can remember listening to my father read this book (a few pages a night) to my five-year-old brother. I was eighteen—I listened through his bedroom door. I loved to hear my father read. It was a side of him I had never experienced as a child, one I did not know existed.

> There were stories in my childhood—mainly stories told by my father and my grandfather about things they had seen, experienced. I think that they each had a sense of themselves as storytellers. When they told stories, people listened. My grandfather told stories of lumber camps, the mill, and the farm.

He mostly told amusing tales of human foibles, lost dignity, heroism. My father also told stories from his travels—travels around town. He told tales in which he had a leading role—buying warts from the little children he knew, ski racing against well-trained and well-equipped professionals, hoeing corn in a rocky field at the age of sixteen.

Mother read stories, told stories—the best were always in response to "Tell me about when you were little." The favorite was when Van Brunt shot Mother. When Mother had had enough, we heard:

> I'll tell you a story about Jack Anory
> And now my story's begun.
> I'll tell you another about Jack and his brother
> And now my story is done.

Discovering My Story Treasures

The spring my mother retired from teaching first grade after almost forty years, she brought home boxes of workbooks, lessons, and remnants of every kind from her classroom closets. I searched those boxes as if they were treasure chests pulled up from a sunken pirate ship. I was shocked to spot the oversized red fairytale book my mother had given me the year I turned seven. Seeing it, I felt a mixture of joy and uneasiness come over me. I also felt miffed that my mother had "stolen" the very gift she had given me, until it occurred to me that I had already "borrowed" some of my son's books, and he wasn't even grown yet.

At first I just stared at the imprint on the cover, the outline of a boy with a staff in one hand holding the hand of a girl in a fancy pinafore. They were skipping down a road. Some squirrels and a chipmunk ran along too. In bold black letters above the figures I read The Road in Storyland. I felt a shiver as memories came flooding back. This book contained lost pieces of the puzzle of me, a former me, someone I thought long gone who was perhaps still hidden inside the mother, teacher, and storyteller I had become. Images from these tales and the sensations I had felt as my mother read them aloud just before bedtime flooded over me. Some, such as "The Country Mouse and the City Mouse" and "The Shoemaker and the Elves," I had encountered again over the years. Others I had completely forgotten. As I turned the elaborately illustrated pages, my goosebumps multiplied: "The Pine Tree and Its Needles," "The Cap That Mother Made," "The Greedy Woman Who Wanted All the Cakes," and "The Turtle Who Could Not Stop Talking." The experience was like suddenly recalling a string of powerful dreams from the night before.

Oh, yes.

Oh, my.

Each illustration brought back something that I had felt deeply but never spoken about during childhood. There stood the old woman greedily holding tight to her beautiful cakes. I had always felt a mixture of horror and satisfaction when my mother slowly turned the page to reveal the final illustration: the greedy woman transformed by some unknown force, her nose sharpened to a beak, her feet clawlike, and her black dress, white apron, cape, and red cap all turned into the feathers of a woodpecker.

On another page I saw the unhappy pine tree who, ashamed of his needles, wished for leaves of gold, then glass, then the oak's fine greenery, only to discover that none served him as well as his own prickly needles. On still others I saw Midas, Boots, the poor shoemaker, the bunny who lived with his grandmother, and the talkative turtle. Each picture brought back some of the hope and hurt I had felt as a small girl learning to live in the world.

Most of these stories became part of my storytelling repertoire with little or no rehearsal. I knew them already. The hardest part of telling them was trusting myself to go back to what I felt as a child, when I had loved these tales and begged to hear certain ones again and again. My mother's voice had indelibly imprinted their images onto my brain. I looked at them as I would at an old family photograph album: Marygold filled with disbelief as she held the rose that her father, Midas, had turned to gold; the early morning sun angry at being caught in the curious rabbit's trap; the naked elves grinning as they worked the shoemaker's leather late at night. In each "photograph" was a little bit of me.

Unearthing Students' Story Treasures

When I tell students about rediscovering these tales, I point out that I had completely "forgotten" I had known most of them until I saw the book again. I ask students if they can help each other search their memories for stories buried and forgotten. Sometimes, rather than visualizing, we begin by brainstorming lists of titles or even story fragments or images. Sometimes a child will remember a story only a piece at a time. "What's the one about the baby goats getting swallowed by the wolf and their mother uses a scissors to get them out? Oh yeah, then she fills the wolf up with rocks while he's sleeping and sews him back up again. I loved that story!"

As a middle school English teacher, I taught several classes. On a brainstorming day, my first class of the day would list every "story" they could think of that entertained or in any other way engaged them at any point up to the present. Poems, songs, nursery rhymes, television shows—I accepted every suggestion. The time for sifting through the rubble for the perfect story for telling would come later.

When the next class arrived, they read the previous group's accumulated list, and they always laughed, claiming their favorites. Then inevitably they added new names. "What about Rumplestilskin?" "Oh, yeah, I remember *that*." My students also talked about illustrations as well as plot elements and mental images from stories with no pictures. The list inevitably included a mixture of classic stories and others only one or two children could recall: *Cinderella, Snow White, Jack and the Beanstalk*, Frog and Toad stories, *Miss Nelson Is Missing, The Three Bears, Bedtime for Frances, The Rescuers, Jason and the Argonauts, The Velveteen Rabbit*, "Humpty Dumpty," "The Three Little Kittens," *Rikki-Tiki-Tavi, Tikki Tikki Tembo, The Magic Porridge Pot, Puss in Boots, The Five Chinese Brothers*, and *The Twelve Dancing Princesses*. The long lists always amazed my preadolescents, but each year they amazed me less.

My students had no idea that even fragments of so many stories lay buried in their memories. Teachers often say to me, "My students wouldn't be able to make such a list. Their parents [grandparents, teachers, librarians, etc.] just don't read to them." I hear their genuine concern about children who have not been read to, but I don't agree that storyless children exist.

We humans are a storytelling lot. We drink in stories from our walks in the woods, our games on street corners, our small moments with relatives, babysitters, neighbors, and friends. And, yes, we drink in the tales from our electronic tellers—television, videogames, recorded music, and movies. Even if we aren't read to, we are fed stories by the world. Or, feeling a hunger for stories, we grow them in our imaginations and feed them to ourselves. If teachers are willing to be receptive to what is within children, treasures for telling will emerge.

Thinking About Choosing a Story to Tell

My students and I eventually looked at our lists, taking plenty of time to talk about which stories might make good tellings. Among other questions we considered these:

🍃 What stories seem easiest to tell?

🍃 What ones would take some work?

🍃 What might you do to make a story like "The Three Bears," which everyone knows, seem new and appealing?

🍃 Is any story on the list too long for a reasonable telling?

🍃 Can a tale be told in installments?

🍃 Would some stories be too short?

🍃 What could you do with "Humpty Dumpty," "Jack and Jill," and "The Three Little Kittens" to make them tellable tales?

🍃 Could certain nursery rhymes be told just as they are?

Our conversation always fascinated me. Each group pondered different questions.

Students would take their time searching for a tellable story. They might review which stories they remembered well or seek out one they wanted to remember better. They might go home to look at the books on their bedroom shelves or in attic or basement boxes. They might talk with their parents about which stories they remembered reading or telling before bedtime. Maybe their parents would have memories about their own or their children's early attempts at independent reading. Such investigations always provided the students with funny anecdotes about themselves and the first words they could speak and read.

Some would come back bragging, "I fooled my mother. *She* thought I could read, but really I had just memorized the story." Others would smile, knowing they hadn't fooled anyone at all but had been allowed their moment to "read" by wise parents or older siblings. Another benefit of all this conversation was that parents talked about the books they had loved as children. A great deal of family history came out of our story talk.

Again, Please?

I would often tell students of my preschool-aged son Brian's relentless passion for "Play Peter Pan, Mommy?" at bedtime, bathtime, and most exasperatingly during dinner preparations. "You be Wendy. I'll be Peter," the little director would say. When I asked, "Who will be Captain Hook?" Brian frowned as if he feared even the thought of this villainous character. "Oh, you be him too," he announced, sure that his mother would not interfere with Peter's final victory. For my students, that recollection usually brought up memories of dramatizing stories in backyard theaters, in school plays, and in pretend games, and we talked of the phenomenon of wanting a story told over and over again. One boy remembered never getting enough of "Jack and the Beanstalk." A girl had loved "The Little Match Girl" even though it always made her cry. I would tell of the fascination of a friend's daughter for the video "Rudolf the Red-Nosed Reindeer," and some heads would nod knowingly.

I have since begun to ask other teachers and parents about the phenomenon of children wanting a story told again and again. One woman told of how her four-year-old daughter watched a video of the recent film version of *Much Ado About Nothing* repeatedly and pretended to be its characters and "talk Shakespeare." Hearing such stories, I laugh, certain I would have been addicted to *Bambi* had it been available on video during my childhood. My son's early years were pre-VCR, but he listened to records of "Jack and the Beanstalk" and "Pinocchio" till we wore them out.

Follow the Child's Lead

After their investigations at home and at the libraries of their youth, my students would often come to class with copies of picture books. We would talk about the problems illustrations sometimes pose for the teller because they often subtly tell parts of the story not stated in the text. I eventually learned to trust that tellers would find their own ways of overcoming such problems, but these discussions were always valuable.

Some children would bring in elaborate or lengthy texts from fairytale and folktale collections, such as *The Twelve Dancing Princesses*, *The Snow Child*, *The Nightingale*, and *Beauty and the Beast*. We talked about how book versions reflect one writer's retelling of a story but how originally they were told by the folk in their traditional language. Some students delight in learning long or complex versions of stories. Others become frustrated. I have learned to follow each student's lead. In most cases the teller chooses the story he needs most to tell and finds a way to tell it.

Children with relatives who immigrated to America would sometimes tell religious stories or tales of the humble beginnings of famous artists or political figures born in other lands. These became a rich cultural and historical reservoir for us.

Every year at least one child told of being raised on traditional stories: the Jack tales, the Brer Rabbit or Anansi the Spider stories, the feats of Paul Bunyan, the antics of Pecos Bill, stories of Raven or Coyote or Gluscabe, and of course, ghost tales. For students who hadn't heard of Coyote or Anansi, or hadn't realized how many Brer Rabbit tales exist, a whole new world of reading and telling opened up.

We also talked about the place of "story" beyond books. Our lists contained several movie titles, and while we wrestled with my concerns about retelling a movie, students showed me again and again that they had learned important stories from movies and even recordings. We listened to video and audiotapes of storytellers, and some students retold, without rehearsal, stories they had heard from tellers at libraries, festivals, museums, and birthday parties. Many students had never encountered a "professional" storyteller, but they did remember a camp counselor who told ghost stories or a grandparent or older neighbor who told tales of bygone days.

Some students described "homemade" tales. David's father settled him into bed each night with "The Adventures of Davey the Lion." Ralph said he believed every word of his uncle's scary story about a hitchhiker and another one about kids in a graveyard until he found both in a paperback he later encountered. At moments like these, we would talk about the nature of various oral traditions and how stories are borrowed and changed. I have always encouraged students to know and share with listeners the sources of their tales, and I reminded them that even professional tellers did their share of borrowing and that it was all right.

I would tell about my friend, Tom Weakley (1994), known for taking tall tales from many different regions and setting them in Vermont. Listening to Tom, you think he is telling a true tale about a real Vermont character. The next thing you know he has bamboozled you with one whopper of a lie. He gets your goat, and you can't help but laugh.

Just the mention of a ghost story would get students listing the many they knew, and someone's recollection of a family tale would bring up more of those. I might play a storytelling recording, such as Jay Stailey's "Sawhorse Stallions" or one of Jay O'Callahan's Pill Hill stories about a boy growing up on a street in Cambridge where all the doctors lived. Students would begin to see how ordinary events in their lives could make for rich storytelling material. We would observe that everyday family life tales are surprisingly like book tales containing characters, plots, and themes, once you start to see them as narratives. Yet, I would caution students with a grin, "Once life moments turn into stories they begin to shape-shift in big and little ways. Next thing you know they're fiction." At that, some couldn't wait to start telling.

Memory Speaks When We Listen

Our memories of certain tales were blurry at first, but they cleared the more we talked about stories and retold them conversationally in and out of school. Today, working with preschoolers through senior citizens, I've learned that memory continues to speak if we talk and listen to each other.

Sometimes when I visit classrooms, teachers look worried if I get students talking. "Oh, don't let them get started. They'll never stop." At senior groups I will meet a teller who recollects an abundance of detail from childhood or young adult days, but the others roll their eyes when that person begins to speak, as if to say, "There she goes again." Many of us are hungry to be listened to.

I don't believe that talk gets in the way of school learning or that it should be silenced because one person has more to say than someone else. Sometimes we need strategies for limiting their tellings, but mostly what they need is the kind of listening that honors their truths. At storytelling festivals and swaps, which take place around the country, facilitators establish guidelines for those who have gathered to tell. Often these guidelines include a time limit and the facilitator gives the teller a warning signal before time is up. Cautioning young or old tellers to be aware of time is often all that is necessary to keep a swapping session from feeling out of control. Tony Toledo, a storyteller from Salem, Massachusetts, taught me that running a good swap, one in which tellers *and* listeners are honored, takes an honest but gentle invitation to both groups to respect each other and remember that time is limited.

Remembering gets easier with practice. The poet Georgia Heard (1989) writes that poets stay open to catching images that might grow into poems. The same is true for storytellers. They catch bits of memory that might turn into stories. Robert Harris, a teller from Western Massachusetts, taught me once to keep a memory column when taking notes at a workshop or listening to other storytellers or speakers. Now in the margin of my notes or on a small pad I keep in my purse, I record the memories triggered by the tales or comments I hear. A child's recollection of her first visit to New York City reminds me of mine: a visit to my Spanish-American roommate's house at age eighteen, where I was introduced to anchovies and sweet vermouth. A woman's mention of her mother's rules reminds me of my aunts' nickname for my mother, their older sister: Mother Superior. I've continued this practice of listening for memories as I read, take part in conversations, go for walks, and hear speakers and tellers during my travels. Our memories collect our experiences; we need only develop the habit of retrieving them to remind ourselves who we are.

Rereading and Retelling

Teachers can help students build a reservoir of story memories by *rereading* and *retelling* stories. Children will be choosy about the tales they want to hear again, but when the practice of returning to stories becomes established, children jump at the chance to hear certain tales again. In Elena Davis's third-grade classroom at P.S. 123 in New York, I saw a chart-sized list of stories she had read aloud that year. Check marks next to titles showed how many times she had returned to the story, and asterisks showed the number of times a child or group had dramatized or in some way brought the tale to life. The children proudly showed me the list and pointed out which stories they obviously loved the most.

In Kathy Oboyski-Butler's first-grade class in Guilderland, New York, I began to set up some of the books I have learned stories from on the chalk tray. I heard several voices murmuring, and one child, pointing to Robert Munsch's *Love You Forever*, blurted out, "*We know that story already!*" "Wonderful!" I replied, "then you can tell it to me." Right away we decided to divide this favorite into parts, creating a spontaneous story theater production. It was clear to me that the story's rhythms, images, and feelings were theirs for the shaping. The child who took the part of the mother acted out the tenderness of rocking a newborn as well as the silliness of rocking a teenage boy. The little girl who played the teenager looked like a miniature rock star holding a pretend microphone, grooving to "strange music." The class chorused almost every bit of the text along with the leading tellers. Clearly, children can retell and make up stories with little or no rehearsal if they have played and worked in an environment that honors rereading and retelling tales.

In both these classrooms the teacher was excited about books and saw clear reasons for returning to certain ones. Whether her purpose was to familiarize students with certain vocabulary, grammatical constructions, or the architecture of narratives, whether she believed the stories carried important themes or information, or whether the children simply loved the story, the teacher had established the value of returning to a work of literature.

I had lost that value myself until a wise teacher gently returned it to me. Though I had loved hearing my favorite fairytales again and again, somewhere after second grade I discarded the notion that one might find delight in rereading a book. Perhaps I associated it with the childhood I was moving beyond. Then in tenth grade I overheard Ms. Butler, our young and lively English teacher, say to some girls, "We'll be reading A Tale of Two Cities. I can't wait to read it again." Horrified at the thought, I blurted out, "They make you read it over every year?" She laughed and reassured me that she reread it because she enjoyed it. "It's a love story, you know." I pondered her reply over the weeks I struggled through Dickens in search of that love story. Her delight in rereading has stayed with me for years.

Tales Housed in the Library

After my students had searched their bookshelves and memories for stories, some knew the ones they planned to tell. Still, I wanted them to be aware of other possibilities for tales so we headed for the library. In the end, about half my students decided to tell a tale from our memory search and about half chose to learn a story from scratch. I usually spent one or more class periods just reintroducing students to the 398.2 section of the school library. In middle school at that time, few teachers used that section of the library. Over the years librarians had purchased collections of Anansi tales from Africa and the Caribbean, Jack tales from Appalachia, Norse and Mayan myths, Cherokee and Inuit tales, and more, but readers rarely signed them out. When I "found" storytelling as an adult, I had very little knowledge of folk literature myself except for the stories in my red book and the Greek myths I had met under duress back in ninth-grade English.

With the help of wonderful librarians, who gave book talks about some of the collections—admittedly not easy reading for some of my twelve-year-olds—I would try to give my classes a sense of the wealth of folk literature from around the world. I shared my own sense of wonder at discovering tales from so many other lands. Some students jumped in. They had enjoyed returning to the tales of their early childhood, and they wanted to explore new territory now. Some were fascinated by tales written in dialect. Others were amazed at the many creation myths from different cultures. Still others found the behavior of gods and other mythical characters "weird." My reaction in ninth grade had been similar, I admitted, explaining that back then the myths contained little more than names and events to memorize for a test. Today, however, I saw the lives of the mythic characters as symbols of the struggles all people face. I promised to help students find their own meaning in what might appear to be "strange" stories. Betty Rosen's (1988) book *And None of It Was Nonsense*, lively writing about introducing the power of ancient stories, helped.

I never tried to sell any students a story that clearly didn't interest them. We simply read excerpts aloud to each other, talked with the librarian about her knowledge of tales, and discovered whatever treasures we could find on those dusty shelves. The librarians reserved certain collections for us over a period of about two weeks, so students continued to return to browse, sample stories, and talk with the library staff, each other, and me about what they had found.

Today, with the resurgence of interest in folk literature, beautifully illustrated versions of folktales and myths from many lands crowd the shelves of bookstores, inviting young readers in a way that the pictureless collections in my school library didn't. I can't keep up with the ongoing supply but know of many by reading the *Horn Book* and other periodicals that review and discuss children's literature. Because of their art work and the limited amount of text on each page, these picture books were more appealing to my middle school readers than thick anthologies. Unfortunately, most middle and high school libraries steer away from purchasing picture books because these books appear to be for young children only. Although my students' interest in folktales convinced our librarians to order a selection, my visits to secondary schools tell me that this practice is not an easy one to change.

FOUR

Choosing a Tale to Tell and Learning to Listen Well

nce children realize how many tales are available, the task of choosing a story to tell can become easy or troublesome. Some have an instant certainty. Others find that picking one is like choosing one piece of candy from the glass display case in a candy shop. For still others, especially if they are tense about performing, commitment to any story is difficult.

When I ask students to select a story for telling, my main advice is to choose one that matters to them. Some tend to pick what they believe will please the teacher or visiting storyteller. Some choose what they think will entertain their friends or please their parents. Those reasons work if the story grabs them too. I advise them that it must take them by the hand (or the throat) and say, "Tell me." They laugh at this, but in time they at least half-seriously admit, "It told me I had to tell it."

Sometimes, looking for the easiest route, students grab something short or familiar but not particularly important to them. Eventually they discover their mistake. While others are working with the stories they love, experimenting with telling styles, and having great fun playing with voices and faces, those who have not chosen well become bored or frustrated.

In an attempt to prevent false starts I tell students about others who have had similar problems in choosing well. George was one of the few kids who resisted looking back at tales he had liked at an earlier age, and he didn't put much effort into browsing through the various books of myths, legends, and folktales we collected. He wasn't a strong reader and kept complaining that the stories were "stupid." Remembering my own youthful distaste for lengthy written versions of Greek myths, I sympathized—briefly. I tried summarizing some tales I thought he would like and offered him tape recordings of various tellers. When it came time to commit to a story, however, George just shrugged and said he would tell "Little Red Riding Hood." He guessed he liked the wolf and the idea of "tricking the girl and the grandma."

I worried that he needed more than his connection to the wolf for his telling to be successful. A tale so familiar to listeners demands newness—or at least high energy—from the teller. George didn't seem able to promise either. Most middle school tellers figure this out without ever being told. If they select something as common as "The Three Pigs" or "Goldilocks and the Three Bears," they usually do a spoof to make it interesting or exaggerate the characters in some unusual way.

George was one day away from his scheduled "final" telling. He had half-heartedly completed our rehearsal tasks, but I could see that he didn't want to risk trying a take-off, nor did he seem to be getting much satisfaction from telling the story straight. The day before he was scheduled to tell his story he asked to switch stories. I allow students to exchange one story for another at any point *if* they show evidence that the new tale is a better choice. (No jumping ship without a life raft.) George approached me hesitantly but with a kind of energy I hadn't seen previously. "I remember a story I heard in fifth grade when some storyteller came. I just found a book of it. The book's not the same, but it helped me remember what I heard. *Please* can I switch? I promise I'll be ready." George's *The Stonecutter* took our breaths away. I recognized bits from the version told by a local teller I knew, yet I could see that George had made the story his own. Although I was surprised that he managed to get so comfortable and tell quite dramatically after just deciding the day before, he reaffirmed my belief that selecting a story that matters makes all the difference. I also saw irony in George's choice of *The Stonecutter*, a tale about wishing to be someone other than who one is and then finding merit in being oneself.

Many students struggle in making their choice, and I encourage that struggle. We take our time exploring possibilities, and everyday I ask them to jot the reasons they are considering or eliminating a story so they can get to the heart of what is important to them. One boy had discovered the character of Anansi. He was fascinated that there were many Anansi tales, but he couldn't find the story that definitively said, "Tell me." He decided to return to a Brer Rabbit tale he had loved as a young child. The experience of exploring and dramatizing a tale he already knew helped him begin to see the connection between the two tricksters, but he didn't find the right Anansi story that year. What he did find was an admiration for the spider whose web spread from Africa all the way to the Americas. I have no doubt that in time, when he begins to see a reflection of himself in Anansi's character, a tale that matters will find him.

Learning Logs

In the early years when I offered the oral reading unit that eventually grew into the storytelling unit, I paid less attention to student choice. Intuition more than informed belief made me stress that students needed to like the work they chose. It seemed obvious. Once story-telling became a significant chunk of our language arts work, I introduced the practice of keeping a learning log, partly to help students think through the act of choosing. Initially, I wanted students to write during what was otherwise an oral language unit, but the log became much more than just a place to do some writing. It evolved into a valuable record of students' thoughts about choosing, shaping, and rehearsing stories. By the end of the unit they had written about their thinking or their reactions to almost every aspect of storytelling.

As we were reading and choosing, I very casually posed a number of questions for reflection. Some students answered every query, while others wrote briefly about only those questions that interested them. Each class's log responses differed according to how their choosing was progressing. I didn't want the writing to be a chore or to seem like busy work; I was interested in what was going on in their minds. When we shared log responses aloud, they could discover each other's strategies.

Among the questions I asked at different times were these:

✒ Describe your process as you've looked for a story to tell. Have you mostly looked through books you own? talked with relatives? read library books? sought out stories from your earlier years in school? Who, if anyone, is helping you make your decision?

✒ Did watching videotapes of tellers or listening to audiotapes in class influence the kind of tale you wanted to choose? Which ones did you like best? Do you have a sense that what you saw or heard another teller do will affect the way you tell your story?

✒ Did the librarian's book talks give you an idea for a story or show you how to tell one in an engaging way? In what ways was our time in the library of value to you in general?

✒ Where are you now in your decision-making process: all set? torn between two tales? totally confused? (If you aren't close to a choice, try to say what bothers you about a certain tale or what you think is making you hesitate to choose.) What could you do to get some help if you are undecided?

✒ If you have already settled on a tale, what is there about this tale that makes you think it is the one for you? Are you considering whether to make your telling participatory? Have you considered using a prop of any kind, or a musical or rhythm instrument? Will you stage the telling in any way? Does your story lend itself to standing? sitting? Do you need help in making a very short story longer or editing one that is many pages long? (See Figure 1.)

I must stress that my questions to each class came directly from the work we were doing at that moment. I would never ask every

Figure 1 *Log assignments*

1/28	Experiences you/family have had with storytelling.
1/29–2/1	Eavesdrop and watch—describe people in the act of telling stories.
1/30	Jay Stailey tape—"Cowboys" and "Sailing"/"The White Horse Girl and the Blue Wind Boy."
2/1	Writing a personal moment (detailed) after hearing Annie Dillard's snowball scene from *An American Childhood*.
2/5	Make a list of favorite childhood stories you remember hearing (told or read).
2/6	Your thinking about choosing.
2/8	"The Crack of Dawn" and other video reactions.
2/11	Might have a "Why I'm choosing this story" entry.
2/12	List/sequence of events.
2/12–15	What I learned by…
2/15	Mapping the story.
2/25	Visualize story beginning. Write what you discovered—visualize beginning/middle/climax/end.
2/26	Partner telling.
2/26	Mirror practice/tape practice.

What was it like to tell the story in front of the group? Surprises? Easy/hard—why? Go back inside the memory.

---

question of any one group. My point was to raise the level of thought students put into choosing and to get feedback on my teaching strategies and students' understanding. Later in the unit, after various rehearsal activities, such as listing the story's key events, exploring one or more characters, connecting the story's tension or events to those in our own lives, and so on, I asked questions about the teller's sense that the story felt "ready" to tell. I never wanted students' writing about their internal work to get in the way of their enjoyment of the story. I threw out these log prompts one—or a few—at a time.

Learning From the Logs

Holly let me in on her planning. "I think that for my second telling I will do the poem 'The Highwayman,' but I want to cut out a little . . . I don't really want to copy anyone, but I sort of got the idea from *Anne of Green Gables*." Holly didn't end up reciting that poem for her second try at storytelling, but later in the year during a poetry unit she quite dramatically recited "Casey at the Bat," much to her classmates' amazement and delight. I found it interesting that a fictional character's rendition of a lengthy narrative poem helped Holly consider taking on such a task.

From Beth's log I learned that she was mostly worried about length. She didn't say why but kept referring to stories that were "too long." Reading her entries reminded me to show students how a long story could be made shorter by finding its skeleton, or basic structure, and eliminating literary detail. Many students wrote, "I want my story to be funny." As I have discovered, the way a tale is told is often the secret to making it funny. Such entries showed me that we needed to explore as a group what makes a performance funny. We ended up considering the pace of delivery, unexpected moments, teller asides, repetition, exaggeration, and other aspects of humor.

I wanted students to consider their own enjoyment first in choosing a particular tale, but I also tried to tactfully suggest that they consider their audience too. Holly did that, I believe. It's possible to "wow" listeners with just about any work if you put your heart into it and work to engage them through eye contact and pacing. However, some pieces, in all honesty, just work better than others. While it is entirely possible to engage a group of twelve-year-olds in "The Highwayman" if you tell it well, I think Holly sensed that what was appreciated in Anne of Green Gable's time might not be accepted in hers. Students sometimes surprise me in the way they take to a performance, but overall, if the teller is well prepared and engages the audience through her own love of the story, any story can work. One day, Owen South, a retired colleague, came into my class and masterfully told Edgar Allan Poe's "The Tell-Tale Heart," but I have also seen students tune that story out when the speaker doesn't have command of Poe's language or a sense of the time listeners need to make the images in their minds.

Some students picked a story that they loved but the audience wasn't ready for, and they just didn't have the experience to pull it off. I understood that problem well. Once in my college oral interpretation class, I read John Dryden's poem "A Song for St. Cecilia's Day, 1687" about Orpheus taming the beasts with his music. The reason I chose such a poem? We had sung a choral arrangement of it during my senior year in high school, and finding the poem in my English literature anthology had soothed my freshman homesickness. I thought if I read it well, everyone would hear the music I heard (that of Orpheus and of my high school chorus). I was wrong. "What the heck was that?" and "Why on earth did you pick that?" Our kind and generous teacher jumped all over the naysayers and helped me save face, but in all honesty, I hadn't been very realistic about my audience. I had spoken classical music to kids attuned to rock and roll, and the critics had killed me.

Telling my students this story and others like it helped them choose with a sense that they had to consider both their own and the listeners' needs. I emphasized, however, that the audience would most probably value anything they really loved and worked to deliver in an engaging way. Consideration of the audience is important, but the storyteller's, like the writer's, first allegiance must be to the work she feels called to create.

Trusting Children to Choose the "Right" Story

After I have announced that students should choose a story that matters, I have to trust their judgment. The first year I did storytelling, Gautham wanted to tell the original *Curious George* (Rey), about George's coming to America. I discouraged him at first because it seemed to me that the story's essence relied too much on the illustra-tions. I was afraid he wouldn't be able to bring those pictures to life for listeners. But Gautham begged me to allow him to tell it, saying he was sure he could do the story justice. That was all I needed to hear. I even took a photo of him practicing to some cardboard boxes in a corner. I look at it often to remind me of how hard children can concentrate when their work is meaningful. He was "into it" as the kids say. Every moment of his telling came to life. In retrospect, I realize that Gautham *was* George. In school he regularly managed to find himself in the midst of mischief. Also, I believe, his ethnicity at times made him feel different from most of his peers. While George came from Africa, Gautham's family had emigrated from India; he had been born in Schenectady but traveled occasionally to India for family visits. Perhaps in George he found a kindred spirit.

From that experience I learned not to worry too much about illustrations. Even very young children understand that illustrations often tell a part of the story not conveyed through words. In most cases they instinctively know that a storyteller must be both author and illustrator. When a young teller stumbles onto a tale in which illustration seems essential, the problem-solving is actually wonderful to watch.

I remember two examples. Erin, a pretty and popular middle school girl, wanted to tell her favorite picture book, Margaret Wise Brown's *Goodnight Moon*. I feared the "cool" boys would laugh at this beloved rhyme, which was more lullaby than story. But Erin, cool in her own way, had complete confidence that she could do justice to it. She simply introduced the setting and asked the class to imagine a young child before bedtime looking around the room at her treasures and out the window at the moon. Erin's love of Brown's gentle poem melted the hearts of even the toughest boys, or if not, her unquestionable confidence subdued their desire to make fun. Later, it occurred to me that Erin, who seemed to be growing up pretty fast, might just be finding in *Goodnight Moon* a way to hold on to her childhood a little longer.

In a school I visited, a sixth grader worked on a telling of a "Sesame Street" book in which Grover pleads with the reader not to turn the page because of the monster at the end of the book. I remembered my own son's love of the humor in this silly tale. Grover builds a brick wall so the reader cannot turn the page, he locks the page, and he does a number of other things to keep the reader from the feared ending. The problem for the teller, beyond the translation of pictures into words, is how to give some variety to Grover's repetitive begging, "Please don't turn the page. There is a monster at the end of the book!"

The young teller, in rehearsal, was clearly dramatic and creative, but unlike Gautham and Erin, he wasn't so confident that he could make this rather childish book work as a performance for his peers. By then, I was. I had had enough experience coaching student tellers to know that my job was mostly to encourage him and help his teacher believe in his ability. Having watched him rehearse, I could tell that he would pull off this feat once he got before an audience. The day he told his goofy tale, teachers and students alike loved it as much as any four-year-old. We saw every antic, and we heard the repeated entreaty spoken, cried, moaned, ranted, raved, screamed, and whispered. We were transported to another place and time.

Choosing a story well does take time, especially when a teacher is first introducing storytelling; various problems inevitably turn up. One year I taught only social studies and limited storytelling to mythology as we studied Ancient Greece. There were plenty of tales to go around, but some stories—"Theseus and the Minotaur" or "Persephone and Demeter"—were popular choices. I explained to students that even if they chose identically worded versions, their tellings would give us a lesson in interpretation and style, and they did. No two tellers approached a story the same way.

The last two years I taught in middle school, I made time for two consecutive rounds of tellings because I had seen so many benefits result from our work. The second selection process was much easier. Students had learned a great deal from watching the first round. Many had picked out their second choices before we had even finished the first set, and most had already gathered a wealth of material. They all seemed to have a keen sense of how storytelling works.

Can a student make a poor choice? Sure. But that depends on the way a teacher looks at learning. In Chapter 13 I address some of the problems storytellers encounter and the subject of "critiquing" storytelling. Basically, I see the teacher's role as encourager, helping tellers or writers of any age to continue to learn without leaving them feeling they have "failed." Some tellings shine more than others, but every story selection will lead to both the teller's and the teacher's growing understanding of how to choose well.

Teaching Listening

Children are asked to listen a great deal in school. It is a place for taking in. Even the giving back too often takes the form of a one word or one sentence response. School doesn't offer children many chances to be listened *to*. One problem, of course, is the ratio of teachers to children: so few of us, so many of them. Some children might find a good listener on the playground, or maybe in the library or the nurse's office, but many never get "heard" in school. Another problem is that the old "wisdom," "Children should be seen and not heard," still lingers with many adults. They grew up deprived of respect for their own child-voices and have no idea what it would be like to listen with reverence to a child.

If you aren't listened to, you don't learn the art of listening. You might be *coerced* into listening through scoldings or glaring looks, but coercion doesn't engender a desire to listen. When I teach storytelling, I try to help children experience the joy of listening to stories, as when one listens to beautiful music. Yet I ask them to step into the responsibility of listening as well, to see it as an art to be practiced with care, as an offering of respect to another human being.

We begin to talk about listening when we tell stories spontaneously or when everyone rehearses at the same time. It is actually quite simple, but it is a step that I can forget even now if I'm not careful when I meet a new group of children. If I ask them to turn to a partner after a visualization or after I tell a story to elicit theirs, I need to remember to say, "Please just listen for the *full* three minutes while your partner talks. Nod or smile or look confused as you naturally would, but let them talk. If they get quiet, keep giving your full attention. Maybe say back briefly what you heard; that usually gives them a moment to think of more to say. But let the focus of storytelling stay on them and see how well you can listen. When three minutes are up, I will tell you to switch."

It *is* possible for all the children in a room to talk at the same time. I usually observe this talk for at least the first few minutes until I see that everyone is engaged in telling and listening. I see my job as a combination of benign crowd control and demonstration. If everyone is talking, I eavesdrop on various conversations and model attentive listening. Or I may move toward a twosome that looks "finished" to help them see what else they could say. "So, what came up for you?" is often enough to get them recounting their stories and adding to their initial versions. If a child seems frustrated by the fact that so many others are talking, I show him how to fully focus on one face and voice in order to tune out the other voices. Most children can easily ignore the sounds of others, as they might on the playground or when absorbed in a book or a television program. Some younger children are startled by the din of many voices, so with little ones I make a point of mentioning before we begin that soft voices and, even more important, looking into the eyes of your partner, are essential.

My middle schoolers and I talked about the expressions on the faces of audience members that help a teller stay in the story when she is before a group. A genuine nod of affirmation, a look that says "Yeah, I get this" or even one that says, "I'm not sure what you mean" lets a teller know you are with her. A hearty laugh or an "ah" in response to a line of description or dialogue helps the teller know her tale is working. The teller needs the audience's faces and verbal responses. This is not to say that listeners should fake a response, but often the gift of our listening, despite the teller's hesitation or lack of skill, builds her confidence, and the story gets better as she goes on.

In their logs students would write about how even one friendly face "kept me going." They would mention distractions too. Listeners accustomed to television, movies, rock concerts, and lecture hall professors, tend to think they are invisible in an audience and can clean out a notebook or whisper to a friend without being seen. But no one is invisible to the storyteller. We would share such thoughts from both the teller's and listener's points of view. Listeners would help tellers know they needed to look at their audience to help them stay with the story. We would talk about the courage eye contact takes and about its relation to emotion, especially confidence. We recognized the teller's responsibility to keep going, to stay with the story and ignore distractions. I would tell about my own experiences during shows with fussing children and rude adults and explain that I had learned to look for the supportive faces in a crowd or to direct part of the story toward a distracted listener to bring him back.

As teacher, I realized that I had to model the kind of listening I expected from students. That meant letting go of student distractions that might otherwise have caught my attention. Sometimes I would take notes on a student's telling as I listened, the way my college oral interpretation teacher had, but when I did, I maintained the stance of an enthralled listener not of a judge looking for errors. I watched for the teller to excel and then jotted a word or phrase to help me remember. At the story's end I marveled at every nuance of artistry and in doing so taught my students to look for each other's finer moments. Other times I put down my pen and let a story completely pull me in because I wanted students to see that kind of listening too.

Students would note that listening well is intensive and tiring, and I agreed. I taught them how to take a brief "inattentiveness" break without bothering any other listener or taking up a distracting activity, reminding them that the teller still sees them clearly even when they tune out. I also warned them that the price of inattention could be missing important moments of the story, perhaps adding to the teller's nervousness. We noticed that having patience with nervous tellers and staying with them helped them improve quickly. Listeners learned to tolerate each other's struggles as well as watch for each other's strengths.

I encourage tellers to look at the audience as much as possible, but I never grade eye contact or criticize a student who is having trouble maintaining it. I have learned through my own experiences with adults that even for "expert" tellers, the emotional work of getting into a story and staying there makes eye contact difficult, especially during a first telling. Eye contact adds a layer of intensity in the dance between teller and listeners. If a teller gets comfortable with a story, offering it to each member of the audience is quite a thrill, but that might not come till a third or tenth telling. Rather than fault tellers for not making eye contact, I just provide them with as many chances to see it as I can. Usually, they improve as they get more comfortable with their stories and see others looking back delightedly.

Jack wanted to tell about Medusa. He was one of those good talkers I thought would shine during the storytelling unit, but unfortunately he never actually learned the facts of the tale. I think he mostly liked the idea of Medusa's snakey hair turning people to stone. A master at looking as if he were working during rehearsal activities, he got up to tell his story and in moments it was clear that he didn't know it well enough to fake it or clown his way through it. He bombed. No one shot tomatoes, but his ego took a blow. Later, he and I spent some time together learning about the Three Grey Women and their single eye, the gifts of the Nymphs, and the other details of Perseus's adventures so he would have the basic sequence of the story.

I didn't want storytelling to leave a bad taste in Jack's naturally talkative mouth, so I took him along with students who had volunteered to tell stories at a local elementary school. I watched him with a fourth-grade class. He still spoke from an emotional distance and with a somewhat shaky voice, but he got the sequence right despite some hesitation. He made little eye contact with his listeners but this was because he was focusing on seeing the story in his mind. I didn't get to observe his next two tellings because I was standing in the hall, but in a while, Jack emerged from a third-grade room with a look of triumph on his face. "I told them the story was scary in my introduction," he said, "and the teacher said we could turn off the lights. *They loved that!* Then I just talked real slow so they would get what was happening, and I told 'em how Perseus was invisible because of the helmet, and how Medusa's head would've turned him to stone if he hadn't polished his sword . . . It was great! I had them right in the palm of my hand." Jack held out his hand. "Turned 'em to stone, eh?" Jack just grinned. He had found the power in looking directly at the audience. I think he also learned that he can ask for help when a task is difficult. He certainly taught me something about how a student's struggles can go unnoticed.

Asking students to write in their logs or talk about which scenes had touched them or what kinds of artistry they had noticed in each other's tellings helped them develop as listeners. Active listening made them more conscious of the choices storytellers make. Yet I wanted them to experience the aesthetic *pleasure* of listening for its own sake and the sensation of really being listened to. For the teller, telling a story to a truly engaged listener is exciting and empowering, if a little frightening at first. And for the listener there is an excitement and a power in being pulled into the world of the tale, especially by a peer.

Ten-year-old Tanya seemed to be honoring herself as she told the story of being eight and seeing her first baby cousin. "Can I hold her? . . . I can do it standing up," she told her aunt with a touch of both timidity and daring in her voice. The eyes of every child in the room fixed on the scene Tanya created. Their faces told me that they identified with both her caution and her certainty as she spoke and held her arms out to accept the fragile infant. Judi, another fourth grader, described in her newly learned English the details of her first sleepover. She bragged about how she played the Spanish teacher during a game of school and how the others begged her, "No, don't go to sleep yet!" I couldn't help thinking her listeners saw their classmate with new eyes. Not only did their minds actively create the scene Judi described but they saw her as like themselves, despite her unfamiliarity with English. They identified with her by remembering feelings associated with their sleepovers or chances to play "Teacher" with their friends.

For too many years I tried to teach listening by demanding it. I got children to be polite to each other and to me, and undoubtedly I taught some to listen that way. But when we listen to each other's stories we listen to hear our feelings spoken by others, to hear characters we knew well brought to life, to return to our childhoods and look toward our futures. It is a whole different kind of listening.

FIVE

From Performing to Telling

t first, my own work developing stories and the inclusion of storytelling in my teaching focused primarily on *performance*. The workshops I attended basically promoted the refinement of performance skills, which was fine with me, because I'd always enjoyed dramatics but had never found time for community theater. Also, I had never liked auditioning. As a child I had known enough competition in the realms of swim meets, school grades, and sibling rivalry to last me a lifetime. I also liked the personal control that storytelling offered. I could become any and every role I wanted: actor, director, and producer all in one. And I didn't have to be sad when the play was over. I had grieved the loss of community (and probably the feeling of stardom) after every show during childhood and even at the end of the one local play I had performed in as an adult. But in storytelling, you never have to say good-bye to a work you love. It filled my need for a performance art in my life.

Naturally, I took a performance focus for my students. The oral interpretation assignments from my college years, basically graded performances, were my model for the storytelling unit. I believe students at every age need opportunities for dramatic play, and our school didn't have an established drama club. Occasionally teachers would volunteer to give one a try, and lots of students would show up at the first few meetings, but the effort to put on a full-length play or keep even an improvisation group going was enormous. I figured that storytelling would give at least the students in my four classes the chance to explore dramatics, and maybe storytelling would catch on with other teachers if word got around. So for a while I focused strictly on performances in my English classroom. Then a number of experiences led me to see storytelling in a new light.

The Problem with Teaching Acting

First, I noticed that my students were trying too hard. In my attempt to help shy and self-conscious students, I had modeled exaggerated gestures, facial expressions, and character dialogue. "Make the story *big!*" I heard a boy say, echoing my words as he responded to another's rehearsal. Like a scolding parent whose words come back as the child chastises his teddy bear, I felt terrible. This wasn't a generic message I wanted to pass along. Yet sure enough, the students who were really dramatic, the ones whose stories were already "big," picked up on my exaggerated movements and overplayed their stories.

I understood being overly dramatic all too well. I was quite aware of moments when tellers, including me, were just trying too hard. "Less is more," a friend and fellow storyteller had once told me after watching me dramatize "The Mountain Whippoorwill." "Don't forget that it is a *poem.*" It took a while to translate what he meant, but I came to understand that listeners need room to make sense of a story in their own way, especially in the case of a poem. A teller doesn't need to bash them over the head with her interpretation and "acting."

Another time, I tried to correct the habit new storytellers have of looking only at me or at one trusted friend while speaking. "Look at the audience slowly before you begin. Find a few faces sprinkled throughout that will support you." The next thing I knew, some students were scanning the audience in a forced, artificial way that was just as distracting as the earlier problem. In addition, I attempted to help tellers place conversing characters in a scene. Using an example from Arnold Lobel's Frog and Toad stories, I showed students how to turn from one character to the other so the audience could imagine the two facing each other as they conversed. I also suggested that they keep in mind the difference in height between the taller, somewhat wiser Frog and the smaller, more childlike Toad. After watching a few children leap from character to character with bobbing heads, which made us laugh but distracted us from the story, I knew another kind of instruction was called for.

Other young tellers had just the opposite problem. On the playground with friends they were naturally dramatic, but performance paranoia set in once they walked through the classroom door. I decided maybe we needed to look at *real* storytelling, not like what the professionals on videotapes did but the kind we experienced in our lives. Perhaps we would benefit from noticing how naturally people tell stories every day.

Seeing Storytelling Everywhere

I assigned people-watching for homework. Students were to catch others in the act of storytelling. "Watch how people use their faces and their bodies, their movements and their stillness, when they tell a tale, right in the middle of a conversation. Listen for variations in people's voices," I said. "Remember, no one rehearses lunchroom or busride conversations. People just tell stories from their lives; their feelings help them find the words for that moment's version. They may exaggerate. They may entertain. They may have told the story before and figured out what makes it entertaining, but unless they become overly self-conscious, there should be a naturalness to their telling."

I also asked students to think about the people they consider "good" storytellers in this "natural" sense. "Do you have friends who recreate moments in class or events from the playing field? Do you have a relative or neighbor or family friend who everyone agrees is a good storyteller? Find out all you can about 'natural' storytelling in the world."

Jarka wrote in her log: "The person in my family with the most experience in storytelling is my mom. When she lived in Czechoslovakia she was a kindergarten teacher. Naturally teachers have to tell stories to keep the children entertained. My dad has not had that much experience with storytelling, but he has had some . . . My dad changes his voice and uses his hands a lot, and it really makes you listen to him and not pay attention to anyone else. My grandmother changes the volume of her voice and uses her hands also. I usually use my hands and sometimes even use an accent. I think that accents not only pull you into the story but they make it fun to listen to and fun to do. Whenever I tell a story I always try to use an accent . . . All of my family knows how to keep people paying attention to them. I think that the most popular way that they keep their audience is by using their hands."

Meghan wrote: "The teller I listened to made me picture the story in my mind." Beth noted: "My friends keep our attention by imitating people and acting funny." Many students simply described the stories they had heard or heard about. Beth added, "My mother's parents told her stories about growing up in the Depression and also what it was like living during World War II. My grandfather told stories about being in the war and my grandmother tells stories about what it was like living in New York City during the war."

Anne wrote about her dad telling Bible stories: "He tells them so we really get interested and don't want him to stop." Alex observed, "When announcers on TV tell about the game they usually have a deep clear voice. They make everything interesting." He added, "When my dad talks at the dinner table we listen. He uses his deep powerful voice. When he gets mad at *me*, everyone pays attention."

At first I didn't think the assignment had accomplished what I had hoped for. They might have been thinking about natural storytellers, and observing them, but I wasn't sure they were becoming conscious of all the "hows" of everyday telling, the techniques people apply without even thinking about them.

I tried something else. I told a story about a minor childhood trauma, the time I dived off the high board, at age "four and three quarters," and hit the water flat on my back. That generated spontaneous storytelling about other swimming pool mishaps, playground accidents, and more. We simply began recollecting the unforgettable moments of life and started telling stories with no rehearsal at all. Just by observing each other we were able to make note of many aspects of natural storytelling, and we saw that it doesn't have to mean performing.

What I eventually came to understand was that noticing natural storytelling and trying our own conversational tales helped us *relax*. We let go of much of our anxiety about performing. We had all seen people of every age just giving stories away—blurting them out because they had to be told. By observing the naturalness of everyday story-telling, we started to notice which storytellers on audio and video-tape seemed most natural when they were performing. We were gaining a new perspective about storytelling and about performance art in general.

We had each chosen to tell our stories because they mattered to us. Our prepared stories reflected our deepest selves in the same way that our cafeteria and hallway tales or our bus and playground gossip reflected our questions, struggles, and desires. About the latter we had never stopped to ask, "Am I telling this well?" We simply looked for response from our listeners at the moment of telling. We got feedback from their faces and adjusted our style of telling to make ourselves understood. We might have wanted to be entertaining or to evoke a feeling of empathy, but we managed that without really practicing. The secret was staying connected to the story and to the listener. In conversation that connection usually comes quite naturally. Students noticed that some people don't listen, don't connect, when they talk to each other, and those insights added to our work as well.

Just becoming aware of each other as storytellers, of the stories we had heard from friends, family members, TV characters, or people in public places helped us become better tellers. We stopped trying so hard to act out our stories. Just as infants mimic the talk they hear, proficient speakers sometimes imitate what they see and hear around them. But unlike infants, who copy sounds and words indiscriminately, my middle school students were quite clear about what they wanted to imitate. Each found a style that was partly original and partly borrowed but which felt natural or right. I realized my job was not so much to teach strategies, such as scanning the audience or placing the characters, as to help each young teller find the way that best fits him.

Just as I had encouraged all of the children to choose a story that mattered personally, I could trust that they would find a style of telling that fit them uniquely. I had learned years before to honor student differences as I taught writing. Now I was rediscovering that idea as I "taught" storytelling.

Be Dramatic? Not Me!

Another problem with my focus on performance became clear in my teacher workshops. Hoping to encourage teachers to give storytelling a try, and hearing the echo of voices from childhood to "put your best foot forward," I started most of my workshops with my most well-rehearsed stories. Teachers seemed to enjoy my performances of tales and poems I had learned long ago and of folktales I had newly discovered. They seemed genuinely interested in the story of my rediscovery of this art and in my anecdotes about student tellers. In most workshops the teachers seemed to have fun unearthing their own storybook memories and recollecting personal experience tales. They shared them with a partner or a small group of listeners without hesitation. Yet I often sensed a reluctance in many participants to retell their stories to the entire group. At first I assumed that it was because many didn't know each other. Then I started running into workshop participants sometime later, maybe at another teacher gathering, and when I asked, "How's it going? Have you tried some storytelling?" I would hear something like, "Well, not exactly. I haven't decided what story I want to tell yet," or "I'm still *thinking* about it," or "Oh, *I'm* no storyteller. I just came to hear *your* stories."

I soon figured out that my *performing* was leading many teachers to view storytelling as something they would never do—or at least not without lots of training. They were comfortable having a conversation with a partner or two across the table. In their classrooms, they felt secure reading aloud with children or staging class plays, but they had the impression that this thing called storytelling was demanding and scary.

The culprit? Stage fright, or what I think of as the public speaking and performing baggage many of us carry around from our own store of embarrassing moments. Even those of us who have had good per-forming experiences still feel tremendous nervousness when it comes to speaking publicly in front of peers and colleagues. Storytelling is a performance art, my workshop participants told themselves. It requires a naturally dramatic personality. If they didn't see themselves as dra-matic, they figured storytelling was better left to the visiting artist, someone with the "talent" for it. In my workshops I had *promoted* storytelling as natural, as what the storyteller Leo J. Kwiatkowski calls "living-room" telling (personal correspondence), but I had *modeled* it as dramatic or stagelike. Teachers wouldn't tell me directly, "This isn't for me." They may even have gone away inspired to try, but in no time their workshop enthusiasm would be quashed under the weight of an already full curriculum and their own fear of performing.

I began to think seriously about this issue. The last thing I wanted to do was to turn people off to storytelling. How could I help them see that because we are human we're *already* storytellers. How could I invite them to draw from their own natural storytelling skills? If I had needed the little teapot song as a signature "story" as early as age five, and if I had continued unconsciously to find poems and other tales that helped me express my inner self over the years, didn't others have that need as well? Didn't we all need to tell our stories in our own way?

A Continuum From Conversation to Fine Art

One afternoon I saw Cloris Leachman in a stage production of *Grandma Moses* (Pouliot). For most of the play her character talked directly to the audience. Like an old friend, she strode across the stage telling about episodes in her life as an artist. I remember feeling I was in the presence of a lively conversationalist. "*This* is storytelling!" I said, grabbing the arm of the stranger next to me. Leachman, though costumed and grease-painted, surrounded by props and backdrops, and

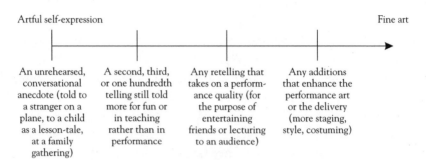

Figure 2 *It's all storytelling*

Artful self-expression				Fine art
An unrehearsed, conversational anecdote (told to a stranger on a plane, to a child as a lesson-tale, at a family gathering)	A second, third, or one hundredth telling still told more for fun or in teaching rather than in performance	Any retelling that takes on a perform-ance quality (for the purpose of entertaining friends or lecturing to an audience)	Any additions that enhance the performance art or the delivery (more staging, style, costuming)	

A person can consider himself storyteller at any point on the continuum. From talk to perform-ance a teller tells. Stories move from left to right because the teller chooses to return to the tale. He may never want to tell it anywhere beyond the kitchen table but it becomes more artful in each retelling, though even a first telling can be quite artful.

clearly working from a script, nevertheless had stepped inside her tale. My seatmate nodded, smiled oddly, and went back to viewing the play.

Watching Leachman "storytell" I could imagine a line of stories from the most casually told conversational anecdotes to the fanciest of rehearsed performances. It wasn't a hierarchy lying on its side, it was a continuum of possibilities (see Figure 2).

I thought about how, without a moment's rehearsal, we embellish stories for perfect strangers. At the grocery store we begin by griping about the long checkout lines and end up swapping hilarious tales about what the kids are probably up to at home while we are trying to get out of the store. People tell stories in hospital waiting rooms, barbershops, and lunch lines, at ballgames, conventions, and funerals. Stories emerge whenever people want to make sense of their lives or offer a moment from their lives as evidence.

The continuum seems a way to convey that storytelling is first of all *natural*—something we all *already* do. While it can be a perfor-mance art, it doesn't have to be. Strangers as well as close friends tell me wonderfully funny and touching stories with little or no hesitation. Such tellers maintain eye contact, use gestures, change the volume and pace of their voices, and do unconsciously what professional tellers work to become aware of. Clearly, humans have storytelling skills. It is our anxiety about performance technique that gets in our way.

On the continuum, a story moves from left to right because we long to return to it. As we retell it, for whatever reasons, we learn about its multiple meanings from the responses of different listeners. We begin to understand its unique and evolving interpretation for our individual lives. We shape the story a little differently in each subsequent telling and perhaps begin to see that, like any narrative, it has a structure. The left side of the continuum represents the most unrehearsed, natural self-expression, yet even a first-told tale is often told artfully. Moving to the right, as we retell and hone and manipulate the tale for different kinds of listeners, we make fine art out of our expressive art. It still might not be a performance per se, but it is artful.

Sharing the Continuum

I began to offer teachers exercises in spontaneous storytelling just as I had my middle schoolers. The teachers told wonderful stories in the workshops with no rehearsal at all, and our talk of the continuum helped them let go of their fear of speaking aloud to the group. By admitting that the last thing I wanted to do was to scare anyone away from storytelling, I encouraged them to become less self-conscious. They began to see their own naturally told stories as evidence of a sophisticated knowledge of narrative and of how to engage an audience. I assured them that their students' stories would also inspire such insights if they listened well and had a little patience.

If the workshop allowed time for teachers to retell their conversational tales to a second listener or to the group, they began to see how naturally revision takes place from a first telling to a second and how the experience of retelling might help students better understand revision in writing. They became aware, as well, of different techniques or styles of telling. One person's story might be straight narration while another's was peopled with lively characters. Some evoked humor through a "dry" delivery while others drew laughs from the tiny and very real details of life that most of us notice but rarely mention. Some found themselves telling a story within a story. Afterward, many teachers admitted that they had felt more naturally dramatic than they imagined they could be. "Telling to one partner helped. Telling to a group of adults—now that's a different story," one teacher quipped. That led a group to discuss how *telling* a story creates an awareness of audience; in writing, in contrast, the writer must imagine the audience.

Thoughts About Stage Fright

One day when revising my workshop handout, I found myself typing in "Thoughts about stage fright." Here is what I wrote: "There are two ways to look at telling: performing and sharing. We've been conditioned to believe that when we perform, our work will be *judged*. Knowing we are being evaluated makes us self-conscious and distracts us, throws us off center. Conversely, when we choose to share something of value, there is joy in the giving. We focus on the recipient, not on ourselves, and there is a spirit of generosity in our action. A well-loved tale can remain a treasured keepsake as it becomes a wonderful gift in the telling."

The idea of letting go of storytelling as a performance to be evaluated and imagining it instead as a gift to be offered occurred to me in that moment of writing. I hoped the image of "gift" would help me address with teachers an issue I knew obstructed my own as well as my students' development as storytellers: stage fright. I'd seen too much of it in my classroom and in my teacher workshops. I knew my own inner fears were mostly the result of old societal messages about "measuring up"—messages that never helped me perform any better as a child or an adult, messages I really didn't have to heed any more.

I was coming to see the telling of stories as self-expression. Whether unrehearsed or retold countless times, oral stories were giving me a window into myself and the children and adults with whom I worked. Students often seemed unconscious of what they were saying about themselves, just as I had been unconscious of what I was saying to myself and the world through the songs and recitations of my childhood. But in my classroom I could feel a power, an unmistakable though often unnamed sacredness, in the moment just after a student's telling. In that moment the teller seemed to be saying silently, "See who I am?" even if she didn't realize she was doing so.

I saw a similar awareness in teacher tellers as they recollected moments from their lives or returned to the fairytales they loved. A simple tale about a father's advice or a child's antics offered both teller and listeners a kind of "ah-ha" when we realized how much that story was saying about life and about us. I am aware of a similar phenomenon as I observe even polished professional storytellers who tell their tales again and again. They too seem to say, "Do you know me—do you know yourselves—a little better through this story?" The idea of storytelling as a gift shifts the focus from the teller to the story offered to listeners.

There is a sense that through our stories we are telling *truths*. We may be telling them through metaphor and symbol, but they are truths nonetheless. In "Killing Me Softly with His Song," Roberta Flack describes a singer who "sang as if he knew me." My middle school students both knew and didn't know each other. They were struggling with the physical and emotional changes of early adolescence. Sometimes they felt painfully alone, yet they shared similar fears, expectations, and enthusiasms. When they listened to each other's stories there was often a collective sigh that said, "Oh, I see that you are wrestling with ———— too." Any of a number of difficulties, such as unattractiveness, the weight of responsibility, unrequited love, and the need to feel powerful could fill in the blank. My middle schoolers had no corner on the desire or the reluctance to be known and understood.

I don't mean to imply that I moved storytelling from performance art to true confession. I simply began to see that once my students and I felt storytelling less as a performance to be evaluated than as self-expression to be shared—in the same way that painting, sculpting, dancing, and making music are considered expressive as well as performance arts—our anxiety about performing lessened. Oddly enough, our storytelling seemed more polished not less.

As our focus shifted away from performing we saw myriad other benefits to our oral language experiences. The literary language of folk-and fairytales offered us new vocabulary and some history of grammar.

Rehearsal activities gave us more awareness of narrative structuring. Improvising and revising orally taught us much about composing. We learned about interpreting literature when we stopped occasionally to argue about a story's meaning, discovering that listeners take away *many* meanings the teller never intends. We did sharpen our performance skills, but that was a by-product of our work, rather than its purpose. My students became much more aware of what made a tale well told, but used that awareness as a way to entertain or mesmerize each other with the stories they loved, not just to get a better grade. After the first few years, I stopped grading storytellings just as I had stopped grading individual pieces of writing. I did give oral comments or written ones by using carbon paper, the way my oral interpretation teacher had taught me. But at the marking period's end, students completed extensive self-evaluations, producing their logs and reflecting in writing on what they had learned. With all of that at hand, we negotiated a grade. My students and I became less self-conscious and more aware of the artistry of our work and its effect. I relinquished my role as drama director and found the multilayered role of storyteacher.

SIX

Personal Stories—One Place to Begin

eeing how my students' experiences during the storytelling unit strength- ened the feeling of community in the room and enhanced so many of our language activities, I decided to intro- duce the idea of telling personal stories on the first day of school in September. Our tales would be informal and spontaneous, and about small but significant moments in our lives. Later, during the storytelling unit, we would make time for recollecting our buried treasures, exploring stories from the library, and rehearsing and shaping tellings. Then we would schedule storytelling ap- pearances with various community groups. The September stories would just warm us up as a community and serve as a foundation on which we could build our work together. I knew whatever story I told would serve as a model to get us started, so I looked for a memory that would tell students something significant about me but remind them I had once been a student too. This is one I told some Septembers.

Every June, when I went to Catholic school, my friends and my brothers and sisters and I faced the dreaded Diocesan Exams, one in each subject. The nuns would threaten us all year with "This information may be on the *Diocesan Exam!*" to get us to pay attention, study hard, and not forget what we'd memorized for weekly tests.

One memory is from fourth grade, the year of the Diocesan Exam Disaster. It was geography test day. Our teacher ceremoniously opened the thick envelope of test booklets and distributed them. When she said, "Begin!" she wrote the current time and the finishing time on the chalk board. I quickly glanced at the entire test, looking at Part II to see the map question. Something was very wrong, and suddenly some children began to make small gasping noises. Even Sister Clement Marie coughed, and when I looked up I noticed that her forehead was all wrinkled and her mouth tight. She got up from her desk. "Continue working," she said, noticing that many of us weren't. We soon realized our test wasn't the only problem, because either a child messenger or a nun from another room came to our door and whispered something to Sister. It turned out that someone—either a diocesan employee or one of our own teachers, we never found out— had failed to order the new series of textbooks for *this* year's geography units. We had studied all the wrong places.

The map question focused on some peninsula near China. "Vietnam?" we all buzzed later on the playground. Francis, the fourth-grade genius, had heard of it but even he didn't know any of the answers. The year was 1961. Our class had mistakenly studied the Iberian peninsula in the old book. We knew all the Spanish and Portuguese seaports, the Mediterranean seasonal climate, and the imports and exports by heart. We didn't find more than one question about Spain on this Diocesan Exam. All that threatening down the drain. We still had to take the test, answering whatever we could. The teacher said, very seriously, that we could guess at the rest. What fun! I can still see everyone grinning at everyone else. Sister laughed too, but her face turned red.

I took my last Diocesan Exam in eighth grade. Every year I looked forward to the part of the English test called the com-po-si-tion. I just loved that regal-sounding word: com-po-si-tion. I always felt smart, rather powerful, during that part of the test. It wasn't about getting the answers right, not really. It was about choosing a topic, deciding which one I had the most to say about, and then saying it. I liked to pick a challenging topic, one I could argue about, or one where I could describe what I saw in my mind. I would look out the window to think it through and list some ideas the way my mother had taught me to organize my thoughts. Then with my fountain pen, in my best Palmer Method script, I would set my thoughts on paper.

In eighth grade I chose the topic "The Famous Person You Most Admire." I sat in the second to last seat near the window and looked out to organize my thoughts. Our teacher that year was a thin, fragile-looking nun. My brothers called her "Fossil" because she was so old and wrinkled. She seemed far away up at her desk in the front. Anne Marie Sugar, my best friend, sat right next to me; her nearness gave me courage. But I worried that whoever graded this test at Diocesan Headquarters probably expected us to write about "famous" people like Marilyn Monroe or Ronald Reagan, movie stars. I didn't admire them. I didn't admire much of anyone "famous." President Kennedy was gone. It was the spring of 1965. I might have written about Martin Luther King, Jr., but in a small town in upstate New York, Dr. King's path and mine had not yet crossed.

I knew the person I wanted to write about but had a feeling the diocesan testers wouldn't consider him "famous" enough. Anne Marie would probably choose a movie star. She read up on the stars in magazines and was always trying whatever new shades of nailpolish and lipstick they recommended. But she would applaud what I wanted to do. I looked up again toward the teacher. She had warned us, "Stick to the topic."

Will I lose enough points to fail this test if I don't choose someone really famous? Oh, who cares? Eighth grade's almost over; next year I'll be in public high school, and they probably won't give a hoot about Diocesan Exams.

Glancing up one last time at Anne Marie (my occasional partner in crime), for a last boost in confidence, I wrote the title: "My Father, the Famous Person I Most Admire." Right away I began to persuade the examiners of my reasoning. "He may not have been famous in the eyes of the world, but he certainly was to the people of Fulton . . . " I looked at my scrap paper list:

built city pool

gave diving and swimming lessons to kids and grownups

annual Elks Swim Show

> director

> clown diving act

> difficult dive exhibition

good skier

Men's Chorus bass

Knights of Columbus

big city junior high vice-principal

working on Ph.D. at Syracuse University

dad of six kids

Yes, he was famous enough. I was sure I could convince them. I would save till the end the part about how he died in a car crash in September on his way home from a faculty picnic in the fog and about how I would never forget him. That would get them. Sister always said to save the strongest point for last.

Composing From the Heart—Beginning a Year Together

When I found that memory it reminded me how little room there had been for my stories in school—or for those of my friends or my teachers. I think I loved that composition exam every June because it offered the only moment of self-expression during an otherwise anxiety-ridden week. The memory also showed me how important it had been for me to express this particularly weighty story. I hadn't been encouraged to tell it anywhere. "Just keep him in your heart and go on" was what the adult world had told me. But I needed to tell his story, both the story of his death and the story of his life. I needed to tell it to myself before it disappeared, as he had, or before I disappeared under the weight of it.

"Throughout this year we'll be sharing stories," I would say each September. Then, after a pause, I would add, "stories from the heart." Some of my new middle schoolers would grimace or roll their eyes. That was fine. I would smile too. I had learned early on that, while most of my young adolescents would resist opening up till they trusted that it was safe, the majority were hungry to speak and write from the heart, of their bewilderment and delight, of their slowly formulating opinions, and of their utter certainties—just as I had been at their age.

Whatever story I told each September would set most of their fears at ease. I would tell about the Diocesan Exams and the eighth-grade girl who saw a composition exam as an outlet for her feelings and a way to rebel against authority. Or I would describe smacking my back on the water after my first high dive. Or I might journey back to my first experience of getting in trouble in school—for *talking*. In that story my public school kindergarten teacher grabbed my arm and yanked me out of the bathroom line, telling me to sit in the classroom till all the others had finished. Why had I talked? To get a daydreamer (who argued with me) to see that it was her turn to "go." That story, a mixture of humor and horror, told from the viewpoint of one who has survived school and now understands how it works (and fails to work), revealed to my students a great deal about their teacher and her values.

Some student would inevitably ask, about whatever story I told, "Is that *true?*" and I would admit that time and repeated tellings might have enhanced the memory. Then I would add that any story contains Truth when told from the heart. Even if exact details are changed or made up because the memory is fuzzy, the story can still contain truth. All our rememberings help us build a bridge between our personal truths and universal truths.

Even if they didn't quite get my meaning, they would see that their teacher remembered being a kid. Like all kids, she experienced episodes of trouble and triumph. Whatever childhood memory I shared would show my newly forming community that the teacher knew about dreams and desires, hurts and humiliation. She could look back at trouble and even laugh at it. I hoped my stories would show them something about my view of *learning,* that it is bumpy but eventually satisfying and, yes, ongoing. Different students would see different messages in the stories, depending on who they were and their feelings about schools and teachers. My story would trigger memories in them, and we would begin our year with storytelling.

Why Begin with Personal Stories?

Beginning the year by sharing recollections shows students that memory is important. Eliciting memory moments establishes that even small experiences carry significance. Not only will we talk and write about memory, but we will interpret it, and recollecting our experiences helps us make sense of the works of others, works of literature, music, dance, art, and architecture. We will also read and talk about the life experiences of authors and other artists, of historical and "famous" figures, of family members, and of the people in our neighborhoods and extended communities in order to draw conclusions about people, society, and history, one of these being that people are individual, and uniquely different, despite the way the world tends to categorize them. Their experiences help us see them as individuals, not as abstract types, and realize what we share in common.

Our "casual" tale-telling the first day also establishes that *talk* is the foundation on which literacy is built. At first our talk seems to be simply a way to get to know each other, but when we listen carefully we see that talk teaches us about voice and rhythm in writing, introduces us to new vocabulary, allows us to explore opinions, concepts, and processes, and even offers us a chance to know ourselves better. Our listening and our reflecting eventually reveal new understanding about composing with and interpreting language.

By admitting to students that my stories have grown richer with each telling, and by describing how details have come and gone or been adjusted, I show that even in our talk—our oral composing—we are reinterpreting and revising. I want them to know how fine the line is between reality and fiction. During our year together they will work and play at bending and shaping experience through the words they choose and their tone of voice, and they will come to see how new meaning can be extracted from an experience in each return visit. They will encounter stories, poems, movies, plays, advertisements, news broadcasts, and historical accounts with new eyes because of our discussions of how language alters experience. If my students become conscious of how their words recreate their own experiences, they will learn to notice how writers interpret experience.

This first week of school students begin to see that, whether they write poetry, fiction, fantasy, opinion pieces, humor, or research reports, their teacher will encourage them to approach the task honestly, from the essence of who they are, from the heart.

Eliciting Stories

Telling my story triggers theirs. Yet each group reacts differently. In some classes, students are bursting to connect their remembrances to mine. Those student stories trigger other student stories, as happens in normal conversations. Your tale reminds me of mine, which may in turn remind you of another one or of more of the details in your first one. When I tell stories in primary classrooms I notice little hands shoot up before I even finish. Their faces say, "That happened to me too!" Not all middle schoolers are ready to jump instantly into the pool. Like reluctant swimmers, a few are afraid. They have learned along the way that school is *not* a place to reveal tender feelings, not a place to expose the heart. In some middle schoolers in September the fear of exposure is like a steel trap holding fast to all the life stories and the feelings within. I don't force it open.

If stories don't surface easily, I ask students to travel with me back to "childhood" to look for the tiniest details. Now, I realize that most middle schoolers are in the process of leaving childhood behind: some have just recently turned away from it; some deserted childhood years ago; others leave it for a few days and then race back when the mood or some young-adult responsibility strikes. Not many admit right away that they remember much about childhood, but small details can take them back.

I share a string of mine: my cigar-smelling grandfather rocking me on his ankle and singing "giddy-up, giddy-up, giddy-up, whoa my po-ny boy"; sitting like a queen on my own rocking horse singing that same song for hours; Nana Walsh always having Chicklets hidden in one of her pockets on Sunday when she wore her fox stole with the little mouths that could bite; an evergreen tree, hollow in the center, where my friends and I sat hidden from the world; the unfinished cellar of our house, which my father equipped with a battered couch and an old TV in the days before "family rooms." Even the tiniest memories can jar the details in their memories loose. We don't worry if a memory is a whole *story;* we just savor the hilarious and touching tidbits from each other's lives.

I have tried this kind of detail recall with students as young as kindergarten, but again, each group's memory gathering offers distinct challenges and surprises. Young children vary greatly in their ability to listen to each other and to take turns, but remembering images can move along quickly and helps them develop those skills. In one kindergarten I took the children on a journey through the house I grew up in. I decided to offer three images. In retrospect, I talked too long. First, I told about my Grandmother Gillard's china closet. Besides her dishes, it contained a tiny glass well with a bucket that could be raised and lowered. Under the watchful eye of a grown-up I was allowed to play with the well and with a few other tiny ceramic figures, mostly animals, which she kept there. Then I walked my listeners up the stairs to my room, where a picture of Alice, the Mad Hatter, and the Cheshire Cat was painted on the plastic light-switch plate. I gave them a glimpse of the rest of the room, which contained a bunkbed, a crib, and dressers, but first I had them focus on the light-switch plate, which I had loved looking into as if it contained a magical world.

Then I walked them across the room to a picture lamp that hung on the opposite wall. The lamp was a glass painting of a ballerina. When the switch was turned once, a lightbulb behind her feet would go on. A second turn made her legs and tutu light up. The final turn illuminated the entire ballerina, on pointed toes, looking as if she were dancing on a frozen lake. I asked the kindergartners to close their eyes and see if they could walk through their houses in their mind's eye and find a favorite object or place they liked to go. Their descriptions ranged from a rocking chair under which the dog rested to very special dolls, a few fragile figurines—some large, some tiny like mine—a closet for hiding in, some video games, and a piano bench that was fun to climb on and "opened up like a jewelry box."

Near the end, one very dramatic little girl, whose attention had not strayed for even a moment during anyone's telling, took a deep breath before beginning. Clearly she had been waiting for her moment. She launched into a fantasy like experience of getting off the school bus and being met by a clown. He told her about her upcoming "adventure," walked her up the sidewalk and front porch steps, and then handed her a bouquet of balloons. Next, a ballerina in a pink tutu stepped out to greet her. The story went on complete with dialogue. The teacher just grinned. Whatever image the next little boy had held in his mind's eye dissolved. "At my house we have a clown and a ballerina too" was all he could say. The last two children both had clowns and ballerinas.

The teacher and I thanked the children, and we all got up and stretched. Later, she and I had a chance to laugh about the incident, agreeing that the exercise had been successful, even though the little girl's fantasy images had overpowered those who followed her. The teacher was amazed that her kindergartners had concentrated for as long as they had and looked forward to returning to their images, which she had recorded as they talked. I learned about a kindergartner's ability to match my modeling: if I wanted children to be brief, I had to demonstrate brevity.

If students want to move from images to stories, one way is to begin with "I remember the time . . . " If they turn to partners and simply talk for three or four minutes, they see that many "times" come to the surface. If they turn up a big memory, such as the time the family drove across the country, I encourage them to look for one or a few related highlights. If what they remember seems too small to be a "story," I ask them to back up in time to what preceded the moment or to background information, so the moment's significance becomes clear.

Timelining elicits many stories. I began timelining my own life when I attended Lucy Calkins's Summer Writing Institute at Teachers

College in the early eighties. Marge Boyle, my section leader, asked us to find the moments, positive and negative, when writing had been "important" in some way. My memories began with writing letters on the floor next to my grandmother's wheelchair. She would let me pick out the stationery for the day from the shelves of scented, ribboned boxes she had ordered from catalogues. I think she sometimes folded one of my scribbled sheets into her envelope before letting me lick the flap and the stamp. I have returned to that timeline often over the years, discovering more memories and adding significant events from my present-day writing life.

I have since made writing/reading timelines with students from middle school through graduate school. The memory gathering is a mixture of pleasure and pain. More than a few students describe negative reading experiences: being told they couldn't read when they believed they could; being moved to "lower" groups or asked to leave the room to work with a "special" teacher. For some, even the "honor" of being taken out of class to read with students in a higher grade made them feel "different." Years later, these experiences still affected their self-image and their feelings about reading. A few recall reading contests with pride. Others tell of ways kids cheated and how the contests took away the joy of savoring a book slowly or rereading it. Some remember being assigned books they "just didn't get." Yet almost everyone remembers one book whose words or pictures transported them to another world. Most can name a teacher who read aloud with passion or told stories that *sounded* just like books.

One year my middle schoolers and I invited parents to come to our classroom and tell their stories of learning, the kind of learning garnered outside as well as inside school. We heard about college memories, getting started in businesses, developing hobbies, earning promotions, finding mentors—oral stories all. The images those tellers left with us resounded for the rest of that year.

In a workshop I gave for adults, one participant made a timeline of the cars in his life, describing both the vehicles and the memories associated with each. In subsequent workshops, I have told about this car timeline and invited tellers to look at repeating themes in their own lives. Among the ones I have heard are, "the gardens of my life," "junkfood junky to macrobiotic nut," and "mothering my friends and family from the age of four." Arlene Brown, a member of my local story circle, developed a wonderful memory piece about front porches, which included tasting her first kiss.

"Whole" stories don't always come quickly. Some students, regardless of age, need to talk their way into a memory, or at least into its significance. Sometimes a student is telling one story, perhaps less than wholeheartedly, when he interrupts himself, "Oh, *I* know what I want to tell about!" I have learned to trust that change-of-mind. I also hear quite often, "*Now* I see what this story is really about." Journeying into the past can take time, but it offers more delights than students ever suspect. Though we start with stories, we often work our way toward essays, projects, and connections with other school subjects.

Drawing is another way to elicit stories. If a storyteller sketches a house or yard or playground, or any place she has spent time and associates with memory, just the act of sketching can bring details to the surface. I don't encourage students to draw carefully, as if for an art project, but rather to sketch in order to remember. When I look into the attic of my house I see the shape of my mother's dress form, the headless figure she used while fitting a dress under construction. My siblings and I always laughed to hear my mother call it "my sister Eileen." By the time my mother had a house full of children, she didn't sew much, except to mend, so we played with Eileen in many odd ways. This image helps me see the rest of the attic in my mind and remember games of hide-and-seek, dress up, and office. I don't need to draw the rest. Sketching the basic outline of the house and looking down into it is enough to bring me memories from both the front and back porch, the yard, each room in the house, and even the roof, from which we jumped into piles of snow on days off from school. Looking at my sketch I see the rock garden out back and the tulip and poppy garden along the side of the house. I hear sidewalk games and shows performed behind a clothesline curtain. My students all have such stories. There are no haves and have-nots in the world of memory.

SEVEN

Triumph and Trauma Tales

o matter how I elicited memories, I noticed that children's and adults' unforgettable moments often fell into one of two categories: triumphs and traumas. Many stories focused on moments of heroism or delight: achieving a goal in sports, helping during a family or neighborhood crisis, reaching out to make a new friend, completing a task, being recognized for a quality or skill, winning a trophy. I encourage tellers to celebrate the small as well as the grand moments of childhood: building forts with tree branches, making hollyhock dolls with toothpicks, imagining being a princess, pirate, principal, or president. In the richness of those creative endeavors students' future actions as members of their local communities and, in time, of the global community, will unfold.

Student stories also include surviving traumas: nearly drowning, becoming lost or being abandoned, getting burned, falling down on a stairway, or crashing on a bike, skateboard, or snowmobile. Children's trauma stories, I have come to believe, teach them as much about how to be brave, kind, generous, and ethical as do their stories of creating and completing. Both are important. I always honor that.

It is clear to me, as I listen to children's stories in classrooms and adults' stories during workshops, that people need to tell about their traumas in some form. Many of my own stories have a trauma at the center: my eighth grade composition, my teacher's scolding, my first back-slapping high dive. In telling about them, we begin to make sense of our accidents, errors, disappointments, and losses, or gain some control over them. We see that whatever we have struggled with is now in the past, at least chronologically. People say, "I'm here to tell the tale" in a sadder but wiser voice.

Lessons are embedded in the stories of painful experience. Each time we return to a trauma we learn more about it, perhaps even how to avoid it in the future. I remember "morning-after" stories told in college. Sometimes they sounded like bragging: who had done the dumbest, most daring, or most embarrassing deed. But I don't think we were bragging, really. I think we were naming our carelessness, lack of caution, and stupidity, often behind the mask of humor, and resolving (however weakly) not to act quite so stupidly in the future.

Children's accident stories are sometimes quite funny, but again I think they tell them for the lesson as well as for the laugh. Some emphasize the gory details of accidents after which they got stitches, earned scars, or wore casts that brought them lots of attention. They find humor and delight in being the star of such tellings, which almost always conclude with their being wiser and more physically agile. Both tellers and listeners find the drama in these stories exciting and the resolutions comforting. The stories usually contain a helpful adult, in a small supporting role, who took action to soothe or mend their physical hurt or rush them to one who could. Wounds to the skin and bones generally get attended to.

Wounds to the spirit, to the inner child, however, are sometimes missed or dismissed by the adult world. Bad scares and deep hurts don't always get the attention they require. Broken hearts don't get stitched together again. More often than not hurt feelings get scolded away by adults who want to quiet the child. "I'll give you something to cry about." They get "tissued" away quickly and even praised away by well-meaning adults who want to calm a child. When my son was hit by a car, all the helping professionals told him how brave he was not to cry. For hours, until I received word of the accident and

arrived at the hospital, he held his hurt inside. Upon seeing me he
cried and cried.

Tears

Feelings held in, sometimes for years, resurface with certain kinds of
stories. Both children and adults occasionally find themselves suddenly
crying in the middle of telling a story. The hurt or sadness from a
recently experienced loss or long buried trauma arises unexpectedly.
Noticing this phenomenon, I looked for ways to deal with it that
didn't add more trauma to the tellers' lives. Often just alerting a group
to the fact that stories carry emotions, and that tears of sadness as well
as relief might come along, prepares them.

Tellers always have a choice of what story to share. Triumph-
centered tales or funny memories make easy tellings. Others involve
more emotional risk. Knowing this might be enough to prevent emotion from taking a teller by surprise. Sharing a story of my own about
crying also works.

I had already been telling stories publicly for several years the
first time I stumbled upon my own tears in the middle of a story. My
kindergarten "scolding" story had started life years before as a piece of
writing composed during a week-long institute. I decided to resurrect
it as an oral tale one evening while leading a story-swap for teachers
at a summer conference. I had had no trouble reading the piece aloud
to my writing group, although I remember tearing up as I drafted it in
the wee hours one morning during the institute. I had written "Nancy
Was a Good Girl" in the third person as a kind of parable for teachers
and parents. Taking the role of narrator had given me distance from
the original hurt. (I had named the protagonist "Nancy" because I
remembered envying my friend's name. Her cursive N seemed so much
prettier than my cursive M. Recalling that silly detail helped me see
into my young character and bring a sense of humor to what was a
trauma tale.)

Resurrecting "Nancy" at the story-swap without ever having told
it aloud in public brought me onto unfamiliar ground, something I

didn't realize until I was well into the telling. The story begins comically. We see "Nancy" at home practicing *not* talking because she took literally her teacher's requirement that everyone be "completely quiet" the day of the doctor's visit to school. During that part of the telling the adults in the room and the adult in me enjoyed looking back at this young kindergartner. However, when I began to narrate the scene in which the teacher grabs Nancy by the arm, yanks her out of line, and scolds her loudly in front of everyone for having "the audacity to talk on the day of the doctor's visit," I accidentally slipped into first person, saying "She grabbed *my* arm and . . . " Suddenly, I *was* Nancy. I had lost my emotional distance. The original humiliation came flooding back, and I burst into tears. I had to hold up my hand as a way to request patience, sob for a second, laugh at how ridiculous I felt, and take a deep breath in order to finish. Though I was embarrassed, the audience's faces—some tearing up remembering similar childhood hurts and some smiling because the lessons of childhood *are* funny to look back at—supported me. My tears, in turn, supported others in that room of "first-time" tellers, reminding them that crying in public is not fatal and showing them this was a safe place to risk telling a tale "from the heart." They all told wonderful stories, and we laughed at how "The First Time I Told 'Nancy . . . '" would now be a story in itself.

When an adult or child begins to cry while telling a story, I have to make my best guess at what to do at that moment. It hasn't happened often but each experience has taught me to be observant of what the particular teller seems to need and then to follow my instinct. As every teacher knows, there is no one right answer. Sometimes very briefly recounting the story of my "Nancy" surprise gets everyone laughing and takes the focus away from the person in tears. My story diffuses the embarrassment around public crying. However, simply honoring the tears of a teller by giving a look to the class that says, "We need to take a time out here," is often more appropriate than stealing the spotlight away from the teller.

Traditionally school is a place which demands that everyone keep emotions in check, and some children who begin to cry want no mention made of it. But often tears simply need to be honored. Then whatever caused them heals a little. Tears erupt in tough kids as well as in sensitive ones. Simply remembering that it *can* happen makes it a little easier to handle. Sometimes a physical gesture of support such as a hug is appropriate, but I am *very* careful to read a child's or an adult's body language. In most cases that will tell me what would be helpful and what would feel intrusive.

What I don't believe in doing is discounting the child's tears by sending him out of the room, suggesting he go wash his face, or handing him a wad of tissues and separating him until he is "under control." Such actions send the message to everyone present that tears are bad. The good news is, tears heal. They wash clean or at least begin to cleanse a wound that may be deep. Even though I cried privately during the drafting of "Nancy Was a Good Girl," I had not completely recovered from the psychological wound my first public school scolding left. Tears are important to the inner child in all of us. If we allow tears and gently honor them instead of forbidding them or turning from them in embarrassment, we teach each other, at every age, how to care for the self and the community.

In "The Poem as a Reservoir for Grief," Tess Gallagher (1986) writes:

> It is important that the inner nature of our beings be strengthened by the wisdom of our grieving. The scientists may tinker, the politicians may instruct us in the various ploys of moral unconsciousness, the physicians may delay death awhile with yet another treatment, but, until individuals maintain a responsible relationship to their own losses and changes, there will be no such thing as a hopeful future. For, as in the Taoist description of the wheel in terms of the strong, empty spaces *between* the spokes, one's future depends not only on the visible spokes of the present, but also on those invisible elements from the past—those things we are missing, are grieving for and which we have forgotten and left behind in order to recover them again as new meaning, new feeling. (116)

There is no age too young to be haunted by "our grieving." In one of my earliest workshops with children in a school other than my own, I asked pre-K children to think back to the first thing they could remember. I told of some of my earliest memories in a low voice and asked the children to see a picture in their minds of when they were "little." They took a quiet minute to think and then turned to a partner to tell whatever pictures they had seen. Several other adults were at hand helping the children group together in partners. I looked down at a pair near me and noticed a little boy sobbing. I crouched next to him as he told of his mother stopping the car because he wasn't behaving. She made him get out and then drove away. She circled the block and retrieved him, but the trauma of that momentary abandonment remained.

I have since learned that most people's earliest memory *is* traumatic. It represents the loss of innocence in some way. Michael Meade (1993) says that such "initiations" occur at various moments throughout our lives, when we move from one stage of understanding to another. From a distance the experience might act as a teacher, but first we must be willing to face and feel its "wound" in order to see it in a positive light. The hurt in some memories remains a long time, but returning, through storytelling, is one way to heal the hurt.

I am not suggesting that we have some duty as teachers to take children back to their wounds or run therapy sessions. On the contrary, I steer children toward positive memories, the big and little triumphs of their lives, because telling such stories reminds them of their power and builds their self-esteem. Still, they love to tell their "scar" stories because in these, they triumph over the giants in their lives, over their fears.

In a third-grade classroom in Iowa I mentioned at some point in my introduction that my dad wasn't alive anymore but that telling stories about him kept him alive for me. I told the story of my first high dive, in which he has a central role. I see that story as a triumph because it got me over my fear of the high board, even if I still had a lot to learn about diving. When I had finished, the third graders sat silently for a moment in order to find a story within. Then each turned to a partner and the room filled with talk. The teacher and I usually spend the first few minutes making sure everyone has a partner. Teachers have the choice of experiencing the activity by partnering with a child or of observing their children storytelling. Each role has advantages.

This time the teacher had a partner, so I took the role of observer and right away noticed a girl whose shoulders were shaking. Then I spotted her tears, but saw that she was talking away. Her partner, a boy, listened attentively to her but looked a little unsettled. I didn't want to draw the entire group's attention to them so I slipped unobtrusively through the crowd seated on the floor and wedged myself down into a space next to the girl. I put my arm around her shoulders for support, alert to whether that helped or hindered. She seemed comforted and continued telling her story.

Her cat had gotten loose and had never returned. I didn't catch when this occurred, but whether the memory was distant or fresh, it was clearly unresolved. My talking about the loss of my dad had probably triggered it. She cried quietly but bravely told tales of the cat as we huddled close. Few, if any, in the room were aware of us. Her partner and I didn't shun her tears, but we didn't advertise them either. We simply listened and by doing so made it safe for her to tell her story.

The boy seemed aware of his role. Once her voice and body language told us she was finished, he and I reflected back the essence of the tale. I knew she was not requesting that we fix her hurt, just hear it. "So, your cat never came back," he said sadly. "Nope," she said, still teary but visibly calmed. "That was a *great* story," he said. She smiled, "Thanks." The boy asked, "You want to hear mine now?" She smiled again and nodded, ready to relinquish the stage. I returned to my role as observer. The three of us had momentarily occupied a private island in the middle of a sea of talking children. I knew this two-person craft was ready to slip into the sea again, and I moved away.

When it came time for volunteers to tell their stories aloud to the entire group, the now smiling girl shot her hand up in the air. I didn't hesitate to call on her. She bounced to the front of the room like any young star claiming the spotlight. I suspected she knew she wouldn't cry this time and had determined she had a story worth telling. What came out was a collage of cat slap-stick comedy—the cat's stealing her sister's undershirt, jumping from a high front porch, sliding sideways down a laundry shoot, and bolting between the legs of an unsuspecting visitor. The audience squealed with laughter. The young teller didn't need to tell us that the cat was gone now; she grieved his leaving by celebrating his life, no small lesson for a pair of third graders and a traveling storyteller a long way from home.

Storytelling has not turned me into a therapist. It has simply taken me to the heart of oral literature. All teachers struggle with hurt feelings in our classrooms. Many of us have trouble reading certain books aloud because they touch us or our children deeply. But we seldom discuss the issue of crying openly and what it means in the lives of children. Storytellers are beginning to talk about tears because we encounter them. If we teachers talked more about them, asking questions about "grieving," exploring what is behind our own tears, and reading what psychologists can teach us about healing the hurts of the inner child, we just might make our classrooms the safe havens children need in order to grow healthy and learn.

Helping Tellers Find Resolution

Finding a resolution for a traumatic memory allows us to turn it into a comedy or a hero tale. In almost every case, if listeners are patient, the teller will see the resolution and the triumph once she's told the story. Often the triumph appears in the form of a lesson learned. Jennifer Johnson, a young adult teller I met at a community story-swap sponsored by the Gathering Place in Norwich, New York, told of finding a robin's nest containing an unhatched egg when she was much younger. She fantasized the bird's hatching and its becoming her close friend. She imagined it would travel to school on her shoulder and sing into her ear. In her excitement to share her discovery with a neighbor, she dropped the nest and the egg broke. Even a trip back to the park with her mother and a ladder in hopes of finding another nest had not consoled her. Jennifer stopped and that seemed to be the end of the story. But story listeners, like concertgoers, wait for the resolving chord before applauding. We knew there had to be another "ending," a reason Jennifer was telling this tale. We waited. "I hadn't thought of this moment for many years," she said. "Then last Christmas, after my first college semester away from home, Mom and I talked about it." Jennifer looked across the room toward her mother, Juanita, seated among the evening's storytellers. "She told me that that was the day she knew we were truly kindred spirits." Jennifer found her triumph in the frame she gave to her memory, rather than in the memory itself.

I had to frame my kindergarten story of being scolded for talking in line to find resolution in it. The conclusion of the story comes later that night when my mother reads the hurt in my face and asks me what happened. She sits on her bed with me and explains that teachers, and other people, sometimes act before they get all the facts. She instructs me in the art of tactfully speaking up for myself should I be unjustly accused in the future. However, her advice doesn't quiet my righteous five-year-old's pride. Another child might have bad-mouthed the teacher or sought revenge on the girl responsible for calling the teacher's attention to her. As a somewhat older child, again in trouble for talking, I used these options well. But as a too-good kindergartner, I saw my resolution in the actions of the adult I believed I would become. "Nancy" decides to be a teacher who will always ask the questions that get at the Truth of trouble. Adults, including me, enjoy the irony of this ending, knowing as we do the *many* truths that trouble wears and how stories help us forgive grievances as well as heal griefs.

However, the death of a pet or family member, the loss of treasured belongings (in a fire or theft), the experience of being teased—any of these can leave an unresolved hurt that gets in the way of our learning and our self-esteem. Yet they all make good stories. We have to expect the unexpected when children tell us their stories. It isn't easy, but it is important.

The Issue of Privacy

In my early years of teaching I worried about putting children in the position of exposing hurts. My mother valued privacy above most other personal rights. During a visit home in my second year of teaching, she asked me in a rather accusatory tone, "You're not one of those teachers getting children to write about their private lives in journals where just anyone can read about their family's dirty linen, *are you?*" A teacher herself, she had read about this "trend" and wanted to voice her disapproval. As a relatively new teacher and still compliant daughter, I respected her advice and feared her censure. I tried not to blush and simply replied, "Who me, Mom?"

I had, in fact, been troubled earlier that year when some eighth-grade boys had picked up a sensitive girl's journal and broadcasted excerpts of it to classmates. I had handled the situation by talking seriously with the class about respect for privacy and by establishing a new method of notebook collection. But I had come away from the incident unsure that I could prevent such a thing from recurring. My mother's warning hit home. After that visit, I stopped using journals in my teaching for three years, something I still regret. It wasn't until I began to write again myself and saw the value in telling my own stories, that I realized the absurdity of trying to teach language arts without personal writing on some level. By then I had gained enough experience with middle schoolers to address privacy issues firmly at the beginning of the year.

My mother's caution helps me understand teachers' uneasiness about opening the Pandora's box of children's lives through personal storytelling and writing. There is a risk of hearing more than we want to. But I tell teachers and parents to remember that Pandora saved Hope when she released the darker aspects of life. Yes, we take the chance of seeing what ongoing traumas interfere with, or at least influence, our students' learning. We may feel inadequate in helping them deal with some kinds of troubling issues, but knowing about these issues is better than not knowing. We can seek outside support for children whose stories reveal serious problems.

Talking openly with students, even those I am meeting for only a short time, about the sensitive nature of personal stories is key. I talk in a way that invites them to take our storytelling seriously, to know that stories are powerful. I do not encourage the public display of private family "linen"; rather, I want children to see that everyone's stories require our respect, regardless of whether they seem funny or serious. Jennifer was able to find the resolution for her robin's egg tale, but sometimes children and adults need a gentle hand to find at least a temporary resolution to a tale that appears to have no triumph. I say "gentle," because it is easy for teachers to take over a troubling story by asking probing questions or pushing for an adult resolution. The urge to fix someone's story is tempting. We must resist it. What helps most often is providing wait-time, attentive silence, and a reflective response that simply says back what we have heard.

A fourth grader I will call Janice told us that her dad went to a bar one night and "only had one coke and lots of beers." Her tone made the children laugh and she seemed to delight in holding their attention. She described dashing into his bedroom the next morning, where she found him sitting on his exercise bike. Since she hadn't had a chance to say good-night to him the previous evening, she ran toward him, anxious for a good-morning hug. "He fell right on top of me! It really hurt." The tone of Janice's voice changed and we could see that she still hurt. We waited, allowing her to find her own important truth, whatever that would be. She continued, "My mother said to him, 'You're still drunk.' And I cried for about half an hour."

I waited to see if Janice wanted to say more; I could see she was hunting for a resolution. I glanced toward her teacher, whose face seemed to say, "I want to see how you handle this." I looked back at Janice and simply reflected key points of the tale back to her and shared my genuine response. "Gee, you were looking forward to a hug and got squashed. That must have hurt." In such circumstances, a tiny bit of humor sometimes helps break the tension by exposing hurt feelings. My use of the word "squashed" in this case did help Janice and her fellow fourth graders giggle, which relaxed us all. It didn't help her resolve the story, however, or find the words to bring a sense of closure to the event.

So I tried a question. "Did you get a chance to make up? Did your dad apologize?" I realized I was offering an adult band-aid, which I don't like to do, but I wanted to help this child reach some kind of resolve so we would not leave her with an unfinished tale. Janice's face told me the resolution wasn't that simple. "Well, he sort of did at lunch," she said rather begrudgingly. I believed she could find her own answer. Finally, our waiting—still one of the hardest things for both teachers and children to do—helped Janice create her own at least temporary resolution. She grinned. Then she ended her story: "Later that night he went on his motorcycle and he was still hungover and he skidded and got all scraped up."

Her tender grin was not mean-spirited, yet it told us that, at least for now, Janice was finished. Someday the tale might take on a new ending or even fade in comparison to other moments. For now this ending provided some comfort.

Do I get uncomfortable when children tell such stories? You bet. I write about such incidents as a way to continue to search for an understanding of my role as teacher and teller. Before I left Janice's class I made a point of talking with the children about how important it is to respect the privacy of her tale. She was brave to tell it, I told them, but it is not our story to retell casually to others. The children's faces told me that they understood the seriousness of what I was saying. Honesty usually comforts people's uneasiness. If they giggle in the face of truth-telling it can mean they aren't taking what I say seriously; more often it simply means that they are uncomfortable.

Later, Janice's teacher and I got a chance to talk, and I was relieved that she felt it had been important for her student to share such a tale and for her class to hear the tale and then my talk about the sacredness of trauma tales. She believed the morning's work had brought them to a new place as a community. Because such stories help us to know each other at more than a surface level, I am committed to staying with this work. What is more important, stories like this help us know ourselves and see that we are not alone in our pain and fear. Through stories we make sense of the sometimes messy moments of our lives. The injury Janice experienced is going to remain and fester within her regardless of whether her teacher taps it through writing or storytelling. Released through language or drawing or dance, it has a chance of taking on a positive meaning. If it stays inside, however, the unresolved hurt will distract her from the opportunities for learning around her.

A Tale You're Not Ready to Tell

Children sometimes make it very clear that they do not want to share a particular story. It is important to respect their wishes. After they get settled with a partner, a quick check of body language clues me in to someone's need for help. "I can't think of a story" sometimes means the story surfacing is not one the child wants to share. Some students can actually articulate, "I can think of a story but I don't want to tell it." In either case it is a matter of guiding them to another choice, helping them see that there are countless options, even if one particular story has risen to the surface first.

"You can set that memory aside. It will probably make a good story one of these days for the right audience," I joke, if that seems appropriate. Or I might say, "Let's see if we can find a memory that would be easy and fun to share right now." Happy recollections exist in all of us. Asking a reluctant teller about what he likes to do, or interviewing him about siblings, neighborhood friends, responsibilities, or pets often leads to a memory. One or two open-ended questions, combined with attentive, patient listening, can help just about anyone find a ready-to-tell tale. A listener needs to leave pauses between questions. Rephrasing them or asking more too quickly doesn't help the teller. Adult attention may not help either. Sometimes it is best to leave the child alone until he has time to think or guide him to a new partner.

My last resort is completely excusing a child from the activity, because nothing separates a child more than giving up on her. My belief that every child has stories and wants to tell them is what keeps them coming. A sense of humor in the face of resistance—I don't mean sarcasm, but the gentle cajoling that allows a person to let go of fear—helps too. Unflinching optimism, like truth, makes some people giggle, but it tends to be contagious. Then the act of writing or telling gives the resistor a feeling of accomplishment and of belonging to the group, even if the story seems small or unimportant before it is told. Speaking about a memory to listeners gives it significance.

Occasionally however, a storyteller's block is something to honor. One middle school boy in a class I visited refused to be a partner with anyone. That sometimes happens, so I walked over, crouched down so we were eye to eye, and began to talk with him in a friendly way. He told me that the only story he could remember was the time he went fishing with a group of men and boys. Everyone caught a fish but him. None of my conversation could take that story away or help him resolve it. It was as if he needed to sit with it, not tell it publicly but come to own it privately to figure out what it meant. I thanked him but walked away discouraged. It is an old habit of teachers to measure the success of our efforts by how positively children respond. The boy's teacher, who knew his history, told me later that she was surprised and happy he had shared even that much with me, a stranger. I believe in reassuring children that they can put one memory away for another time and take out a different one. Writers and tellers do that all the time. But in the end, it is not for me to choose what stories they will tell or not tell.

Recently, a fourth-grade girl began to tear up as she was beginning her story. "Maybe I better tell a different one," she said, "This one's sad." I told her that was fine. Then she grinned. "No, I think I want to tell the one about my grandpa." And she did, smiling through her tears and teaching us many things by savoring an important moment in her life.

Telling and learning from their personal stories, whether triumphs or traumas, children strengthen the voices that will allow them to speak their personal truths all through their lives. By encouraging them to do so, teachers help them honor the ways in which they are different as well as alike. Today, their attention to television, movies, recorded music, and advertising draws them into conformity in the ways they act and talk and desire material things. When they tell of their own unique and fascinating lives, they travel into each other's worlds. Their stories contain families different from those on the sitcoms and definitions of heroism and wealth different from those in the media. Their stories open them up to each other—and to learning about language and life.

EIGHT

The Personal Tale as Teacher

he ancients told stories about what they didn't really understand: about the moon and the sun's light and the pictures the stars made in the sky. Their stories answered questions: Why is the sea salty? Why would a mountain erupt with fire? They told stories in an attempt to make sense of the world.

The stories we tell and retell about significant moments in our lives serve the same purpose. We tell stories to return to an experience that marked us in some way, to search for a moment's meaning, or to repeat its meaning to ourselves or others. Our stories become advice to others and, very often, to ourselves. Retelling the tale may reveal new layers of meaning as we grow and learn more about the world.

The more personal tales I hear children tell, the more I see that they grow out of the life-questions children have formulated as they experience or observe events at home, on the playground, at the houses of friends or relatives, at camp, or at school:

Why are some children bullies and others meek?

What will happen if I ride my bike at full speed down this hill?

Can I swim from one side of the deep end to the other, and what will happen if I can't?

Will I score a goal in this game, and what can I learn that will help me score more in the future?

Where do warts come from, and what does it mean to have them removed?

What was I like when I was younger?

Who in the world sees me as smart/funny/good-looking, and why do they?

Why do grown-ups like my sister/my brother better than me?

. Why is my sister/my brother the way she/he is and I am the way I am?

What were my parents or my grandparents like as kids?

Can grown-ups and kids be friends?

I watch children probe these mysteries when they recreate and sometimes elaborate upon their memories. They relive their lives through their stories and in subtle ways reinvent reality as they would like it to be or believe it should be. Whether they revisit the pain or joy of a particular moment, they take some control over it by telling its story. First they choose the memory; then they choose what to tell about it. By shaping it they give it meaning, and in doing so they create what I have come to think of as their own personal fables, which help them know how and how not to act.

Aesop's fables, mostly about animals in nature, exposed human predicaments and foibles yet spoke a useful truth. The crow's thirst moves him to fill a shallow pitcher with pebbles so the level of water will rise. The story reassures us that necessity will give birth to invention. The sun's warmth persuades away a traveler's coat while the wind's bullying force cannot. Fables represent the human condition.

Fables fascinated me as a child. I felt a shiver when the lion laughed at the mouse's offer to help it someday, but deep satisfaction in witnessing the mouse's humble heroism later in the tale. When the milkmaid drifted further and further into dreaming about what her earnings would bring, I winced knowing she would have no chickens to count in the end. Many fables reminded me of myself in some way, and the caution they offered was more palatable than the advice offered directly by parents and teachers. To this day, a story-based sermon is more likely to linger with me than a lecture.

Like fables, the memory tales I hear include characters who make errors in judgment or let loved ones down, but tellers almost always find sweetness or satisfaction at the end when the moral or lesson shines through. Tellers of every age often smile or nod near the story's end, especially if they are discovering the story's message for the first time. I have heard many stories about tellers who discovered that they were able to accomplish something they hadn't believed possible or who delighted in something they had thought would be distasteful.

Children tell coming-of-age stories in which they realize they aren't indestructible and figure out that grown-ups aren't infallible. Adults tell tales of children's wisdom and resilience. They also tell stories that honor the child within themselves. All these stories emerge tender and tentative but clearly filled with lessons. What they lack in polish, they make up for in freshness and depth of feeling. Telling a story for the first time, a teller often works out its meaning in the moment of creation. Getting a chance to retell the same story, the teller beams with the confidence of being its creator and the owner of its insights.

Neil, a kindergartner, trembles as he begins his tale about an older cousin who dunked him in the deep end of the pool. Eventually a grin comes over his face as he remembers sneaking up on the cousin later from underwater in the crowded shallow end. There, on his own territory, the smaller Neil was able to dart away unseen. The story rings with the triumph of the underdog. How much is real and how much fantasy is unclear, but telling the story seems to be Neil's way of teaching himself to be brave in the face of future bullies.

Ryan, a plump third-grade girl, tells of first dreaming about and then finally getting to go to a hockey game at the college fieldhouse near her home. In her excitement to enter the giant building she pushes past the tickettaker only to be stopped by a security guard. Later, her enthusiasm distracting her, she runs head-first into one of the thick glass doors to the rink and falls down. A large hockey player retrieves her, lifting her up in his arms. The next day a friend offers her money for the shirt the hockey player touched. "No way!" says Ryan. "I earned that shirt." The other children delight in her exuberance. Her tale seems to reassure us all of the magic and the safety that still exist in the universe. There is something in a child's storytelling that says, "Hear my story, I am teaching myself about the world."

Just as I wanted to hear "The Lion and the Mouse" repeated, students will long to return to their favorite personal fables. When they do retell and relisten, they have a chance to move to a story's deeper layers of meaning, to see its characters, including themselves, as symbolic of human behavior, just as the characters in Aesop's fables are. Through retelling, children grow more proficient with narrative structures, they learn about composing for an audience outside themselves, and they internalize the meaning of revision. Retellings change stories in significant ways.

Discovering the Moral Within the Fable

I first began to think about how personal tales teach the teller lessons during a workshop at Teachers College a number of years ago. The presenter asked us to tell a partner a story we had already found ourselves telling at some point in the past, one we might have told only once before or found ourselves retelling often for its entertainment value or its lesson about life. My partner told about when, as a brand new driver, a permit-holder, she pulled into the driveway and accidentally drove right through the closed garage door, hitting the accelerator when she should have pressed the brake. Her sister and mother, sitting in the back, began to scream. Her father, seated next to her on the passenger side, told them to calm down and go into the house. The young driver steeled herself for the berating she was certain would come.

Her father was a very authoritarian parent, and she feared that his lecture would rip to shreds any dignity or confidence she had left. However, he placed his hand gently on her shoulder and said, "Look,

you just had an *accident*. Even experienced drivers have accidents."
He assured her she would be a good driver and that insurance would
cover the damage. He hugged her and said he would take her driving
the next day. That story, she told me, has become more important to
her since she's lived away from home. It has given her an important
perspective on accidents, but, more important, it has reminded her of
the depth of her father's love. Clearly it was a personal fable she would
carry through life.

The Tale Belongs to the Teller

When I began visiting schools, starting with personal stories was one
way to invite children and teachers to begin to see themselves as
storytellers. I could tell just one story about a time when I felt smart
or confident or pleased about something that had happened, and
inevitably it triggered similar memories in my listeners. Often my tale
focused on a first-time experience or accomplishment. Then students
would help me list other possible "firsts": first bike ride without training wheels, first day swimming without adult support, first recital, first
fight with a bully or a friend, first overnight away from home, first
money earned, and so on. I began to see that almost all these personal
tales had a spoken or unspoken message. My visits don't allow me to
see children return to stories, but as they discover meaning in a first
telling, I wonder how it might grow with repeated reflection.

Matt, a fifth grader, told of the day he learned to tie shoelaces
after practicing on the workboots of a man named Oscar. The story
described Oscar's giant golden workboots and his patient and gentle
teaching style. We could all imagine Matt at a young age with chubby
fingers struggling again and again to get the thick leather laces to
behave. Matt finished the story beaming with pride. I knew there was
some important lesson in his tale that wasn't obvious to us. I silently
wondered what moral he attached to this memory: Stay with a task?
Don't be afraid to ask for help? Little fingers learn best on big objects?
After a few moments' pause, when I was sure he had said all he wanted

to say, I asked, "Why do you think this story, of all the firsts in your life, came up in your memory right now?" Matt replied, "I don't know why I chose *this* story, but I do know what I learned that day." Ah, here comes the lesson, I thought. "I knew that day that Oscar wasn't just my dad's friend, he was *my* friend. Grown-ups can be friends with kids, you know." Matt paused and we waited. "I got a whole bunch more stories about Oscar: the time we caught our first fish, our hiking trip to the mountains. . . . " Clearly, for Matt, learning to tie his shoes was steeped in significance.

I don't believe a moral needs to be teased out at the end of every personal fable, but I do believe it is important for a child to connect to the story's meaning if it can be found with a gentle touch of encouragement. We all laughed with Matt, sharing his delight at discovering what could be called "The Oscar Tales." My "Why do you think . . . " nudged him to voice his own meaning. Often the children listening will bring their own meaning to a teller's tale, and that can be an important part of savoring stories. But neither another child's nor the teacher's response should drown the teller's moment or his understanding of his own tale.

Jeri Burns, a member of the tandem-telling Storycrafters in Philmont, New York, shared a story from her childhood with me. At twenty-two months of age, Jeri's younger sister, Jodi, had still not taken her first step. Jeri's parents were growing concerned and had arranged to have Jodi X-rayed by specialists. On the afternoon that Jeri's mother went to get the X-ray results, both sets of grandparents and some other older family members were caring for the two girls. Jeri told me she remembered the room as full of elders all focusing attention on Jodi and all because of something she *couldn't* do. Jeri, just a three-year-old herself, looked directly at her sister and in a firm voice insisted, "Jodi, get up and walk!" The smaller girl put her hands to the floor, pushed herself up, and walked. Jodi's mother, just arriving home at that moment, was shocked to see her little girl finally walking. When I first heard this story I saw it as a hero tale for Jeri: clearly she must be a miracle worker in her family's eyes. But Jeri said it is still retold in her family as a lesson tale. "Today, 'Get up and walk!' is an expression we all say whenever someone is hesitating or stalling when they should be taking action. I return to it to get through difficulties. I tell myself,

'Come on, Jeri, get up and walk.' It works every time. The expression carries a measure of truth for us the way 'sour grapes' or 'slow and steady' does for others."

Layers of Meaning

Telling my own personal fables has reinforced for me that we must find our own meanings in our tales. I've often found myself retelling the story of a car accident I had two years ago. It contains many subthemes, and I tell it for different reasons to different listeners. It can be about rushing, about toughening oneself before a blow, about facing death, or about quieting the mind after a scare by forgiving oneself and one's fellow traveler. It is a women's story with women but less so with a more diverse audience. I have told it in a serious way to my sixteen-year-old and in a funny way to peers who, like me, tend to "run late." It gathers more meaning as I continue to tell it casually to acquaintances and small groups. I haven't used it as a performance story, but I wonder how it would change if I did. Out in the world, what lessons would it teach and to whom?

Both children and adults often have secret reasons for telling stories. Sometimes those reasons aren't clear even to the teller, but if the story resurfaces from time to time, new meaning shines through. Various members of my family used to tell the story about the night my older brother, Dan, and I, teenagers babysitting our infant brother, got him to stop crying by feeding him toothpaste. Dan smeared one of his thick and already hairy fingers with the sticky, minty cream and let the baby suck on it. We both felt quite proud of this problem-solving. It had been a *long* night of incessant crying. I remember telling the tale to friends when we swapped sitter stories. I even used it as an example of creative thinking during an interview for a high school award. For my older relatives the story was about a quirky teenage solution. But I secretly liked it for its image of my brother and me as equals. Three years my senior, he had never been an equal from my perspective. The story showed our camaraderie, a closeness I longed for but that our age disparity prevented at the time. I liked hearing others tell the tale. I would picture myself at my brother's side laughing over our success. By savoring that image, I was teaching myself how to be my brother's friend.

I have heard stories about the time a child didn't quite make the touchdown or win the ribbon. In some of those, young tellers reach for the joy of almost getting there even if they didn't really feel it at the moment of loss. I have heard a story from a boy who won a 4-H contest despite the fact that he was officially too young to enter. He seemed to be confronting both the unfairness of linking skill with age and whether or not it was fair for him to participate. I have heard family love proudly displayed through the depiction of a Fourth of July party splashed with impressions of the day's and night's highlights. I have heard children describe their relationships to important adults through personal stories. Rebecca, a second grader, thought her story was about the day her uncle Phil fished her out of the pool, but as she kept talking, it turned into one about how her uncle honored her more than her dad did. Mindy, a fifth grader, described helping her dad with the construction of a garage, a day-long event that included getting covered with paint and hosed down with her dog as the sun set on her weary pleasure. Allowing children to tell about such life moments regularly and encouraging them to return to tales and to talk about those return visits, helps them see the multiple layers in their tales.

Learning to Savor Personal Experience

In *Care of the Soul* Thomas Moore describes an uncle he used to visit each summer. A farmer, the uncle told and retold many stories about growing up. Moore says that, as he grew older, the same stories began to seem more like real stories: his uncle was turning his boyhood into a tale from which his young nephew could learn.

Works of literature can also serve as models for students' personal fables. The snowball scene in Annie Dillard's *An American Childhood* is a favorite I first heard told by the Burnt Hills, New York, storyteller Becky Holder. Dillard frames the incident by recalling that, during neighborhood football games, she learned from boys how to throw herself wholeheartedly into tackling the ball or its carrier. One day, throwing snowballs at cars, one in her gang of friends hits a man's windshield. The driver stops, gets out, and for many blocks chases Dillard and another child, who appear to be the most catchable culprits. The chase takes all three in and out of snow-filled yards and around corners, until the man catches them and breathlessly lectures them on the stupidity of throwing snowballs at cars. Dillard remembers the chase as thrilling and admires the man for exhibiting what the boys's football games have taught her, that you have to throw yourself at something wholeheartedly in order to gain it.

I look back at the log entries students made the day I read this story aloud and realize what I didn't do. I read Dillard's story in the hope of triggering a personal story during the choosing phase of our storytelling unit. It would give them a further possibility, along with our childhood treasures and library finds. I also wanted to offer them a personal story other than my own. However, we didn't talk about the story and our reactions and connections immediately afterward, the way we did when someone in the room told a personal story. Since I had read "literature," I skipped the talking and had them write in their logs immediately. I really hoped they might freewrite their way to a detailed memory that could serve as a possible oral telling.

Nick wrote what I would call only the outline of a story: "the time me and a friend threw glass on the road. A car ran over it and the tire popped."

Jeff wrote a much more detailed account: "About 20 kids from the neighborhood came over and we had a snow war with shovel catapults and prisoners and igloo forts. We built a real life igloo with a sunken floor with all the things you think about putting in a snow fort but never do, like an ice moat in a ditch we dug and secret tunnels and simple kinds of booby-traps." That was as far as he got when the bell rang, and since I gave students a choice of whether to use this story or not and we didn't go back to talk about their triggered memories, Jeff never even returned to the entry to finish it.

Michele wrote quite a detailed entry, which included being "eight, young and curious." She followed her eleven-year-old brother and his gang "deep in the woods at the end of our neighborhood." There they found railroad tracks. "A tall skinny man jumped off the train. Our hearts pounding we started running as if the world were going to end in a moment. The man chased us all the way up the winding dirt path not stopping at all for the thorn bushes or swinging twigs. Not stopping to look behind us we just kept going, our hearts in our throats. We hopped on our bikes and rode off before he could catch up to us." Michele's story clearly had potential as a performance piece, but she too abandoned the story after that day because we never talked about them.

I am certain that if we had talked the stories out first, these stories might have become lesson tales to be told and returned to. The responses were simply jotted into journals. But letting stories surface, if nothing else, may mean that they will surface again sometime. The returning that Moore talks about, however, will probably not happen unless students are given the time to hear and honor each other's tales. Then their exploration of meaning is more likely to happen.

Jane Yolen's *Owl Moon*, the story of a father and child who go owl watching in the cold, dark, early morning hours, is another multilayered tale that can elicit children's experiences. At a teacher's request I read the story to her second graders. I read slowly, asking the children to picture the tale in their minds. I did not show them the illustrations. At the end we sat in silence for a short time to savor the quiet mood of the book. Then I asked if the story reminded them of any experiences they had had and requested that they listen carefully to each other's memories. Few had ever been owl watching, yet every child in the room made a connection to the story, many in the form of lesson tales.

Some told of times alone with their fathers when they learned a particular skill. Others told about being in the dark or out in the cold, and almost all concluded with what the experience had taught them. Some described times they had had to be very quiet for an important reason. Their memories floated over the afternoon like the distant train whistle that broke the quiet of the young character's journey. Although I heard them years ago, before I had developed the habit of taking notes when children tell stories, I distinctly remember that, like Yolen's story, the children's tales each centered on some important truth about quiet or darkness or cold or childhood in general.

Every time I see students make connections between their lives and the stories they have read or heard, it seems clear that the exercise helps them think. Their faces reflect some inner work of connecting the known and the unknown. It is an active look, and I am learning better all the time how to wait for what will emerge. I see this same look in adults. One young woman at a story swap raised her hand, but once she was acknowledged she sat for a moment thinking. Finally, she said, "I've never thought of this as a story. It was just advice my father gave me many times. Now, well . . . ." Then she began.

> My father grew up in a small town in Wales. Mining was what everybody did. When a boy turned fourteen he went into the mines. That was that. My dad said that as a boy he watched the miners come up covered with soot, and he listened to them cough. He promised himself he would never be a miner. But when he hit fourteen, his father said, "Today you're coming to the mines with me." He hated the thought of it, but he went that day. That night he lay in his bed crying. He had always dreamed of working with horses in the fields, in the bright sunshine. What could he do—leave his family, run away?
>
> The advice he's always given me is, "It's okay to be afraid of what you don't know about. It's even more important to run from what you know is a terrible thing." My dad ran away that night. He did find work with horses, and he never went to work in the mines.

After a pause she repeated, "He's told me that many times." I wondered how many times she would retell it to herself and, perhaps, to her children, and they to theirs. I felt certain that many others that night took its lesson away as I did.

Some lesson tales step forward rather tentatively, as if they have been hidden away for a long time. Others carry the mark of having been enjoyed and savored many times. Another woman at that same swap delivered her story with a flourish. She said she had not had an easy time coming to America from Argentina as a little girl. One of her favorite early memories of living in America included smelling some delicious-looking meat, which street peddlers were selling in a park on her way home from her new school. When she asked her mother if she could try some on her next trip, her mother was adamant that she never purchase food sold on the street. "Why?" the girl asked. "It will kill you," her mother told her firmly. The next day, the girl took a little money she had saved to the park. She looked around for an appropriate place to die. Having chosen a comfortable tree to rest against, she walked over and purchased what we recognized from her description as a hot dog with all the fixings. She sat down, took a big bite, and waited to die. After the audience stopped laughing, she told us she had learned that day that there was something in America worth living for. She also discovered that her mother didn't always tell the truth.

Some adults' personal fables are sad. When they look into their childhoods they confront buried anger and fear. Yet even when a story seems to reopen some emotional wound, it begins to heal the wound, as if the balm of learning is applied whether or not it is spoken. At one of my first storytelling workshops for teachers, a woman told about when, as a little girl, she had begged her mother to make her older brother take her downtown with his friends. The boys didn't want "anyone's bratty sister tagging along," but her mother convinced them to take her. When the boys got halfway across the bridge leading downtown, they lifted the girl up over the railing and held her out over the water, promising that if she ever begged to go with them again, they would drop her. She said she learned to fear bridges that day and, though she hadn't told the story often, those feelings still lingered with her whenever she drove or walked over a bridge. We had little but awe in response to her powerful tale, but she seemed grateful just to have an audience that would listen with reverence.

This teller, a school librarian, wrote me that she recently retold the story to fourth graders as a prompt for their personal tales. Her children, who usually loved reading scary tales, "gasped when they heard my story. Perhaps because it was real, it truly horrified them. After weeks, some still ask for another detail, and I'm finding myself reassuring them all . . . I guess because I've lived with the memory, it has lost some of its impact. This incident and others from my childhood have helped shape the person I've become. But I rarely think of it now and was honestly surprised by the reactions of the children." She said she thought she would never tell the story to a young audience again.

Sometimes our stories do seem too powerful for our children or for our peers. We can be good judges of that. I asked participants in a teacher workshop to sketch their childhood homes, looking for a memory or bits of story connected to a certain room or object or space inside or outside the house. After a time I suggested they stop drawing and find a partner with whom to share the story or stories they had "seen" in the picture. One man, sitting apart from the group, continued to painstakingly detail the front view of a large building. He didn't seem interested in moving toward any partner or talking. Hoping he would participate, I walked over and whispered, "The idea is just to look down into the building or the surrounding area to see the memories stored there, then to *tell* them." When he didn't respond right away, I looked more closely and noticed that the structure didn't look like anyone's home, not even an apartment building. The man didn't look up; he just continued to draw line upon line, detailing what I now realized were many small windows on the facade of a building about three lots wide. I waited and admired the picture, wondering if he needed more time or simply didn't want to talk about it.

Finally, he looked up. "I don't have any memories worth telling about this place."

I tried to hear in his silence all that his statement conveyed. We both looked down at the picture. After a time I asked, "Is this where you grew up?"

He nodded. Then his face changed. I imagined he was trying to bring up the positive meaning from what must have been a very negative experience. Finally he said, "You see this window?" He pointed to one on the top floor. "I crawled out that window many times and went to the park down the street." His face broke into a grin. "*That* place I've got *lots* of stories about."

I smiled and waited, but he seemed to want to keep those stories to himself for now. That seemed right, but I couldn't help asking, "Do you tell your students those stories?"

"You bet," he said, smiling broadly now. "I tell them about the orphanage. Some of them don't have lives that are so great either, and the stories help them see that there are others as bad or worse off than they are."

Those personal fables I didn't get to hear, and I suspect that most of them had never been told to his colleagues, who sat at the other tables in the room. We can't always tell our stories, no matter how much wisdom they may hold. But imagining him telling his orphanage stories to children in his inner-city fifth grade gave me comfort.

Some personal stories I heard in a correctional facility where I was invited to tell stories to students working toward their GEDs. I tried to think of the job as just another school visit. Previously, I had taught remedial reading for two semesters as part of a junior college's correctional program at a different facility. I had felt a little uneasy at the beginning of that experience, but had come to like my students and respect their determination to succeed. I told myself that telling stories in a similar setting would not be difficult.

It didn't take long for me to realize that my personal stories were not exactly scenes all my listeners identified with. I wasn't even speaking the language a third of them spoke. I remember feeling very lost.

But, little by little, the men's faces began to show their response. A few chuckled at the images of the young me, and some seemed genuinely touched by my humiliation when the kindergarten teacher yanked me out of line. I told them folktales and poems as well, but having promised to run a workshop, I knew that in the short time available, it was easier to draw out personal stories than folktales or other story memories. By the end of each session, at least one listener had offered a powerful story in return. When I asked for their stories, only about half of the men were willing to turn to a partner to talk. I had brought paper, so a few drew pictures or wrote. One young man, who spoke to no one when I asked the men to partner up but wrote steadily after I distributed paper, handed me his writing as he left the room. "I hope you will like my story," he said.

> Hello, my name is Steven and I have a story to say when I was young. Well here it goes. When I was four years old I was into martial arts. My godmother had put me in martial art classes. For self defense, self control and self discipline. As I was growing up I saw a martial arts movie star and his name is Bruce Lee. So I always loved to see all his other martial art movies. Never did I miss one. I wanted to be just like Bruce Lee. So whenever I go to martial art classes I would practice hard and pay attention to what is being taught and said. I would leave from martial art classes and work out three hours a day in stretches and other workouts for my mind, body and spirit. I was growing up stronger and stronger and moving on to higher rank belts in martial arts and I was winning first place in tournaments a lot and my sensei loved me and I still do martial arts and I want to do the best of the best. Goodbye.

I am still humbled by all I heard that day. I have thought many times about what this one story encompasses: the desire for self-discipline, the nature of martial arts, finding a hero, being loved by a teacher, having one's dream supported by a godmother, growing stronger, and doing "the best of the best." I have wondered what my stories, even my presence, said to those men. I think about the look on the face of the teenager who handed me his paper and remember the teenager I was, desperate to write my father's story to anyone, even diocesan testers who would judge it for adherence to topic, supporting details, and spelling. At the top of his paper the young man wrote both his name and his correctional facility number, as if to say, "You meet me here in this prison, but this story is about who I really am." A brief but powerful glimpse of his life, it seemed to me a personal fable, one he was telling himself and one that might teach a visiting storyteller.

I heard two other stories that day that have lingered with me. They were not personal stories that focused specifically on moments in the life of the tellers. However, as I have said earlier, I believe we find ourselves and our lessons in any literature we choose to speak aloud. It seemed to me the men conveyed something about who they were and shared some truths they had learned from life.

To one group I told Benét's "The Mountain Whippoorwill," the long narrative poem I had learned in ninth grade. I had hoped that at least the rhythmic language and my gestures might offer an aesthetic if not a comprehensible narrative experience to those for whom English was not a native language. When I finished and asked listeners if the story reminded them of any other work or of any incident in life, several looked respectfully toward an older resident. Most in the room were in their late teens and twenties, but this man had gray in his hair. He smiled as if grateful for their acknowledgment. I had relied on his face during my telling; he had smiled and nodded regularly. The teacher who had set up my visit nodded toward the man as if approving what the others seemed to be requesting of him.

The gentleman stood, taking the floor with a clear stage presence. He began to recite a long and rhythmic narrative in Spanish. His voice was fierce at times and gentle at others. He shook his hands, knelt, and concluded with a bow. The men applauded wildly. I felt as if I had heard a great aria sung by a Pavarotti locked in a prison facility in upstate New York.

The teacher, as moved as the rest of us, seemed daunted by the task of translating such a work of art. "Well, it is a poem he learned as a young man. It is basically about respect for women and their gift of new life." He went on to say the poem told the story of a young girl who had an illegitimate child. The village wanted to ostracize her.

Her grandfather, the narrator, bade the villagers remember that all life is sacred and that a most sacred child had been born of an unwed mother whom some might have wanted to ostracize long ago. The villagers agreed to take in his granddaughter and help her raise the child as one of their own.

I couldn't know what the story meant to that man's life, but I could see the passion with which he delivered it. It may or may not have been his personal story, but it was one the other men clearly associated with this elder in their midst. I witnessed how powerfully it touched them. I couldn't know what illegitimacy, ostracism, a sacred child and his mother, or even what speaking boldly and beautifully one's native language in that setting meant to the teller or to the other men there, but like them, I felt the power of the tale.

The final story has stayed with me since that day and been a reminder of how we make even a traditional story into a personal one. I recount it here with respect for the teller and offer what my ear and heart remember. A man, who I believe came from the Virgin Islands, told it in an entertaining yet cautionary tone. "I have a story. I hear this story many, many times when I am a boy. You hear this story too I think? 'De Billy Goat Gruff'?"

I nodded and smiled. Some of the other men nodded.

"He try, he *try* to cross the bridge without paying the toll." He looked around at his fellow inmates as if to ask, "You know this story too?" They all laughed.

"He try to sneak across at night, but the Troll, he *catch* that billy goat." More laughter erupted from the listening men. "He try to barge past the Troll; he try to butt him with his horns." The man paused for their laughter, now, like a call and response. I was laughing too. "But no, the Troll, he send him back." All the men grinned and shook their heads. Apparently they knew this troll. "Finally"—the teller's face got instantly serious, he was no longer joking—"Finally, the Troll, he gobble up the billy goat." He nodded and paused to let the image sink in. He spoke the next two lines very slowly. "One must pay the toll. There is no escaping it." Some of his listeners grew somber. Some nodded. Some chorused, "Ah" in affirmation. I added my "Ah" and my nod.

Whether we choose to explore the moments of our lives or the tales told us in childhood, the stories that live within us are our teachers. If we voice them, we are likely to live out the lessons they teach.

NINE

Poems and Songs for Telling

o talk of story memories and storytelling is complete without considering the rich repository of language that comes to us in poems, songs, riddles, proverbs, prayers, nursery rhymes, and the like. When we are young and first learning to make sense of the world, the music of our language is an especially potent force. Our first image-language connections may come from rhymes that adults or siblings, the radio, television, or recordings have sung or spoken to us.

Some of us, for a variety of reasons, may have lost our love of rhythmic language as we grew older. More than a few teachers tell me they don't do much with poetry in their classrooms because they don't understand it well. Somewhere along the way they fell out of love with poetry and haven't found their way back yet. I returned to poetry, after being scared away from it, by speaking poems aloud with children and by remembering a connection to poetry I forged in childhood. My early enjoyment of poems and songs paved my road into storytelling. Earlier, I mentioned my delight in the little teapot's cry to "Tip me over . . . !" As I examine my story history and meet with groups of both school-age children and adult tellers, I am amazed not only by the numbers of poems people recall from childhood, once they start unearthing them, but also by how fondly they enjoy remembering and reflecting on them.

Singing and reciting have been intertwined for me since I first proudly mastered "Twinkle, Twinkle Little Star" at about age two and sent my silent wishes into the night with "Star Light, Star Bright." I believe that at every age, by speaking poems and singing songs, we release potent emotional energy hidden from the world and sometimes even from ourselves. I have watched my son sing in a high school rock band like an ancient priest chanting from the depths of his soul. I have seen shy, awkward sixth graders and tough, cool eighth graders speak their truths to the world in loud, clear voices through the medium of a poem or song. After such a performance a kind of cosmic shudder moves through the room before the adolescent speaker returns to "normal."

One poem comes to mind when I recall my initiation into poetry spoken aloud. Looking back, I realize that through her dramatization, my mother may have been releasing something secret and precious about herself. At the time, my siblings and I simply giggled spellbound under her enchanting performance of Laura E. Richards's "Eletelephony."

> Once there was an elephant,
> Who tried to use the telephant—

She would recite these lines in the most matter-of-fact way, then pause and correct herself as if she had just accidentally misspoken.

> No! no! I mean an elephone
> Who tried to use the telephone—

She would begin to look puzzled, as if she were losing control, and my face would break into a grin.

> (Dear me! I am not certain quite
> that even now I've got it right.)

I would finally start to giggle, so delighted by what I knew to be feigned perplexity.

> Howe'er it was, he got his trunk

She would speak this first line of the second stanza as if she were now calm and quite ready to proceed, but "howe'er" always foreshadowed the fun ahead.

> entangled in the telephunk;

For this line and the next two she plugged her nose, which sent all of us into hysterical laughter.

> The more he tried to get it free,
> The louder buzzed the telephee—

She would grow more frantic-looking with each line, and then, when our laughter subsided, gather her composure and speak the final two lines with happy resignation.

> (I fear I'd better drop the song
> Of elephop and telephong!)

I remember vividly the deliberateness with which my mother said each phrase and the way she paused after certain words so we could savor their funny sounds. She acted as if nonsense words were quite normal. I so loved watching her pretend. I figured out early on that grown-ups enjoyed pretending with children but they did not play in the same way with one another. It taught me that, regardless of age or sophistication, one can play, finding humor and perhaps solace in a poem spoken aloud.

Finding the Poetry and Song Within Our Lives

Not all of us remember liking poems and songs, and for some the memory may even carry a bitter taste because of a particular experience—a poem was forced on us or we were made to sing a song or asked to mouth the words instead. I remember being filled with fear at having to recite Wordsworth's "Daffodils" for a grade in the teacher's book. I feel sad to think of the mechanical way our teacher drilled the poem into us. We certainly didn't feel the lonely poet's wonder at coming upon "a host of golden daffodils."

If there is a formula for bringing ourselves and our children back to poetry, it is simply that, as teachers and parents, grandparents and neighbors—as the guardians of language and story—we first touch children with the language we loved over the years. To do that, we must reexperience our own early encounters with the music and the wonder of language. If we retrace how we came to a love of sound and rhythm, we will discover methods we can adapt to help children hold onto their instinctive love of language play.

I'll take out a few of my own memories. Some surfaced when I stumbled on forgotten poems in the children's section of the public library or leafed through the children's literature texts my mother had saved from her college days. As I talk with fellow teachers about their recollections of poems and songs, memories are continually jarred loose: "Oh, I haven't thought about these in *years!*" they exclaim, and I feel the same amazement. Each tells me a little more about how I came to love language, despite the negative experiences I had analyzing poetry or singing in public.

Earliest Memories of Song and Language Play

Most of the extended family who cared for me during my earliest years "spoke" in song. I am fairly certain, because I watched them do it later, as my younger siblings came along. My Grandfather Walsh's arrival at our house was marked by his loud singing. "Goodmorning goodmorning goodmorning and how are you today?" he bellowed goodheartedly, regardless of the hour. His equally tuneful "Gotta gotta gotta gotta gotta gotta gitalong" signaled his departure, and, of course, we in turn sang our way in and out of his house.

All through my youth, Grandpa Walsh was the patriarch of song in our extended family. One of the youngest of a large Irish brood that had come to America poor, he had made and lost a good living more than once in his youth in the twenties and thirties. I had a sense that prayer and song sustained him. Grandma Walsh, "Nana," a local church organist at one point, claimed him as her favorite soloist. All their children either sang or played the piano (my mother both

cherished and resented her lifelong assignment as family accompanist).
I remember that Grampa encouraged his adult children and any of his
grandchildren who sang at gatherings around the piano to "Tell the
story. *Tell the story*," as if the song said nothing until the singer felt its
meaning. Grampa sometimes cried when someone sang. I watched
how the words of the song and the passion of the singer touched him.
His tears filled me with wonder.

My mother's singing was always playful. As she dried us off after
baths in the kitchen sink she would croon, "Hey baby, it's *cold* outside!" or "Put your arms around me, honey, hold me tight." She rubbed
the thick terry cloth on our skin to the rhythm of radio tunes and
hugged and tickled us afterward. I don't remember her playing finger
games with me, but as a three- or four-year-old I enjoyed watching her
play them with my baby sister. "I see a mouse . . . ." She would pause
and then run her fingers in a tickling gesture up my sister's arm or leg
or bare belly during diapering time. "Now he's crawling up your neck!"
It was a way to distract my sister from fussing and teach her words at
the same time. When I mentioned this memory once during a workshop, a young teacher cried out, "That's the way I learned "The Three
Pigs"! My mother used to draw it on my back with her fingers as I was
falling asleep." The teacher turned to the back nearest her and showed
us where each scene of the story took place.

My father sang bass in a men's chorus. I picture him practicing
his rhythmic though not-very-melodic part as he shaved before an
evening rehearsal. Once or twice a year I would attend a concert of
the entire chorus, seventy men all dressed in tuxedos with red cum-
merbunds. I liked trying to pick out the bass sounds, which sometimes
contrasted with the rhythm of the melody. I also remember Dad
singing along with the car radio, a beat or two behind the singer, as
if he knew the entire song. I thought that was so clever. Today I
employ a similar technique while rehearsing a new story or learning
a poem with the help of my car tape player.

My dad's father, Papa Gillard, was assigned the job of dressing me
each morning during my preschool years because of my grandmother's
arthritis and my parents' jobs. He would stand me on the dining room
table, which thrilled me, and teach me my prayers. "Angel of God,
my guardian dear" ("Reach for the sky, Honey" and off came my pj

top), "to whom God's love commits me here . . . ." He'd pull my T-shirt with its too tight neckhole over my head. Each movement of my pudgy arms and legs accompanied a line of praise, petition, or thanksgiving. The rhythm of the spoken word, my movements, and the words' meanings were imprinted upon my psyche. When Papa ate his late morning breakfast of soft-boiled eggs and cream-colored coffee, he allowed us "pigeons" to "buy" bits of food. We sang our ABCs and recited "One, two, buckle my shoe" or showed off our knowledge in some other way. Now I see that those playful moments were exercises in language assessment. I borrowed his technique when, as a teacher, I took note of what my students' reciting and storytelling told me about their knowledge of words and grammar.

Long car rides to cousins' houses, hikes along the railroad tracks as we picked dandelion greens and cowslips, hours of jumping rope and swinging on swings were likewise filled with songs. "Where have you been, Billy Boy, Billy Boy?" I remember one of my dad's friends, "Slug" Swierczek, teaching us a parody to "Oh dear, what can the matter be?" that included the line, "He promised to buy me a bunch of flat tires to tie up my bonnie blue hair." When some middle schoolers balk at "serious" poetry and beg for nonsense verse or the kind of rhymes that "just make us laugh," I am reminded of how Slug's songs, which made us cry we laughed so hard, remained our favorites right through our big kid years.

Meeting Children Where They Are

We are wise to meet children on whatever language pathway we find them. They travel where they do for important reasons. This is why I think the search for our own memories of learning to like (and dislike) language play, "serious" poetry, or song is so important. At a recent Sharing the Fire Conference in Boston, teachers and storytellers joined me for a session entitled "Poem-Telling." I offered this invitation in the program: "Poems celebrate the little details and momentous occasions of human experience. Bring your favorite poems and memories of rhymes and songs or come browse to find ones that tickle your funnybone or touch your soul. We'll sing, spit, smile, and shout them."

At first we were all a little shy, intrigued by the invitation to spit and shout but unused to letting go of our reserved adult natures publicly. After all, we teachers spend the better part of every day helping children—our own and our students—gain *control*: of their behavior, their muscles, their language, themselves. We believe we teach control in the best sense. Yet what happens is that gradually, the Child within, who sang, shouted, giggled, and at least erupted occasionally with emotion (or desperately wanted to) gets buried under all this control and under curriculum demands and tests and schedules.

Fulfilling my duty as hall monitor when classes passed in middle school, I sometimes felt like a prison guard. Among the staff we often talked of "holding the lid on" as the essence of our teaching on the days before a long weekend or vacation. Yet encouraging poetry and storytelling in our classrooms, in our colleagues' classrooms, during assemblies, and at community gatherings just might allow our students to let go of "control" a little more often and in a way that is constructive. If students actively and creatively display poems, songs, and stories through movement and voice, they are less likely to need to let off steam in the hallways or on the days before school breaks. We might all waste less energy.

At the Boston conference, my "Poem-Telling" participants weren't sure what to expect. Some, seeing the piles of books I had brought, immediately began to browse. Others, who had brought poems or perhaps remembered their teachers' injunctions to "wait until you're invited," sat and waited politely for the session to begin. I opened the program by admitting rather sheepishly that I had offered the workshop for selfish reasons. "I love reading poems aloud and it's lonely doing it without company." I saw knowing smiles. I asked if they too had memories of poems and song-poems that comforted them, made them feel brave on hard days, and helped them laugh. Almost everyone nodded.

I suggested that we begin with our own memory work. Later we would feast on the old and new books of poetry for children and share ideas about professional books that focused on teaching poetry in a natural, playful way. To begin the memory work, I asked everyone simply to relax as I walked down the lane of my own memories. They could let go of my voice occasionally or completely, listening to me only until what I said triggered *their* memories. I asked them to be conscious of their breathing. It would take them back to the rhythms of childhood language and melody. We took several deep relaxing breaths together in order to allow the internal memory-gatherer, like the night-dreamer, to let go of the present moment and find a path to the past.

I talked about my memory of the song "Playmate" and how as a child I sang it over and over, perhaps to comfort myself when no neighbor child could come out and play or when my siblings were off with other friends. I remembered miming, yet also feeling, the sadness of "My dolly has the flu. / Boo hoo hoo hoo hoo hoo" much the way my mother mimed, but perhaps also felt, "Eletelephony."

I talked of "The House That Jack Built" and how I had loved the kissing sound of "the maiden all forlorn," just as I had the kissing "under the bamboo tree" in a song we sang on long car rides. I recalled tongue twisters such as "Bill owned a billboard and Bill owed a board bill . . . " not to mention "Peter Piper's peck of pickled peppers." I mentioned jump-rope rhymes, hide-and-seek calls, prayer litanies such as the string of "God blesses" that my sisters and I said in unison for at least a few years when we shared a common bedtime. I told them I vaguely recalled the story of "the gingham dog and the calico cat" but remembered just liking the sound of that phrase as I had liked the expressions in "The Owl and the Pussycat."

As a child I had adored riddle poems, one about a single girl named "Elizabeth, Elspeth, Betsy, and Bess" and one about "thirty white horses upon a red hill," a metaphor for teeth and gums. I named Broadway show tunes that I had sung at full voice from a neighbor's swingset, hoping to be discovered as the next Annette by a Walt Disney scout. I told of barbershop harmony favorites my aunts and uncles had sung in the kitchen, John Denver tunes played by my cousin Harold, and "Rocky Raccoon," the one Beatles' song even old relatives requested from my brother Dan.

I cautioned them that my memories might not be anything like theirs. My purpose was to encourage them to return to the places where they had encountered rhythm and rhyme and to the people who had crooned, called, recited, sung, or even scolded. The rhythmic phrases I carried with me included Grandmother Gillard's "A stitch in time saves nine" and someone else's "When ya gonna use your head for somethin' besides a hat rack?"

As I looked around the room, some were writing and some appeared to be time traveling. A few were smiling while others were clearly lost in their memories. I allowed time for quiet reflection before inviting participants to share their memory treasures. We conversed first with partners. Adults, like children, discover more than information when they do this kind of memory work. They unearth feelings and appreciate the chance to talk or write privately as they sort through what they want to share publicly.

Marjorie sang us the version of "Old King Cole" she had learned at bedtime: "He called for his pipe, and he called for his bowl, and he called for his fiddling fiddlers three, fiddle dee dee." Someone started us on Sunday school songs, including: "Nebuchadnezzar couldn't sneeza," "Zacchaeus was a little man," and "First I must honor God, second honor His name . . . ." We laughed at our discoveries, feeling ourselves children once again.

Barbara recalled a poem she could say at a very young age that contained multisyllabled words such as *extraordinary* and *superlative*. She sighed. "I loved those grown-up words, loved feeling them in my mouth." Another woman mentioned a recitation that rhymed "winning hearts" with "throbbing parts," a ditty she had learned when she was far too young to have any idea what it meant. This triggered my memory of men and women relatives alike singing a bawdy parody comparing a woman's body parts to places like the Himalayas and Greece. It concluded, "But then I spied my wife and to save my very life, I let the rest of the world go by."

Others in the group recited such diverse recollections as "Liar, liar, pants on fire . . . " and "The goblins'll get you if you don't watch out." Often people remarked that it was more the teller they remembered than the tale. One workshop participant's face told us she was still searching for the memory even as she began to speak slowly. "My mother sang something with the phrase 'pretty baby' in it." Suddenly, three others simultaneously burst into song: "Oh I want a lovin' baby and it might as well be you, pretty baby, pretty baby . . . ." Her face flooded with the long forgotten joy of being a tiny girl sung to by a loving mother.

Then other faces lit up with recollections. The songs and word-games of those who truly nurtured our child lives, stored away in our deepest selves, began to surface. Mothers, fathers, great-aunts, big brothers, camp counselors, Brownie leaders, choir directors, school custodians and lunch ladies, playground attendants, librarians and television storytellers such as Captain Kangaroo joined us in the room. Our discussions focused as much on the memory of those relationships as on the words. Our power as teachers and storytellers to touch the children in our lives with the gift of language became very clear.

By recollecting these relationships, we were suddenly aware of what is at the heart of the work we do. It isn't so much a matter of choosing the proper poems or tales, although certain poems and songs and stories had been important to each of us. What is vital, we concluded, is the combination of enthusiasm and authenticity that accompanies our "teaching." Whether we share our favorite poems or help children into their own for solo or group performances, we need to let feelings be a part of our work. As a child, I hadn't been scandalized by adult relatives singing a raunchy song in praise of womanly body parts because I had sensed the free-spirited humor and the camaraderie that filled the room as everyone, male and female, chorused it together. Many of us remembered humorous as well as serious works, and we all agreed that young or old, male or female, we needed more humor in our classrooms and in our lives. School, with its many requirements and standards of excellence, can too often be humorless. We admitted that as teachers *we* probably took life more than a little too seriously, perhaps for good reasons. But if we hoped to bring the spitting, shouting, whispering, and singing of poetry and stories into our classrooms, we would have to balance propriety with fun. We would need to allow laughter and even invite tears, like my grandfather's, if we were going to share aloud the poems and songs we loved and help children find the ones that touched them.

Telling Poems with Middle Schoolers

Remembering and browsing, reciting and reading aloud, the methods I used in my Boston workshop, are the same ones I used to "teach" poetry in middle school. We looked and listened within, followed our breathing, trailed along memory lane, and let whatever images, fragrances, tastes, or sounds we could discover take us back in time. For some students, only a shadow of a memory might appear at first, but we learned to give ourselves time and talk. Looking through books of jump-rope chants, holiday songs, nursery rhymes, and poems helped us, just as they did when we searched for story memories. Once we began to relive moments, return to places, and revisit people who played patty-cake, bounced balls, and crooned us to sleep, everyone found treasures. In those moments we found lost pieces of ourselves, the people we were before all the shoulds of grown-ups and peers set in. Sometimes we figured out that those shoulds had made us doubt ourselves or created a stockpile of negative feelings that had long blocked our creativity. Many students discovered that in poems and songs they found more than simple wordplay and giggles; they found echoes of their deepest feelings and blueprints for how to live. Some of my young adolescents saw forgotten connections to adults or to peers they were currently pulling away from.

Their memories, like those of the workshop participants, included jump-rope chants: "Teddy Bear, Teddy Bear, turn around" came up every year. They would smile at the image of their younger selves. Others grinned, remembering the sneers in their voices as they chanted, "My mother punched your mother right in the nose." Some giggled to recall the delicious naughtiness of "Amster Amster sh sh sh" (replacing "dam dam dam"), and some admitted pitying Humpty Dumpty, who couldn't be put back together again.

One student mentioned the crickets outside a tent as a constant reminder of summer. Some recalled early morning birdsong drawing them from dreams. I heard testimony to rock-and-roll music, scratchy 78 rpm records, A. A. Milne and Robert Louis Stevenson, patty-cake, "Jack be nimble," "Georgie Porgie," radio jingles, Billie Holiday, Gregorian chant, and the mournful sound of a cantor.

The channels through which the music of words comes to human ears and hearts are limitless. I continue to be amazed at how many adults still retain long poems they learned by heart in school or even during the years before school. Some laugh at how certain poems made little sense to them at the time but realize how the rhythms or perhaps just one image in the poem anchored in their soul. In an early chapter of *When You've Made It Your Own*, Greg Denman describes the way he gently planted the images of Robert Frost's "Stopping by Woods on a Snowy Evening" in the minds of his students by reciting it, quietly and repeatedly, as they drew in ink on white paper the woods they had stood in moments before. I might have understood my teacher's reason for introducing us to Wordsworth if she had taken us to see a field or even a yard of daffodils.

My middle schoolers never tired of browsing through books and folders of poems. I borrowed poetry collections from libraries and saved copies of student-written verse from year to year. I kept every morsel I could find about poets and the process of writing. Paul Janeczko's anthologies, such as *The Place My Words Are Looking For*, which contained poets' explanations of a poem's history, intrigued my students and encouraged them to find the poet in themselves.

Telling Poems Aloud and Weaving Poems into Stories

Telling poems or singing songs is different from telling stories, but the traditions are closely connected. The bards of old sang stories. My students could name many modern bards whose songs told stories or argued issues. Over the years I experimented with requiring students to memorize at least one poem or song, but in the end I moved toward the idea of simply inviting them to take the words of poems into their mouths, faces, torsos, and limbs. I showed them different ways poems could be interpreted and then they simply played with bringing poems to life. We could learn a small poem, such as Eve Merriam's "Hurry" from *Jamboree*, fairly quickly and explore telling it in different tones of voice. Then we talked about just how we had kept words or images in our minds in order to learn the poem by heart.

Sometimes I would tell longer narrative poems that I admitted had taken more work but were very satisfying to know. Most students wanted in on the fun and learned many more poems than if I had assigned them the task. Everyone found at least some poems they wanted to read aloud repeatedly. They could read to walls or friends as a way to practice. Some preferred mouthing the words in a whisper to themselves, but I encouraged them to "mouth" poetry in order to explore it completely.

"Say it slow. Say it fast. But say it. Don't rush to understand it. Hear it. Try on the syl-la-bles and pause to feel the white spaces. Let the commas invite you to linger and the periods make you halt. Let the rhyme you encounter anywhere in the poem roll about in your mouth. Taste each consonant and vowel. If there's not a hint of rhyme, listen for other tricks of sound within. Poets play many instruments."

When I said such things, some middle schoolers looked at me as if I were crazy. I assured them that poems and songs had kept me sane, that they had helped me name and release at least some of the craziness inside. I had found poems to fit my every mood over the years, and I knew they would too. It just might take some looking. No strangers to moodiness or craziness, my budding adolescents always came around.

I would sometimes take on the persona of oral poet to encourage their own risk-taking, hamming it up as my mother had in her rendition of "Eletelephony":

This is not regular reading aloud.
This is song. This is play.
(Isn't play something usually discouraged in school?)
Shhh! It'll be our secret.

No singsong poems for us.
No memorization just because we *should*.
No talk of "This is booooooooring!"

Find a poem (or song) that l-i-n-g-e-r-s in your mind:
One that tickles till you're giggling silly,
One that brings just a tear to your eye,
One that will help you sob like you haven't done in years,
One that makes you feel so grown-up, so wise,
You want to hold on to it all your life.
Find a poem that makes you want to sing!
Find a poem that lets your spirit soar!

We'll grow a garden of poem-tellings.
We'll toss a salad of them.
We'll create a Dagwood sandwich of poems to chew and savor
and mmmmm swallow and then bite in for more.
Okay, find a poem for dessert too,

Carmelly and chewy or whipped creamy smooth.
Just brush your teeth before you go to science.

We'll find the poems and songs that say
"I was written for *you*."
They won't be hard to memorize.
They may appear before your eyes in dreams . . .
Speak the poems
>**you**
>>need to hear.

From Poems to Tales

For many good reasons, speaking and writing poems and songs can be approached separately from storytelling and writing. But I am intrigued by the many ways in which the two influence each other: when poetic language or form turned up in our storytelling, when our poems took on narrative qualities, or when in some other way the two fed each other.

I would tell students about meeting Eve Merriam (whose influence is recognizable in the invitation above) and about laughing with her over her poem "Schenectady," written in delight at the sounds in our city's name. I would tell them of my shock when Frank Hodge, the Pied Piper of children's books in our area, introduced Eve. Having read much of her work, I had imagined that she would be quite young. And I would laugh, trying to recapture the way she shouted the poem "A Yell for Yellow" as if she were still a kid on the playground and not a poet in her seventies delivering a keynote address from a podium. Within such conversations—and they were conversations—we danced back and forth between poems and stories.

Or I might pick up on someone's mention of a parent's rhythmic call at suppertime and tell about storyteller Tom Weakley (1992) who built a full-length performance tale around his dismissal of his mother's call to supper. As a five-year-old engrossed in the rrrrrrrrrr of the cars he was racing through the dirt, he ignored her call of "Taahhhhhmy, suhhhhhpper!" That is, he ignored it in spirit but dutifully sang back, "Cuhhhhhhming" while continuing to rrrrrrrrr with his toy cars.

Or I might play them folksinger John McCutcheon's song, "Calling All the Children Home," which begins with the memory of his mother calling him and his nine siblings. Though the song begins in his backyard it ends in celebration of the world's children, including such names as Isabelle, Moishe, Mikael, and Kim in the final chorus.

I enjoyed telling students about the first time I wove a song and a story together. I had made the connection between the traditional song "Molly Malone" and my parents' influence on my life as a teacher, and I eventually published it (Schwartz 1989). What the written version doesn't tell is that I composed the story while driving into the countryside the morning of the last day of my first storytelling residency. By then, I had already told the residency participants all the stories I knew. I wanted to spend our last day telling spontaneous personal stories, but I also wanted to model how a personal experience can be shaped or embellished to make it a better tale for telling. In the car I found myself singing the song about Molly being from Dublin, pushing a fishcart like her parents before her, and coming back as a ghost. It occurred to me I could follow each verse with parallel reflections about visiting Ireland, realizing my parents' influence on my choice of vocation, and feeling the influence of their "ghosts" upon me still. I think the fact that I created the story while driving intrigued my students as much as its content.

Months later, when a storytelling friend asked me to speak to her class about personal stories, I tried it again. Since I was speaking on an afternoon close to St. Patrick's Day, I wove fragments from "Harrigan," "When Irish Eyes Are Smiling," and other Irish-American popular songs with short memory sketches of growing up. My students and I had talked about how, once you find a story framework or formula, it is not hard to adapt it to different situations.

Whether my students actually combined story and song or ever told a long narrative poem as a story was not important to me. I simply had a hunch that since poetic rhythms and story images had been so intertwined during my own early language development, my students young and old would find gems among the layers of their early language memories. Discovering and polishing those gems couldn't help but add to the richness of our work and play in language arts.

TEN

Looking Within for the Story in History

mages of people acting out of courage and foolishness, greed and generosity, tolerance and intolerance are found not only in fairytales and poems; they are also found in history. Images are what helps history stay with us. Once it stays, we begin to see its significance. We begin to learn the lessons history has to teach. Telling stories makes history and its lessons ours.

I memorized dates and the names of people and places in history easily as a child. I still recall the year Columbus sailed and when William the Conqueror conquered, but until I ran into an image reflecting how people's lives were changed by a person or an event, I had no relationship to history. I didn't own it, and its lessons were lost to me.

Sometimes presenting a young mind with images isn't even enough. A friend recently watched *The Sound of Music*. She realized that thirty years earlier, when she had first seen it in the theater as a teenager, she had had no idea of who the Nazis were or what the Von Trapps wanted to escape. The uniformed guards had merely been movie screen bad guys. History is one more resource for storytelling material. Once students take history into their mouths and bodies, once they put on and feel its emotions, they no longer remain passive memorizers of its facts.

Now I'll be honest that I haven't heard many children tell historical tales, but watching my son Brian encounter history through an experience of shared reading and writing, I got a glimpse of how important it could be for a child to return to history through his own oral composing. At age seven, new to his school, Brian went to the library. The librarian, Marguerite Lewis, asked him about his interests, hoping to steer him toward books he would enjoy. When he whole-heartedly answered, "Baseball" she introduced him to a collection of biographies that would take him inside the world of professional ball. She promised he would meet Mickey Mantle as a boy and watch the Babe get his start too. Peg Lewis knew something important about people and learning: we gain access to learning—history in this case—through something inside us. Brian could only step into history from where he was: boyhood. But with my support, reading the books aloud with him, he was able to explore the complex world of big league trades, corporate decisions, mentors, the peaks and slumps of a career, the issue of segregation, and all the other aspects of those biographies that were far from his own experience. Our conversation as we read together helped him understand what would have gone over his head if he had read independently (which he couldn't have at age seven).

Soon he was composing, partly by writing and partly by dictating as I wrote, a fictional baseball biography of his own. It included high parental hopes, mentors, corporate decisions, moments of discrimina-tion, and, of course, heroic baseball victories. It didn't hurt that Peg Lewis met Brian at the library door each week and asked him to update her on his discoveries. When I asked him recently, almost ten years later, about his memory of this experience, the images of the history we explored and of himself as recreator were still vivid in his mind, not to mention the memory of that wonderful librarian.

If we want children to step into history through storytelling, we must meet them where they are. What moments or people in history have they already encountered? What characters or events do they want to know more about? Where might history collide with their interests as big league history did with Brian's young dreams of being a ballplayer? If a class is studying a particular period of history, where are the moments or the real-life consequences of those moments that will make the period one worth remembering for a child?

Barbara Lipke (1993) tells her students about her memory of walking through New York City on her way to school in 1934. She saw jobless and homeless people everywhere and adults selling apples for a nickel on nearly every corner. Then she spotted a five-dollar bill on the ground, a fortune to a little girl during those times. All day she was torn between excitement at having found such a treasure and guilt, imagining someone not being able to pay rent or buy food or afford a doctor's fee. Telling this story, she brings her students into the past with her to relive her dilemma and draws out the stories of their lives that will help them connect with the era of the Great Depression and its impact on their present and future lives.

If we want to invite students to tell stories about history we must first do it ourselves. It is not difficult if we think about the images of history that already belong to us from experience or reading. I used to pretend to be Helen Keller after a teacher read us excerpts about her life. Later, I saw the film *The Miracle Worker* every chance I got. I had worn glasses from the age of five because of bad nearsightedness and wondered what it would be like to be blind and to push through that darkness into courage and competence as Keller had. As a young girl attending Catholic school, I often heard tales of Joan of Arc and of the children to whom the Virgin Mary appeared at Fatima. Those were moments in history that came to life because they touched my child's heart. I even tried (at least some of the time) to live the kind of life that might draw a divine apparition my way. History offered me another model in Anne Frank, whose story I first saw on TV and marveled at every time I saw it again. History, in the form of stories, offered me ideals to shoot for.

Later, as a teenager, I peered into history through the keyhole of romance. My mother offered me O. E. Rölvaag's *Giants in the Earth* and a few other historical novels. She never talked with me about the books except to say that she liked them at about my age. Yet just the idea of sharing story images with the girl inside my mother was enough to sustain me through what was difficult reading for me at that time. Rölvaag took me across the desolate landscape of pioneer America in the company of young and idealistic newlyweds from Norway who dared to try to tame Nature. The whine of the locusts swarming over crops and driving the young wife, Beret, to the brink of insanity has never left me. Pearl Buck's *The Good Earth*, set in China, showed me how another culture regards its ancestors and offered me a different look at the hard times associated with romance and the land. Irving Stone's *Those Who Love* lured me into history through the courtship of John and Abigail Adams, again giving me lessons in love and toil, and leading me to think about such adult concerns as law making and political alliances.

I never told any of these stories. I am not sure I understood even a fraction of what they might have taught me. There was no place to tell them or even rewrite them the way Brian did by combining his dreams and his knowledge of baseball. If I did complete some kind of report on the books for school, it was no more than a plot summary I dashed off and eventually discarded. The awe those characters inspired I kept secret in my heart. I wonder now how telling aloud even a fragment of one of those tales of courage might have supported my own budding adolescent courage. Would claiming the words of those women characters have made my journey into womanhood any less perplexing? I bet it would have, just the way the speaking voice in Lowell's poem "Patterns" helped me grieve.

When I helped seven-year-old Brian recreate what our reading had stirred up in him by taking down his dictation of his fictional biography, I saw what pleasure it gave him to voice his interpretation of the history we had studied. His personal retelling revealed the extent of his understanding and a great deal about his inner life: the importance of his friendships, his impressions of his dad and me, his struggle with competitiveness in school and on the field.

I saw that same mix of pleasure and effort again when in fifth grade, at an evening read-aloud for families organized by that same librarian, Brian delivered with intensity two excerpts from L. M. Montgomery's *Rilla of Ingleside*. This is the story of Anne Shirley's (*Anne of Green Gables*) daughter whose teenage years are stolen by the concerns of World War I, a war Canadians impatiently wait for America to enter. In the process of choosing important moments in the text and preparing them for delivery, Brian returned again and again to Rilla's struggles and the light-hearted spirit she inevitably brought to them. By finding a way to combine her humor and her seriousness in his oral reading, he seemed to take her on as a kind of mentor. I too had been mentored by the characters in the historical fiction I read as a teen and indirectly by my mother, who gave me the books, but I internalized my new insights far less because I never shared them with anyone, aloud or in writing.

Bringing Ourselves and Our Students to History Telling

If the stories of history are to bloom in our classrooms, we need to find our stories and the courage to tell them. If we take the time to look just a little, we might be surprised at what is there. The leader at a women's writing workshop some colleagues and I attended asked us each to identify one woman in history we would like to emulate. Speaking extemporaneously, every one of us stood up and described clearly the aspects of the life of the woman she admired. No one lacked for detail and most even told of some significant moment. I was amazed. My friends and I had never spoken of our admiration for these women before, and I doubted that we had told such stories to our students. The experience affirmed for me that history lives within each of us.

What are our connections to history? Perhaps we were told of a relative's journey to America and therefore have a tale that can lead children into a study of immigration. Or we may have been shown old photos of grandmothers in high-collared blouses seated in wicker chairs or boyish, barefoot grandfathers perched on city stoops. In a friend's family photo album there is a picture of his father, a white man, standing with the Negro League baseball players he called friends.

Perhaps as children we found arrowheads or visited forts or heard legends of the native people who lived on the land before us. Perhaps our reading or visits to museums have brought us a new awareness of the people whose land was taken and whose migration was mandated, and we would like to develop that into a tale for telling. We may know of a secret cellar hiding place in some local home that was a station on the underground railroad or own a baseball card from the fifties or the biography of a suffragette. We may have heard of a grandfather whose business failed in the thirties or of an aunt who worked in a munitions factory in the forties. Or we may have met characters in historical fiction, in biographies, or in collections of letters. Any of these might be the key that unlocks history telling.

To Research or Not to Research

"But I don't have time to research a tale, and I wouldn't want to do a poor job of it," some teachers say. Let me offer two pieces of advice. First, not every tale requires research. Publishers today offer many historically accurate works of fiction and nonfiction about people and events from different eras. Teachers can choose an excerpt that moves them and that they believe will excite the minds of their students.

The evening Brian read from *Rilla of Ingleside*, he was preceded by a young teacher whose chosen excerpt was from *Amos Fortune, Free Man*. In a brief introduction he told us that as a boy he had enjoyed singing the songs known as spirituals in his church choir. While reading, he had found one of his old favorites and been reminded of how important these hymns were to the slaves and even to freed men and women whose life journeys had not been easy. Then he began to sing, ever so slowly, in a deep, well-trained voice, "Swing Low, Sweet Chariot." He wove the song's chorus in again near the end of the reading and invited the audience to sing with him.

My first reaction was to be grateful that this young man, one of only two male teachers in the building, had demonstrated that a man could sing proudly, unaccompanied by instruments or other voices, and that he had invited us all to join in. Now a fifth grader, Brian was already getting the message, despite his school chorus's attempts to counteract it, that singing wasn't cool, especially for a boy. Later, I also realized how powerful this teacher's full-voiced singing had been in bringing us into the historical moment of Amos Fortune's life and how his own personal connection to the spirituals had connected all of us to the people called "slaves." Through his singing, he had shown Amos Fortune to be a man he identified with. Although the teacher didn't tell the excerpt as a story, he made excellent eye contact, especially with the children, as he read, pulling them into the world of the tale. When he sang, he lowered the book to his side and for a moment seemed to *become* Amos Fortune. Brian, who had been struggling to combine reading expressively and making eye contact (and who had politely resisted his mother's instruction), paced his reading more slowly than when he had practiced at home and made excellent eye contact with the large audience. The task no longer daunted him after he had watched such a proficient demonstration.

The value of offering history as *story* is that it will linger in the minds of children long after the telling. And telling is different from reading a long text aloud or from memorizing chunks of a book. The experience of trying to read an entire historical novel to my classes one year taught me what *not* to do. I had committed myself to reading *The Man Who Tamed Lightning* to all four of my classes. My brother Dan, a science teacher, had lent me this book about the life of Charles Steinmetz, a genius in the field of electricity. Steinmetz had played an important role in the development of the General Electric Company of Schenectady, the city where I taught. My reading of the book coincided with the publication of a photo biography, *Steinmetz in Schenectady*, by Larry Hart, a local historian. Most of my listeners, fascinated by the actual photos of the man and of the local places they knew, were eager for the reading each Friday. The story included Steinmetz's youth in Germany, his political escape and penniless beginning in America, and his eccentric life in Schenectady. Unfortunately, *it simply took too long to read.* My students met for only forty-five minutes a day, and I couldn't give more than one day a week to such time travel.

Some of the children didn't particularly like the story, despite my attempts at a German accent and the author's account of Steinmetz's idiosyncrasies. I thought I could speed up the reading through storytelling, but I found myself spending hours prereading and editing the book for action highlights. Because I thought the children were used to the author's style, I didn't allow myself to pull out an event or two and tell about them in my own style. Looking back, I realize that I could have used my planning time and our class time more efficiently if I had read the book on my own, outlined a few key moments in Steinmetz's life, and told them in a comfortable style. I could have included moments from his youth and his escape, the flavor of his German accent, and glimpses of the wild habitat he set up in Schenectady. Then I could have moved on to another book. Better yet, I could have encouraged any children who were interested to find their own moments to tell after I had jump-started the book. I am certain that many of the children would have read the entire book, others would have turned to Hart's book, and those who didn't connect with Steinmetz' story about politics and science would have been free to move on to another inquiry that did engage them.

That year, I learned that there are shorter, more enjoyable ways to bring historical fiction to life. I also learned that I can take stories from a written text and tell them in my own words. If I can see key moments in my mind's eye, I can tell those moments for my students, with or without accents, details, or dramatics. What resounds in me will come across to my students and my efforts will lead them to their own investigations of history and their own storytelling.

The second piece of advice about researching a tale is that it is not that hard to do *if* you find a fairly accessible topic and one you care about deeply. Both the historical tellings I have prepared were for "gigs," as my folksinging sister calls them. Schools asked me for a particular story. Gardnertown Fundamental Magnet School in Newburgh, New York, asked me to present an assembly program on the life of Martin Luther King, Jr. What was my connection to that story? Basically an abiding sadness that I had considered myself an "honor student" practically from the time King watched the boycotted buses go by to the day he was shot in Memphis, yet during all those years I was only vaguely aware of the key part he played in Montgomery, Birmingham, Selma, or even Washington. In my small town in upstate New York I was almost as oblivious to the Civil Rights Movement and King's actions as my friend had been to the presence of Nazis in *The Sound of Music*. My sense of having missed such a significant time in my own country's history made me want to know this man now that I called myself "teacher." Wanting to learn his story and share it with children so that they would not ignore the history occurring all around them was my ticket in.

My questions directed my research: Who taught King to lead at such a young age? Where did he find such patience? What mentors in his young adulthood had he looked to? How had he learned to face death so boldly? These questions and others led me to bookstores and libraries. Armed with three children's biographies, one adult history of King's life, and a series of other works about the Civil Rights Movement in general, I dived in, and I loved every late night kitchen table moment.

One day some students found me working on the third draft of a timeline of the events in King's life from his youth through his death. One boy shook his head and asked, his face full of disbelief, "You are doing this because you *want* to?" I just laughed. While the offer of the gig had given me a gentle push, the puzzle was now of my own making. Timelining was helping me sort through events and see some as consequences of others. I was able to locate what to me were the people and the moments that had made King who he was. This was a little more work than telling an excerpt from a biography or historical novel, but, as my student so clearly witnessed, it was mine. I found forgiveness for myself, a child who had not known King or Malcolm X or any of the figures young and old, male and female, who had marked this era. I learned that racism is perpetuated by ignorance. The stories of these major figures in the Civil Rights Movement and its collective action inspired by King, Malcolm, and others, gave me renewed hope in our country's future, despite the residue of ignorance and hatred that still exists. In the end I found more stories than I could possibly tell in one assembly, perhaps even more than in a lifetime (Schwartz 1994a).

My second experience with research was quite different but in its own way enlightening and rewarding. Doris Dunkleburger asked me to develop a story, any story, about the town of Waterford, New York, for her kindergartners. Doris had helped me secure funding for my three-day visit from a General Electric grant for local artists in the schools. Taking my task seriously but not knowing quite how to shape history for kindergartners, I headed to the small but friendly Waterford Town Library. There I found bits and pieces of local history, but nothing that at first seemed appropriate for kindergarten. When the library closed I walked the streets under an Indian summer moon and tried to feel my way back in time. Waterford began to remind me of my own hometown, Fulton, once an important port on the Oswego River, just as Waterford had been a canal stop at the juncture of the Mohawk and Hudson Rivers. When I found myself at the locks connecting the rivers, the story began to form. I knew rivers meant spring floods, and moments before I had been reading about Waterford's greatest flood early in the century. Even small children would be able to visualize the heavy spring rains and the thawing snows that ran off the Adirondack Mountains. I had read that the flooding grew worse because so many trees had been cleared for new houses and farms, so the story could have an environmental theme too. I also thought we might have fun talking about the Erie Canal—looking at how many years ago the canal had been built—and naming the streets in town affected by its flooding. To our story my kindergarten audience added the finger-snapping and hand-clapping sounds of a downpour as well as a chant: "The Mohawk's flowing west to east; the Hudson's flooding down from the north." The entire plan evolved from one pleasant library evening, a moonlit walk, and a slight rush of anxiety about wiggly kindergartners. A little research is not so bad. As my mother used to say when introducing some new food or activity we assumed we wouldn't have a taste for, "Be careful, you might like it."

Models of Historical Storytelling

The National Storytelling Association as well as publishers such as Yellow Moon Press and August House offer historical tales on inexpensive audiotapes so students can hear examples of history brought to life. Syd Lieberman, a high school teacher and storyteller from Evanston, Illinois, was commissioned by the city of Johnstown, Pennsylvania, to write a story commemorating the centennial of its famous 1889 flood. He mixed fact and imagination to tell the story of townspeople whose worries about the dam above the town were not heeded by the wealthy and powerful men who had built it. Lieberman writes about how secondary sources such as books and newspapers provided him with the context and background of the story. Then a primary source, the diary of Gertrude Quinn, brought him a personal recollection of the flood. Lieberman decided to base the heart of his story on the Quinn family's experience of that awful day. The audiotape of this breathtaking story might frighten very young children, but it held my class's attention and provided an excellent example of how to create a lively historical tale.

Joyce Grear, a full-time storyteller from North Carolina, presents live performances of tales about famous African-American women such as Harriet Tubman, Phillis Wheatley, and Mary McLeod Bethune. But Grear includes in their biographies the tales of those individuals, often white, who helped them along their paths of courage. Grear's purpose in depicting "unsung griots" as she calls them is to show young audiences that camaraderie and cooperation have fueled achievement over time despite the divisions that some have fostered between people of different colors. (Grear, and most of the storytellers mentioned in this book, are listed in the National Storytelling Association Directory in the Resources for Storyteachers.)

In a masterful interweaving of histories, Doug Lipman combined the tales of four distinct grassroots movements in a speech at the 1993 Sharing the Fire Conference in Boston. He connected the work of those trying to repeal "separate but equal," with the efforts of the supporters of the American public library system, the birth of Hassidism, and the creation of national folk music in Hungary. His point was to encourage storytellers to consider the importance of both grassroots support and visionary leadership in the advancement of their movement. In his audiotaped keynote address, Lipman ties the tales together, showing how the leaders of each cause garnered support over a period of many years. His speech offers history lessons as well as tales.

At the National Storytelling Conference in Seattle in 1993, California storyteller Sandra MacLees took participants through some of the process of developing a tale for telling. She gave each small group in the workshop a few pages from different books about the life of Harriet Tubman. Each group's reading matter covered a different period in Tubman's life, although some information overlapped from group to group. After giving the small groups time to work on the task, MacLees asked each group to provide a first-draft telling. Not only did we see how the different tellings pieced the facts of Tubman's life together, but each group or individual brought a unique style of telling to the facts. The collaborative process seemed an easy one to replicate in a classroom and one that would offer students insight into the subjective nature of history writing and telling.

When I taught social studies for a few years, before I had added storytelling to my bag of classroom tricks, my students showed me that they enjoyed stepping into history through the projects they did in response to historical literature. They stumbled into a kind of storytelling by creating newspapers that might represent the period of history depicted in whatever book they chose. Some wrote and read aloud from imaginary diaries. Others wrote monologues that explored the inner depths of a story's characters. Many students delighted in such tasks that tapped their creative juices and encouraged them to read for historical detail. Watching them present such projects, I always marveled at how serious some of them were about stepping into the past.

Colorado storyteller John Stansfield found less than a page of information about Julia Archibald Holmes in Gladys Bueler's *Colorado's Colorful Characters*, but it piqued his curiosity. Then, using Bueler's bibliography, he discovered A. W. Spring's *A Bloomer Girl on Pikes Peak 1858*, a short compendium of Holmes's letters, journal entries, and other historical research about her. Stansfield believes a historical telling needs a clear focus so he based his story on Holmes's journey with her new husband and brother along the Santa Fe Trail and up Pikes Peak. Into the story he wove her beliefs in abolition and women's rights, her burgeoning writing ability, her sense of wonder in nature, and her determined enthusiasm for life. He told the story in the third person but interspersed his narration with quotes from Holmes's writings. Stansfield (1994) believes it is important to memorize direct quotes, dates, and important statistics for a historical tale, but he emphasizes that any story should be told in language that is comfortable for the teller. The story will change as it matures. His advice to would-be tellers is "Exercise your creativity, and keep on telling." He adds that it is important to acknowledge sources in some way because it may inspire listeners to read, research, and develop their own history tellings.

In "Recalling Forgotten Lives," Kate Shaw describes the work of many historical tellers, including Rex Ellis, who developed stories for the first African-American history program at Colonial Williamsburg in Virginia. The program evolved from five-minute talks about certain characters to a two-hour walking tour in which visitors heard about George Washington and Thomas Jefferson but also about London

Briggs, Simon Gilliat, and Matthew Ashby. As Ellis remarks, "Story-telling disarms visitors and motivates them to confront the difficult and painful subject of slavery from another perspective."

Shaw also writes about Elizabeth Ellis, a storyteller from Dallas. Ellis contends that the past teaches us about what it is to be human—we can't know who we are unless we know where we have been. She tells about the time Mary McLeod Bethune brought her students out onto the steps of their schoolhouse to sing spirituals until Ku Klux Klansmen, who had arrived to close the school, became embarrassed and rode away. She also describes explorer Delia Ackley, who traveled to Africa around the turn of the century to collect specimens for natural history museums. Ackley asked permission of the native people whose land she crossed and worked in harmony with them throughout her journeys. Ellis believes she counters sexism, racism, and agism in her choice of characters. Knowing that history has most often been told from the point of view of educated white males, Ellis says, "Stories allow us to see history through the eyes of women, children, minorities and the working class" (Shaw).

Many teachers ask their students to interview older family members or neighbors in order to develop an oral history of a local or national event. Children need time and support to develop good questions before they make appointments for interviews. They also need classtime to practice interview skills so they learn how to listen carefully for answers and ask follow-up questions they hadn't neces-sarily planned. With preparation, the experience can be fun and rewarding for both the child and the elder who travels back into memory. Barbara Lipke (1994) writes of a most surprising and touching experience. For her class's Museum of Family History, Jennifer, one of her fifth graders, interviewed her father about coming to America. He told her of escaping from his factory job in Eastern Europe where he had worked as a boy of fourteen making boots for German soldiers. He slipped away by night past barbed wire fences and border guards and walked hundreds of miles to freedom. He came to Boston and a year later went to Harvard. After the class presented their museum stories and artifacts, Jennifer's mother said that he had never told anyone in the family the story before, not even her.

Ed and Gerda Sundberg have developed Ribbons of Memories, a Scandinavian-American Heritage Project that preserves the experiences of Scandinavians who came to the United States during the Great Migration (1847–1917). The Sundbergs offer solid advice on the importance of preparing for interviews in "Documenting True Life Dramas." Barbara Blair worked at Plimoth Plantation, a living history museum of the early seventeenth century in Plymouth, Massachusetts. The historical researcher, Blair says, needs a personal conviction about the period or character she plans to study and develop into a tale: "It has been essential for me to believe in the significance of my story." She too looks for primary sources such as birth and death records and diaries, but she also scouts out paintings or prints of historic buildings from the period to give her a more complete feel for the times.

I ordinarily do not have a strong desire to go looking for historical stories on my own, but writing this chapter has rekindled in me the fondness for history my mother's books brought me as a teenager and the study of Martin Luther King's life brought me as an adult looking back at my teenage years. I have gone in search of Abigail Adams again as a result, and who knows what other people or events I'll bump into once I begin to wander into the past. Maybe we'll meet each other storytelling our way into time.

ELEVEN

Honoring the Interior

tories are medicine . . . . They have such power; they do not require that we do, be, act anything—we need only listen." Those words in Clarissa Pinkola Estés's introduction to *Women Who Run With the Wolves* confirm what I have discovered about stories: they heal us psychologically. When Estés, herself a Jungian scholar and storyteller, says we need only listen, I believe she means that stories will gently teach us, not scold us or shame us into being other than we truly are.

As I have watched students choose and tell stories I notice they have an intuitive ability to find those that seem to comfort them and help them explore aspects of themselves. In *Men and the Water of Life*, a book about the psychology of stories, Michael Meade says we "enter the territory of the heart by going into our wounds and reliving them" through a story's symbols.

I first discovered this healing aspect when I reviewed my memories of the teapot song, the *Gigi* characters, and the young woman in "Patterns." Since then I have looked closely at my other story choices to see what life issues I might be working on. I noticed, for example, that the stories I loved as a child—"The Woman Who Wanted All the Cakes," "King Midas," "The Stone in the Road," and "The Star Dipper"—all dealt with greed and generosity. They cautioned me that a generous heart would be rewarded while greed and selfishness would be punished, or at least bring unhappiness. Why had I asked for stories about greed and generosity so often? What was in me, a well-cared for little girl, that needed healing?

The year I was born my parents agreed to move in with my dad's aging parents, since Dad was the oldest of the two sons that still lived in town. My grandmother, suffering from rheumatoid arthritis, ruled the house from her wheelchair: a loving but authoritarian queen upon her throne. My mother, father, grandfather, and five siblings were her humble (and at times grumbling) servants. I developed a rather greedy side—or, to be kinder, a needy side—having to share the limelight with so many others. I wished for more toys, more cookies, more of my parents' attention, and often more privacy. My elders, however, espoused the values of gratitude and generosity. I was taught to be delighted by the hand-me-downs from an older cousin, grateful for one cookie, and lucky to have two sisters with whom to share a room. By about age five I was already putting my own envelopes in the Sunday collection basket. I was taught through example that giving of myself, from a smile for a passerby to a hug for a tearful sibling, would truly bring me pleasure. Still, the graciousness instilled in me by Saturday confessions, Sunday sermons, Brownie Scout visits to the less fortunate, parental lectures, and opportunities to give of myself only managed to drive underground my basic childish self-centeredness.

Stories comforted me. They played a double role, instilling in me a desire to be kind, obedient, loyal, self-sacrificing, and grateful for small blessings, yet honoring the shadow side of me that was being squashed, scolded, forbidden, and hidden away. In truth, I found my kinship to Midas and yet predicted that his golden touch would only bring him sorrow. I loved the greedy woman who wanted all her cakes to herself (she and I were one), but the fact that she turned into a woodpecker in punishment for her stinginess cautioned me to be willing to share. Yet I found even her transformation, illustrated at the story's end, to be quite beautiful. Her woodpecker self was certainly more lovely than the pointy-nosed old woman she had been. I would stare in wonder at her, at how she had changed, looking back and forth from the earlier pictures of her dress, shawl, apron, and kerchief to her new black-and-white feathers and her red-feathered head. I marveled at the story's mysterious resolution, and I believed it.

Did the tale wipe out the greediness in me? No, but little by little the old woman's fate tamed my childish neediness by honoring it. I tell the story today rather than read it, but I do show small groups of listeners the illustrations that were so powerful to me as a girl. Inevitably, some child comments about how "pretty" the woman-now-woodpecker looks. I nod and smile, remembering.

I have observed this phenomenon—of students finding themselves in stories—for ten years now. It is a mystery, yet it makes sense. Telling stories, students explore their dark sides and confront their fears without having to act on them outside the story's boundaries. They try on personalities different from the one they show publicly: bold, shy, angry, optimistic, naive, worldly. At a time when the influence of the peer group and the media is so powerful, storytelling seems to help them honor who they already are as well as sample who they might or must not be. I have watched them befriend their less-than-praiseworthy sides: meanness, foolishness, bigotry, laziness, greed. When they seem to "listen" to the story in the way Estés describes, I know I'm in the presence of powerful inner work.

Dirk, one of my sixth graders, rarely connected to the boys in his class, a number of whom were tough guys who prided themselves on not being good in school or, at least, in English. He seemed to live in his own fantasy world much of the time, occasionally trying to make friends with another lonely child, but giving up easily if things didn't go smoothly. If anyone spoke harshly to him, he ran from the room and cried, making himself a more inviting target for those already inclined to bullying. I knew from a counselor that at home he was responsible for caring for younger siblings while his mother worked. He spent whole weekends indoors, forbidden to go outside or even answer the door. The few times I had seen him elated he talked about weekend adventures with his father, who had moved out.

During the storytelling unit, as usual, he kept to himself. I observed him reading through books in order to choose a tale and saw him rehearse quietly by himself, making entries in his learning log when prompted by my questions. However, I never actually heard his entire story until the day he told *The Water of Life* for the entire group.

I have a vivid memory of this telling, yet some of what I write here reflects listening to an audiotape and rereading Dirk's process entries. At first Dirk spoke haltingly, as many first-time tellers do, pausing to see each scene in his mind's eye and struggling between saying memorized phrases and telling the story in his own words. He appeared to shut the audience out, "looking" only at the story images he called up. Yet his very serious tone commanded our attention. From the opening lines he seemed to enter some distant land and we, his listeners, were compelled to follow.

Dirk had chosen a classic Grimm brothers story in which the youngest son, a pure-hearted prince, completes the task of finding magical water to cure his father the king and through patience and goodness wins the heart and riches of a beautiful princess. His greedy and jealous older brothers try to cheat him out of his father's gratitude and the princess and her wealth, but in the end the young prince triumphs.

Dirk's choppy opening narration worried me. I was afraid he would lose his audience, but when he used a high-pitched character voice for the old man who appeared in the princes' garden and said, "I know the cure . . . but it is very hard to find," the audience was his. Next, in a stern and kingly tone, his father character refused to let the first two sons seek the cure, saying to each in turn, "No it is too dangerous. I'd rather die!" Dirk's listeners, especially the other boys, were seeing a whole new side of him, a powerful and commanding side.

He still spoke haltingly whenever he returned to the narration ("The prince said how much he loved his father," and "The king *thought* his son's love was pure") but the audience waited patiently for the next lines of dialogue. They laughed aloud at Dirk's characterization of the wise old dwarf who stopped each brother on the road, and they loved the mean-spirited older brothers who in turn shouted foolishly, "Out of my way you idiot!" and "Where I'm going is none of your business, you little midget!" Every listener seemed shocked to hear such voices come from this outwardly shy boy. Later, when the deceitful older brothers connived to spoil the boy's triumph and sought revenge against him by exchanging the healing water for "*bitter* sea water," Dirk's energy soared.

With sinister delight the brothers told the youngest of their misdeed. One brother warned, "If you speak one word of this to our father . . . ." The cruelty in Dirk's voice came from a part of him we did not know, perhaps a part he hardly knew himself. Yet clearly he identified with the goodness of the youngest son as well as with the anger of the older brothers and the dwarf. In a log entry made during a rehearsal exercise (in response to the question "What image in the story strikes you as important?") he had written, "My mind got a picture of the two older princes being wedged between two mountains or cliffs." Clearly he had honored their punishment by the dwarf although he had enjoyed speaking their mean-spirited thoughts. Perhaps he knew what it meant to be wedged between two cliffs.

As Dirk became more involved in the story and saw that we were with him, his narration smoothed out and his eye contact with the class improved. I remember thinking that he was safely *in* the tale now and would increasingly become a more confident guide. Whether they are young or old, when tellers become one with the tale there is a visible shift. They become less self-conscious and more story-conscious. Even very experienced tellers can have difficulty making this shift during new tales or, conversely, during tales they have told hundreds of times and take for granted. Complete engagement with the story demands attentiveness. New tellers don't understand until they experience this intense engagement. At one moment they are working to get inside the story but are distracted by nervousness or a sense of the audience's presence. Perhaps they simply feel exposed and find it hard to relax and concentrate. But once inside, as many tellers report, they feel themselves relax. Then they become guides for the listeners who journey with them through the tale.

Did Dirk's telling change his relationship to his classmates? I wish I could describe some dramatic transformation. I only know that the children seemed to see him differently afterward, and I believe in some deep way his success helped him see himself in a new light. He looked exhausted but very proud when he finished. I felt that perhaps he had voiced some of the anger he felt toward those, young or old, who had belittled or betrayed him. For a brief time he had triumphed over the challenges before him.

He brought his newfound confidence to a second story he learned later in the unit, *Rainbow Crow*. He learned this Lenapé tale from a picture book version retold by Nancy Van Laan and illustrated by Beatriz Vidal. In it the once beautifully multicolored crow suffers the loss of both his colors and his magnificent singing voice after carrying the gift of fire from the Great Spirit to the animal world buried in snow. Dirk had no trouble stepping into this hero tale and keeping his audience mesmerized. I remember especially how he narrated a difficult part of the tale without faltering, "Crow, all alone, flew off to a distant tree where he wept." Dirk lowered his eyes and paused for us all to feel the sorrow of the moment. "Even when the snow stopped," he spoke softly and slowly, "Crow *still* wept." We could see the grief in his face and hear it in the timbre of his voice. Dirk clearly trusted the story, and I think he trusted us or perhaps asked us to know him and his pain through this story. In the end Crow is shown a new way to view his losses. The Great Spirit tells him that, although the "two-leggeds" will one day take fire from the animals, they will never kill Crow for his meat, cage him for his singing, or steal his black feathers. Crow's losses will translate into the gift of freedom, and if he looks closely he will see rainbows beneath the shiny black feathers. Perhaps, by identifying with Crow, Dirk acknowledged some of his own losses, but I also believe he felt the triumph of the story's resolution.

When any child steps into the storytelling circle and holds the attention of classmates, a teacher delights in the confidence that exudes from his or her face and stance. But when an unhappy or "misfit" child experiences that power, it is something spectacular to behold. It is not the bully power we sometimes see such children grab for in desperation, so that for a moment they won't be at the bottom of the pecking order. It is instead an experience of power over whatever circumstances have robbed them of a belief in themselves. It is the thrill of the homerun hit, the marathon completed, the solo performed masterfully, the job well done. I believe it reinforces for the child the belief that he or she can also come to know that power outside the world of the story.

Children Claiming Power Through Storytelling

As I read more books about psychology and stories I see that there is much to learn. I am meeting more therapist-storytellers whose very work it is to help clients heal psychological wounds by working with stories. I don't claim to be a therapist. But I see that the knowledge gained by those in other disciplines, from anthropology to physics, informs our teaching, and those in psychology are teaching me a great deal.

As I visit schools many teachers tell me how difficult it is to work with students who are alienated and unmotivated. Children don't get excited by learning when they come to school discouraged and angry about life, and many more do all the time. Even the children who come well-fed and attended to bring insecurities and problems that distract them. Telling stories in which they can see themselves will not cure all the ills children face, but it may just help them develop the inner strength to go on.

Even in classrooms where I have just met the children and have had no time to dig deeply into a tale, I often observe young tellers own the power within themselves when they stand before the group and tell a well-loved tale or a memory. I like watching their peers and teachers see them with new eyes. Teachers often say, "It was most unusual for Tommy to come forward" or "Katrina is so shy! I didn't think she had that in her." Children's peers might just say, "Wow, great story!" or offer praise in the form of a hand slap or some other gesture, but clearly what they are communicating is that the teller or tale has taken them by surprise.

Within a story young tellers feel safe stepping inside characters to try on feelings they know are unacceptable to adults. Dirk surprised us because he boldly became the mean older brothers. He pushed the dwarf aside with great disdain. He let himself feel the pure jealousy of the two for the youngest one. As the dwarf, he showed how good it felt to punish his tormentors by trapping them in tight mountain gaps. Drama teachers have long known the power of the villain's role, but even if a teacher puts on lots of plays, there are usually only one or two juicy villain parts to go around. In his story Dirk was able to be the king, the good and evil sons, the magic dwarf, even the princess.

Students also tread on territory in which they take risks with their peers. Watching Mercie, one of my middle schoolers, tell Virginia Burton's *The Little House*, a story about a tiny country house becoming surrounded by high-rises and modern factories as the city expands, I imagined that she loved the tale years before when adults or older siblings towered over her. Yet at age twelve, it seemed that she might be exploring her relationship to her friends, changing and modernizing themselves into teenagers while she was holding on to girlhood. She hung around with some "fast" girls who were starting to receive lots of attention from boys. Maybe the story was her way of exploring her uneasiness with change. It's just a guess. I can't be sure what students tell themselves or each other through their stories: they often seem unconscious of story symbolism. But watching Mercie, I felt as if I was learning something important that she wasn't revealing to the rest of the world in any direct way.

Amy did something similar. Extremely shy, yet unlike Dirk in that she seemed quite comfortable with herself, Amy told Eve Bunting's story *St. Patrick's Day in the Morning* about a small boy considered too young to march in the St. Patrick's Day parade. He rises earlier than anyone in the household on parade day, takes his little flute, and proceeds to lead his very own solo parade around the town, marching quite a distance despite what the grown-ups thought about his stamina level and maturity. Amy happened to play flute in the school orchestra, so she used her own flute as a prop and marched in that same quietly proud way as she told the tale. She seemed to be saying, "See? I can do what you all do in your loud and show-offy ways. I'm just doing it in my own quiet, private way." There was an unmistakable look of pride, perhaps even a touch of defiance, in her eyes. Whether she was defying her peers or her parents, or even some voice inside that told her she wasn't big or brave enough, I don't know. But Amy was one more student who seemed to be saying, "See who I really am" through storytelling.

I won't pretend that teachers can control whether this happens, but I believe the phenomenon is related to children's being listened to and learning how important their own listening is to each other.

Honoring Oral Composing

Teaching writing initially brought me to teaching listening and from there to an important connection between writing and storytelling. I noticed that some children struggled to get their ideas down on paper, but once they switched to the oral mode they could more easily formulate what they had to say. Some added and revised as they read their "final" drafts aloud. When this first happened, more fluent writers, who had worked hard to finish their pieces before signing up to read, would glance at me as if to ask, "Is this allowed?" In response, I would take my enthralled listener stance, rivet my attention on the reader to honor the oral composing taking place, and I'd offer a calming nod to my questioners: "We are witnessing *creation*—let's keep listening and not worry if the words aren't actually on the page yet." The audience's attention seemed to be what gave these less-fluent writers the impetus to continue composing as they "read." Eventually the practice became standard, not just allowed but encouraged. We stopped thinking about final drafts as final, recognizing that thinking on one's feet comes in handy throughout life and noting that an audience's presence often helps a writer synthesize, clarify, and expand.

Storytellers likewise compose aloud. Even if they have told the story several times before, they formulate its images anew. Telling is an act of creating as well as recreating. Storytellers search for fresh words and phrases as well as recollect familiar ones. Telling stories and the half-reading, half-telling my students did gave them practice in framing mental images, composing phrases and grammatical constructions, and shaping text.

An Environment Safe for Growth

Like writing, listening to and telling stories require a certain kind of environment if they are to help children develop socially and emotionally. What children need is an environment of *safety*. For my middle schoolers, I believe it came first from sharing myself, taking the risk of telling my own real-life and symbolic tales. Their sense of safety also became more certain when we agreed that being in-process was acceptable and that support for each other's "approximations" (Cambourne 1988) was essential. A final, "finished" product was not our ultimate goal, though excellent products emerged. What mattered most was learning, trying, gaining insight, and most important, honoring each other as individuals. These experiences would stay with students long after the story itself disappeared.

As I worked to develop a sense of safety in my classroom, I let go of some of the critical, judgmental side of my teaching. I didn't lower my expectations, but I focused more on what students did do than on what they didn't. It was clear to me that if I focused on volume and pace, or the number of gestures, or the amount of eye contact, there wasn't time to notice all that their storytelling had to teach me about them as individuals. If I stayed busy giving them points for skills, such as staging and responsiveness to the audience, I could easily miss the moment when teller, tale, and audience became one. There is something unique in that moment. I couldn't record it on a grade sheet, but it always taught me something about the children and how to teach them better.

To encourage their development, I had to create occasions for them to return to their tales, to reexperience that feeling of oneness with a different audience or perhaps to discover something new about the meaning of the story or the rhythm of its language. Each time they found a new audience or ventured into a new story they learned more about how audiences and stories work.

Ellen told stories masterfully from the start. She struggled with math and social studies, like so many of the kids, but when it came time to do any kind of presentation for English she embodied flair. Even after she had moved on to another classroom, she discovered a local storytelling contest and offered to model storytelling for my new sixth graders. The year she went to high school I asked her to co-present at a storytelling workshop for teachers. That day Ellen told Barbara Cohen's *Molly's Pilgrim*, the story of a Russian immigrant child's first experience studying Thanksgiving and pilgrims in an American classroom.

I watched her play each role in the story: the sweet but confused Molly, her determined mother, the mean and powerful class bully Elizabeth, and the understanding teacher who valued Molly's home-made pilgrim doll (resembling a Russian peasant) for its uniqueness. Ellen's confident delivery grew out of her delight in the story, but it was supported by the rapt attention of the adult audience. How wise she was, I thought, to bring a story about school and children to a group of teachers. It didn't occur to me at first that Ellen's own Jewish heritage had influenced her choice.

When a listener asked her what she liked best about telling stories, she said: "I like being different things in a story. I first told 'Chicken Soup with Rice' back in sixth grade. I liked being Christmas and dinner and all the things from the seasons and months. Later, I told a story at the Empire State Plaza in a contest. I got to be a farmer and liked talking like a farmer and imagining myself as one."

"I guess that's why I pick stories. I get to be different people and do different things. I told a story about being a possum and liked being an animal, since I *am* human." The crowd laughed. "In this story I tried to do the mother a little differently. I don't know how to do a Russian accent, but I wanted to make each character clear in some way. I really liked being the character of Elizabeth, the mean girl. That was a blast." Ellen laughed as if she had surprised herself by saying that.

Then getting serious, "I picked this story also because I think it can teach little kids not to be mean to each other. When they see Elizabeth, they'll know she's being unfair to Molly. Adults might not need to learn that, but I think there is a message about racism here." She looked at me as if uneasy to be speaking to adults about what they might learn. I smiled, and she concluded, "I just really liked this story."

"I just really liked this story" is enough. It is all I knew when I chose "Patterns" at her age. Yet Ellen also knows that playing the mean girl is "a blast." She recognizes the cruelty of one child to another and sees the racism underlying the cruelty. She senses her kinship to the adults in the story, both women, and may even notice qualities in them she wants to emulate. Whatever *Molly's Pilgrim* taught Ellen, she honored the many sides of herself by telling it.

"Even in the most broken of times the storyteller's voice makes a kind of order at the center of things," comments Dan Yashinsky, a Toronto writer and storyteller. Yashinsky describes Boccaccio's fourteenth-century work, *The Decameron*, in which three young gentlemen and seven ladies survive the Black Death by sequestering themselves in a villa outside the town of Florence, where they spend ten days each telling one another ten stories. "What makes their sanctuary effective is not the wall. It is the storytelling that helps them keep their courage up, their terror quiet and chaos at bay." Yashinsky, like Clarissa Pinkola Estés, knows that stories heal the spirit because they honor the interior.

TWELVE

Trust the Story

welve-year-old Mercie had worked over a period of weeks choosing and preparing Virginia Burton's *The Little House* for performance. Clearly she knew the story well, but just days before her scheduled "final" telling for the class she had written this in her log:

> I feel kind of self-conscious about telling my story. I don't
> really know my story too well. I really need to practice
> my story. I don't really have characters. The only one is
> "the little house." I'm always forgetting the details. I'm
> embarrassed to tell my story in front of "other people."
> I'm very self-conscious. I'm afraid people will get bored.
> I'm not ready.

Mercie never voiced these anxious feelings to me. I didn't read and respond to that entry, or the one that followed her telling, until I collected her log a day or so later. Her delivery of the tale about a house in the country slowly being crowded out by tall buildings as the city expanded was simple and undramatic but poignant, and very well received by her peers. Her log entry for the next day speaks for itself: "I told my story yesterday! Weird huh? I did great. I'm really proud of myself."

When I read the entries, I laughed and hurriedly wrote back before moving on to other logs. "But you *were* ready when the time came, or at least the story was ready. Always trust the story, Mercie, whether you are telling or writing. It will tell itself if you trust it." That comment says one of the most important things I have learned as a storyteller. Yet looking back I realize that I dismissed her pre-performance jitters.

"Always trust the story" is a truth I am still coming to understand as I invite others to step into stories. I trust that I will choose stories I am meant to tell and draw listeners inside, where they will find whatever healing or delight they are meant to find.

In writing, I am one of those people who writes and talks my way to what I know. It is not that I don't begin with a clear sense of what I have to say; it is just that once I am in the story or the writing, trust leads the way. The work inevitably surprises me. Storytelling actually demands more trust because it takes place in front of people. This may sound a bit mystical, but when I am deep inside a story and feel the audience come along with me, or when as a teacher I watch a shy or self-conscious child go inside a tale she loves the way Mercie and Dirk and Jack did, the experience is beyond mystery.

The uneasiness, the distrust of her ability that Mercie felt, is familiar to most storytellers. Whether they are young or old, "inexperienced" or "masters," they must take courage in hand in order to step out of chronological time into the world of memory or fantasy and tell a newly learned or newly discovered story. The experience reminds me of watching students traverse a "confidence course." Similar to an obstacle course, this series of structures for climbing and learning balance is meant to challenge the individual to his physical and mental limit. The person traversing the course relies on a supportive spotter, someone assigned to catch him should he lose balance. The spotter's job is also to encourage the individual to stay the course, to find his confidence and trust it to take him safely to the end.

If it is a tough audience, telling a story the first time, the first few times, or even the hundredth time can be like that. Mercie knew her story. She had worked hard to explore it, but to tell it before the entire class she had to confront her fear of their criticism, test her ability to concentrate, and face whatever subtext had led her to dig this story out of her treasure chest in the first place. This last obstacle, confronting the subtext, is generally one young tellers face unconsciously, but it adds to their uneasiness. Even an adult may tell a story for a long time before seeing her underlying reason for choosing it.

A teller's "balance" is also tested once she gets fully inside the story and is confidently telling what she has rehearsed. Suddenly the story seems to have a will of its own, as if the teller is only along for the ride. She may start feeling anxious that she will "fall off," or that the story will desert her and she will fall flat on her face—many tellers admit experiencing such a sensation. Yet some let it terrorize them, while others relax and enjoy the thrill of the ride. I think Mercie, like many tellers, wanted the story to be a simple matter of memorization. She was a good student who did well on tests. Our character exploration exercises—in her case the "character" of the little house—and my advice to students to let go of the words and find their own way into the tale, unsettled her. That day in class, however, she did enter the story and bring her listeners along. Her second log entry reflects her euphoria.

The Creative Mind at Work

When the teller, the audience, and the tale become one it is the work of the creative mind, the thrill center, one might say. Practice exercises and rehearsals help the teller know the tale and gain a sense of control over it. These are important aspects of learning a tale. Most tellers have little confidence without left-brain organization of the tale's events. But it is the creative, generative function of the teller's mind that makes storytelling more than saying the lines in a script or reciting a poem. Jack needed to know the events in Perseus's tale in order to feel the power of turning his young listeners to stone. Then, with a little help from dimmed lights, an eager audience, and a supportive teacher who acted as "spotter," he was able to tell the drama of Perseus's meeting with the Gorgon in his own unique way. Ancient as the story is, in that moment he created it anew.

The Influence of the Audience on the Telling

Each audience, and the teller's relationship to it, affects how deeply he can go into the tale at that moment. The audience supplies the teller with various kinds of feedback, or sometimes little feedback at all. Listeners' responses can contribute to the teller's feeling that someone else is in charge. Kristyn told Dr. Seuss's *Yertle the Turtle* to her middle school peers in a proficient but rather controlled way. I encouraged her to try it in a recreation program for four- to six-year-olds. Later, she and I had a great laugh about the difference between the two tellings. "The story changed! I said things like 'And do you know what happened next?'" Hearing that, I knew she had taken the risk of allowing the audience to enter the tale. As a result she knew more about the art of storytelling and about her own creative powers.

I like to rehearse a new story as I walk a bike path with my friend Kathy Ramsay. She hangs on every image and responds in ways and in places I don't expect. What she brings—her understanding of me as an adult, her delight in learning more about my past life, and her fascination with story subtext—influences her reactions. They in turn give me information about the tale's strongest images, its pacing, and so on.

A story about singing morning Mass in fourth grade differs in tone and detail when I tell it to children and when I tell it to adults. In the first version, I tell it more from my child self, remembering the way the world looked from the vantage point of age nine. In the adult version, though the narrator remains nine, the character of my mother and images of the Church in the 1950s loom larger. The audience pulls them out of me differently each time. My best tellings of the story, when I give myself over to the memory, come as a surprise. Together the audience and I discover each moment anew.

Some audiences are easier than others. I invite very young children to look at my face as I speak. Some are still learning to pay close attention, and I need their grins and even their puzzled looks to know whether the story is working or not. Older students are just as hungry to be pulled into a tale as the little ones, but they don't always know it. For me, the most important thing with older school audiences is honesty. They get plenty of honest advice, but they don't get a lot of sheer "from the heart" truth, at least not from most adults within school walls. If I set up a story briefly with the truth of why I chose it (or how it chose me) or ask them a question that helps them find a place for the story within, they usually let their resistance down. Even if they don't, I have to believe the story will pull them in and not let nervous snickers or rolled eyes scare me from going as deeply into its truth as I can. Whether I am working with a welcoming auditorium of teachers delighted to learn more about storytelling or those who would just as soon mark papers, I have to be willing to step all the way in and let go of "Will they like it? Will I be good enough? Will they listen?" The stories will work their magic if I trust them.

Nerves

At many storytelling events, even among very experienced tellers, there is a tension similar to that in ballplayers before a game or dancers before a recital. The teller's ego is at stake. Mercie's nervousness was real. It was based on whether her teacher and audience would appreciate her performance or find fault with it. The strongest tellers I know take time to calm their jitters by focusing their minds on the story, stretching and relaxing their muscles so the story can work its way down into the body. I have watched tellers warm up backstage, in the alcove of a school stairway, and in a faculty bathroom. Some breathe and center themselves; some tell me they imagine one or more characters or the story's opening scene or the moment of climax. Breathing slowly and finding a piece of the story or visualizing the story moving through them helps them set their egos and their fear of criticism aside.

As I mentioned in an earlier chapter, it helps to think of the story as a gift to be offered rather than as a work to be displayed for critique. One summer night, when I was just beginning to tell stories publicly as an adult, I had the experience of telling a folktale to a group of teachers about a girl's magical journey through the woods. I hoped they would delight in this story, one my mother had read so often to me before bed. Afterward, three women spoke to me individually and mentioned completely different reasons for why the story had touched them. Not one of their reactions matched another's or fit what I loved about the tale. That didn't matter. Their diverse impressions taught me that each listener takes away her own unique "gift." They remind me that I am not in charge of what listeners get out of the story. My job is to tell it the best I can.

Even if a teller can't see the faces of the audience, trusting in the story and in the listeners' capacity for delight in the tale brings comfort. In his introduction to *Leaving Home*, Garrison Keillor writes of delivering his Lake Woebegon tale each week before a large audience. "You stand in the dark, you hear people leaning forward, you smell the spotlights, and you feel invisible. No script, no clock, only pictures in your mind that the audience easily sees, they sit so close. You come to be so calm out there it is more like going to bed than going out to work. It is like crawling under a quilt that my grandma Dora Keillor made for me from scraps of clothes worn by my aunts and uncles." (p. xvii)

Look Within for Antidotes to Fear

Performance-consciousness is normal and certainly familiar to me. Competition filled my childhood. Besides sibling rivalry and diving meets, our family regularly made reference to who had a "good" voice, who played the piano well, who got the lead in the school play, and who made first-string and honor roll. Striving and measuring up were constants. Luckily, this spirit of competition was balanced by the advice to go inside a performance for the joy. I see now that my Grandfather Walsh's "Tell the story" meant letting oneself enter the world of the song. He was instructing us to let go of self-consciousness, to bring our being to the song in order to feel it.

When my grandfather and other relatives sang certain solos at family gatherings, they showed how to get lost in the music. One of my Uncle Jacks would reach way inside "Ol' Man River." He would even sweat as he sang, it was such a labor of love. My other Uncle Jack sang "Ave Maria," "Danny Boy," and "I Hear You Calling Me" in the kind of Irish tenor voice that melts the heart. As a little girl I didn't quite understand all the words to those songs, but I was pulled into their bittersweetness by the music and the look on my uncle's face. My sister Maria Gillard, now a songwriter, offers the next generation of nieces and nephews this gift of trusting a work of art on her recordings. Whether singing of old friendships, political injustice, "The Gillard Family," or lost love, she pulls her listeners into the "story" (1992, 1994).

From time to time the old fear of not being good enough still haunts me as I see it haunt my students, young and old. But another diving image, from a college meet, reminds me of a way to think about performing. I went to a women's national diving competition sophomore year. Though happy to have qualified, I was a nervous wreck. I watched the other girls in the locker room asking each other about the degree of difficulty of their dives and heard them talk about where their teams ranked. My team wasn't even with me, only my male coach, my brother. The girls were clearly trying to psych each other out by telling stories of easy wins and unfair losses. One girl didn't enter the conversation. She seemed self-assured and calm. I asked her how she was feeling. She responded confidently but without boasting. "At every meet, big or little, I look at the crowd and remember they love the beauty of a graceful dive, just the way I love the feeling when I nail one." She gave me a look of sisterhood, assuming without reservation that I knew the satisfaction of "nailing" a dive. "So I take a slow breath," she continued, "picture the dive in my mind, and then go for it for myself and the crowd." She laughed, hearing how serious she sounded. "Hey, they want a good show and I give 'em one."

She won that meet, scoring well above the others on almost every dive, even though hers weren't as difficult as some of theirs. Her grace was a gift she offered to the judges and the crowd alike. To me, a very nervous fellow competitor, she offered a glimpse of trust.

Visualization

The practice of visualization, which I described in Chapter 3, has been one of the most helpful tools for exploring and rehearsing stories and for calming nerves. Visualization has received bad press in certain circles because people associate it with mind control. But what it teaches students is that their minds and creative powers are under their control.

Johanna Reiss, author of *The Upstairs Room*, first introduced me to visualization as a composing tool. In Reiss's week-long seminar at the International Women's Writing Guild conference, held each summer at Skidmore College in Saratoga Springs, New York, she asked us to sit on the floor and look up at the furniture in a room from a child's point of view. Then we were to close our eyes and "see" a room in a house where we had lived during childhood and try to recall details from the vantage point of whatever age we imagined ourselves. I was amazed at how clearly I remembered the large dining room furniture, even the feet of the table legs. I saw the rose and green pattern of a rug we had recently purchased and my grandmother's lace tablecloth. This one activity brought up more memories than I could write in a week.

Courtney, one of my sixth graders, told of how her gymnastics teacher encouraged the team to picture themselves successfully completing a routine or a vault. My students and I began the practice of seeing ourselves successfully telling our stories before a receptive audience. The day before "final" tellings began, I would have students sit in the audience formation we used for performance, a standard way of arranging our chairs so everyone was comfortable and knew what to expect. (I usually prefer that listeners sit on the floor, but my middle schoolers preferred chairs, so I honored that.) I would ask them to close their eyes and picture themselves walking up in front of the audience to take their turn. I used my normal speaking voice but paused every few sentences so they could form a mental image. You can't rush visualization.

"See yourself looking confident. That may mean you are excited or calm, but within you is a feeling of 'I'm going to knock their socks off I'm so good' or whatever words describe confidence for you. Now, in your mind, look at the audience. Smile, and breathe. You see that their faces are eager for your story, and you are equally eager to tell it. You have worked hard on the story. You begin with a strong voice. Immediately you see the audience that is with you. You see the images of your story clearly in your mind and through the tone of your voice you invite the audience to see them in their own unique ways."

My words are different every time, but basically I ask students to rehearse their confidence. I lead them through the beginning, middle, and end of the telling, asking them to picture the gestures they will use, the faces they will make, and the places where they will pause or look more closely at the audience. At the end, I invite them to come back into the present. The students then record what they visualized. They don't need to write immediately, but I encourage them to catch the image as soon as they feel ready.

Many of my middle schoolers wrote that they did see a clear scene and told me later the exercise had really helped them believe they could do it well. One time, Bert, who resisted much of our work in English until he could find his own way into it, sat frowning at his desk. When the others were capturing the images in words in their logs, I walked over and whispered, "Did you have trouble seeing yourself?" "Yeah," he grumbled. "Did you see *something?*" I asked quietly, knowing that often just the rewording of the question helps. "Well," he said, trying to find the words. Then he grinned, "I saw myself standing at the plate. I hit a home run." I smiled. "You did just fine. Write down everything you saw." Clearly Bert had rehearsed his confidence in a way that made sense to him. He couldn't imagine himself masterfully telling a tale, but he certainly could see himself a star. So much of Bert's resistance in English was that there he couldn't see himself as a star. This experience gave me a little more insight into the star he truly was. In any visualization exercise the student is in charge of his or her own thinking. I remind them of that every time.

Other writing teachers have offered me very directed image journeys, but I admit that I don't usually care for them. Whether or not I do often depends on the teacher. I wouldn't resist a mental journey led by my yoga instructor, Ellen Sadowski, because I completely trust her gentle and nurturing guidance. Yet I have attended writing and storytelling classes in which I felt uncomfortable going where a teacher's visualization led me. As a result, with my students I use the kind of visualization practice that allows them to construct their own route. I encourage both my young and adult students to follow whatever images seem to come forth. If I suggest something that doesn't seem to fit where their minds want to go, they should trust their resistance and simply *see what they see*. We talk a lot about visualization, how it is simply exercise for the mind and the imagination.

Here are a few log samples:

I saw myself standing there with confidence. Making my face look like the boy as he left the huts to hunt the birds. I then became his mother shaking her finger at the boy and telling him nothing good would come from the birds. At the end I could see myself bring it to a close. Letting my audience know by my voice. And then just standing there letting it sink in.

Kathryn

I saw myself using hand motions more than other things. I told it with good expression also facial expressions come in too. I did different things like wipe my sweat when Anansi said it was hot and point to the ground when the rock part came up in the story.

Billy

I saw myself being a bit nervous. My legs were shaking a bit. My voices were excellent. I could picture myself making strange gestures. I also saw great facial expressions on my face, scrunching up or freaking out. I saw lots of detail. I really went inside my story and could see details of trees or people or houses. When I finished it was a success and I got a big round of applause.

Chris

I stood there for a minute and looked around the room. I saw that everyone was ready and I was too so I took a deep breath and started the story. I was kind of nervous but then it wore off. When I said "the sun was straight above me" I make a little circle with my hands above me. And when I said "the moist ground was covered with these beautiful flowers," I bent down and pretended there was something there. In the middle I got better and felt more comfortable and I had more action in my words and at the end it turned out great.

Nicole

I saw myself getting up from my seat and taking a big deep breath. I paused for a minute and began. At first I was shaky and nervous. I really was not into my story. Then I started to motion and make eye contact and make my voice like the characters. For example—when the mouse came up to Gus (the ghost) and said he was cold with chattering teeth. I could picture myself doing that.

Kelly

Kelly's visualization showed her what I have learned by watching countless tellers: the beginning of the story is often the hardest. The teller must let go of the here and now and enter the tale. Once inside the road becomes clearer and the teller can relax. I find great pleasure in watching young tellers scrunch up their faces, begin to make eye contact, really go into their stories and then bring them confidently to a close. Each new story journey brings me a mystery, a whole set of clues to the puzzle that is me, the listener; to the one that is the young teller, my student; and to the larger one that is humanity. Storytelling is only one way to puzzle out the world, but it is a powerful way and accessible to all who speak and listen.

This Story Scares Me Away

Some stories I have had trouble trusting, even after weeks of work. Something in the story has drawn me to it: some image or aspect of a character, a shared point of view, or a lesson learned. I might be certain why I chose it or baffled by why it whispered, "Tell me," from some library shelf. Then as I am "learning" the tale—telling it conversationally to friends, rehearsing it as I drive or walk, mapping or outlining it—I start to notice things about it. Stories are like new friends. You might take to each other easily and wonder why you never met before. Or you see the possibility of friendship but have reservations that are hard to name. Something in the story might rub you the wrong way. You find yourself avoiding telling it even after weeks together. The attraction may still be strong, but whatever is in the way is powerful too. I tend to shelve a story I am resisting. I give myself permission to let it go—for now. There are thousands of stories. I may grow into it later or discover eventually why it bothered me so. Then I have to decide whether I want to do the inner work of getting over that troublesome spot, whatever it is.

What keeps me and my students from trusting a story differs for each of us. Some of the excuses I've heard more than once:

🍂 I'm afraid I'll forget the words.

🍂 This story is dumb.

🍂 I'll make a fool out of myself.

I'm Afraid I'll Forget the Words

I have to keep telling my students and myself that storytelling is *not* memorizing words, as one would a play script. A storyteller rejourneys through the images of a tale and along the way encounters smells, sounds, tastes, textures, and certainly nuances of the characters. Anyone who has grown up in this culture and been exposed to even a limited number of books or television programs can tell "The Three Bears." You might hesitate if it has been years since you have heard it, but with just a moment of concentration you picture the bears deciding to head out for a walk before eating their steaming porridge. Then you see Goldilocks enter the house and find the waiting breakfast. "This porridge is *too hot . . . too cold . . .* (and finally) *just right!*" It's all coming back to you now, you're *in* the story. You make a cracking sound when the baby bear's chair breaks "*all to pieces.*" Once you get Goldilocks upstairs to bed and asleep, you can have some fun with the bears' astonishment upon returning home. Growling "*someone's been eating my porridge*" in Father Bear's big voice is great fun for most adults and children, and little ones love playing the disgruntled baby bear who whines, "*and she ate it allllllll up!*" Once you get carried into the tale you let the audience in, noting their reactions and playing to what they seem to enjoy. That's storytelling. It is *not* about forgetting the words.

As you speak, you begin to relax. That is what it feels like to trust the story. Your breathing comes more easily. Your heartbeat slows. You walk along with Goldilocks at one moment and the bears the next. The audience accompanies you, enjoying your unique way of telling the familiar story. You might feel nostalgic about your own childhood. You might play to the audience, offering your own special asides or funny characterizations. You get creative and innovative, borrowing from favorite TV characters and from your Great Aunt Mildred, who told you the tale as a child. Trusting the story is really about trusting yourself.

The same is true for any story, even a narrative poem, whose words you have learned but whose images and layers of meaning continue to shift each time you tell it. On more than one occasion I have heard Donald Davis, a well-known storyteller from North Carolina, thank his audience at the end of a program for helping him further shape his stories. Davis tells touching and humorous tales of his boyhood in the rural South. He lets listeners know that their collective laughter and silence convey information about how the story is being heard, and he adjusts his telling as he goes. His stories sound simultaneously familiar and fresh. Although I have heard some of them five or six times, that mixture of the familiar and the unexpected brings me back again and again. It is clear to me that he trusts the stories.

Anecdote-telling reminds us that telling stories is less about words than about returning to a memory or a feeling. You relate an experience you or a friend or a family member had, or recount a story you read in a magazine or heard from a passerby. You retell the story by grasping for it image by image. Maybe you see the face of a person who told it to you or recall your shock, delight, or sadness at first hearing it. You don't worry about forgetting the words. Instead, you reexperience the emotional impact hearing the tale (or living it) had on you. You repeat the story in order to pass on some aspect of it, often the feeling or the lesson it left with you.

Word choices often depend on your audience, whether they can see you or just hear you over the phone, whether you have a lot of time or only a little, and so on. There may be a line of dialogue or a certain descriptive phrase which you repeat the exact way every time.

That phrase feels as right as "Not by the hair of my chinny chin chin." It predictably catches the listener's attention and emphasizes a moment. So you keep it. Otherwise you just walk your way through the recollected images, adding and subtracting from previous tellings.

This Story Is Dumb

"This story is dumb," an expression familiar to those who work with adolescents, is a cover up for something else that is bothering the teller. She may worry that the story is not right for the audience. Or, like Mercie, she may believe she doesn't really know the tale "well enough." (Although this is true occasionally, it wasn't true in Mercie's case; she just needed to face her performance anxiety.) What the teller most likely fears is the criticism or silent, negative judgment of the audience. In some cases the teller may unconsciously fear a character, an event, or a key theme of the story. I have discovered that I subconsciously choose some stories to confront a particular characteristic in myself—say, a fear of bullies—but then I have trouble trusting the story because I haven't let myself all the way into the bully character or into the courage within the hero.

I distinctly remember being a small child and watching my mother tell "The Three Billy Goats Gruff" as she placed colored pieces of cloth on the felt board. Though I had heard her tell it many times I still feared that the story might turn out differently. What if the troll eats the littlest billy goat this time? (I was the third child in our family.) What if he has learned not to be fooled? What if this time the biggest billy goat isn't strong enough or quick enough to butt the troll far from the bridge? Although my fears were a product of my youth, tellers at every age experience the feeling of being simultaneously drawn to and afraid of a story. Opinions about why this is so differ, but if a story doesn't feel right, that uneasiness is as much about the teller as the story. The teller can choose to explore the uneasiness or just select another tale for the time being.

I try to impress on my students that they are responsible for choosing whatever story they tell. I talk with them many times about the importance of choosing a story that matters to them. "My story is dumb" usually just means they didn't choose well. They can choose again or ask for help in making friends with the tale.

I'll Make a Fool Out of Myself

"I'll make a fool out of myself" is at least an honest statement of the fear behind storytelling (or traversing a confidence course or completing any task, for that matter). I would rather hear a teller admit "I'm scared" than hide behind "This story is dumb." An awareness that fear is perfectly natural and that we all share moments of it helps tellers of every age. It is a simple fact but an easy one to forget. I like to poke fun at fear, finding ways to dilute it with laughter.

As an infant, my son Brian taught me the art of cajoling. If he was resistant to some task, often because it was new and he was afraid, I made light of the situation. We turned trying new foods into an airplane game. We sang silly songs when it was time to put toys away. We got through our weekly encounters with the cold water of the YMCA pool by shivering so loud we laughed. I learned to distract him from a bout of temper with tickling or loving-spirited mimicry: I would make a funny monster face and say, "Oh you won't, won't you? Well, I'll gobble you up!" I don't mean to say I never let him feel frustration or sadness; I simply learned that the power of play surpassed the power play.

Cajoling worked just as well with my middle schoolers. I met their various expressions of "I ain't gonna do *that!*" with humor and patience. Brian had taught me to recognize their fear of failure and meet it with exaggeration and gentle mimicry. "Oh I know," I would mirror middle school whining, "this is *so hard.*" Then we would all laugh, or at least enough of us, and we would forge ahead despite the whiners.

Storytelling is about risk-taking. Mercie knew that, and I don't deny it. I just match my students' "do-we-have-tos?" with tales of my own first flops and those of former students who survived storytelling or reading their writing aloud, or whatever horribly unfair thing I required of them. By sharing my own struggle with new stories, I meet my students on familiar ground. Then we can take risks together. First-time-parent stories or tales of my early years of teaching, for instance, are similar to tales of first bike rides, first stitches, and first moments of glory on the playing field. Each year, as students learn a new story I learn one at the same time. I go through the same exercises: sequencing events, sketching scenes or drawing a story map, and exploring characters through point-of-view exercises. My young tellers see me make good and poor choices, feel nervous, and push through my fear during rehearsal tellings.

Each year I also invite consultant teachers to join me so that students can see more than one adult demonstrate what it is like to learn something new. As students share their log entries about how their stories are evolving, we share our discoveries about process. Like apparatus additions to a confidence course, new stories present new challenges to the teller.

As a teller-for-hire I always elicit audience support by declaring, "This is a *new* story." I am not apologetic. Talking process is not the same as apologizing for not being prepared. In my classroom, when the students or I share something new or unfinished, we need the audience's acceptance of the rough edges and their honest response. If I let an audience in on the fact that the story I am telling is new, they know I am placing my trust in them, and I think they listen better. A new story feels awkward, like new jeans until they're broken in. I need all the help I can get and don't want to pretend the story is all polished. I have never forgotten hearing Rafe Martin tell *Will's Mammoth* before a large audience years before he published it in book form. He told us the story was new and hadn't settled down yet, and he was letting it teach him. I had never heard a teller say that before and learned a lot from his honesty.

I am wary of too-polished stories. They aren't alive if the teller is certain of every word and gesture. I don't deny that it is wonderful to sink into a story you have told many times—it feels comfortable, like the old jeans you wear after school. Yet beware the tale that is too worn: if you find your mind wandering to your after-school chore list, it is time to get another story for a while.

Breaking in a New Tale

Lucy Calkins, whose writings and speeches have been central to my evolution as a writer and a teacher of writing, asked me to close a Saturday conference at Teachers College. I was flattered by the invitation and hunted for a new story the way you would buy a new dress for a special occasion. The cover illustration of a picture book in the children's section of the library caught my eye. Marianna Mayer's *The Unicorn and the Lake* seemed perfect. Its archetypal characters, the unicorn and the serpent, were representative of the traditional folktale, yet unlike a folktale, the story's beautiful literary language captured the transformative power of Nature and highlighted the theme of community.

I tape-recorded myself reading the story so I could get the words just the way Mayer had so masterfully composed them. I even wrote to ask her permission, promising I would stay true to the text in spirit. She wrote back, thrilled to hear that people were telling stories again. What I didn't do was learn the story first through mental pictures before beginning my practice recording. I attempted to learn it phrase by beautiful phrase instead of scene by scene. Consequently, I couldn't get the story to settle into a comfortable place. Partly because of early performance anxiety, but mostly because I didn't do what I had learned to do with "The Mountain Whippoorwill"—*just tell the story*—I found myself blocking. Each time I finished telling one scene into the recorder I struggled awkwardly to find the *words* that came next.

This distinction is one I am still coming to understand. I memorized songs and scripts easily as a child. I prided myself on knowing all the verses to long camp songs such as "Found a Peanut." In high school memorizing gave me a kind of power, not to mention extra credit for a Shakespearean sonnet or monologue. Yet, as I have moved toward telling stories through images, I have let that memorizing ability lapse. In trying to learn *The Unicorn and the Lake*, I was trapped somewhere between memorizing and imaging.

A supportive professional friend, Kathy Oboyski-Butler, drove to Teachers College with me early that Saturday morning. She acted as my spotter on the "confidence course" more than once as I told the story in the car. When I faltered, she whispered, "Just keep going." Once I had walked all the way through the journey without quitting, even though I had often paused awkwardly searching for words, I knew the story was mine.

My telling at the end of the day suffered no awkward pauses, although it did suffer the loss of some of Mayer's well-crafted phrases. But my guess is that no one missed them. The beauty of her images filled our minds. What I learned, and relearn, is that it is the story, the power of its meaning, that listeners long for. Finding that power is work and takes time, but the best thing to do is to start telling. Donald Murray (1985) says you have to write bad to write good. The same is true of storytelling.

I am not saying beautiful phrases aren't valuable. Eloquent words have their place in storytelling. Some fine tellers learn long and complex stories in exact words. But a storyteller can only offer listeners the power of a tale when she stops feeling afraid of forgetting the words and allows herself to step inside its essence. I don't forbid a teller to memorize a tale, but I look for a relaxed connection and try to help tellers of every age find solace, not anxiety.

When I think of a teller who got comfortable with her tales, I think of Sally. I first wrote about Sally in *Give a Listen: Stories of Storytelling in School* (Schwartz 1994b), but I have continued to reflect on all her storytelling taught me. "Why that Brer Rabbit, he was just itchin' to play a trick on ol' Brer Bear . . . ." For weeks Sally carried her Brer Rabbit collection with her the way a toddler carries a blanket. Every day during silent reading time she traveled alone over the fields and down the roads to the briar patch. When it came time to tell her story for the class, Sally not only had one tale, she could do an entire Brer Rabbit program. She and Brer Rabbit had been a team during childhood, so finding him again in young adolescence, she had no trouble at all in trusting him.

Still Afraid to Let Go of the Words

"The Mountain Whippoorwill" showed me the difference between saying the words and seeing the images in my mind, but I still have to remind myself to let go of the words on many stories. Although it is getting easier, I include this final story about *not* memorizing because I know it is the hardest hurdle in storytelling for teachers who love words.

Twelve-year-old Christina came to my weekly after-school story-telling club. New to the district, she was trying to find her niche in seventh grade. The first day the club met, she casually summarized a fictional story she had written while attending her previous school. Everyone wanted to hear it in more detail, so the following week she read it to us. We all thought it would make a wonderful story to tell, but Christina knew it would be hard to tell it the way it was written. Like Marianna Mayer, she had chosen her words carefully. She didn't want to let them go for the sake of telling, so she rejected our pleas.

Over the next few sessions each club member settled on one story for "polishing." We had informally told short family tales, discussed the tales we had loved as young children, and browsed through folktale collections and picture books.

Christina couldn't seem to make a choice. I suggested tales other middle schoolers had enjoyed but assured her the choice was hers. I even offered my red book of fairy tales from childhood, but she rejected those, too. She signed out books and tapes each week but came back undecided week after week. Finally, it dawned on me to ask what she *didn't* like about each rejected tale.

One was too long, one too babyish, one had an unsettling ending. I was especially curious about why she had turned down Eve Bunting's (1984) *The Man Who Could Call Down Owls,* because at one time I had tried to add it to my own repertoire. It is a haunting tale about a mysterious bird-healer and a boy who learns from him. I had been drawn to the book initially by Charles Mikolaycak's black-and-white shadow-filled illustrations as well as by the teacher-learner relationship in the story. "What's wrong with this one?" I asked Christina.

"I'm a little afraid of it. I can't say why."

Hmmm. I told her about my struggle with, and eventual abandonment of, the story: "I didn't feel I could get it right. It still draws me." I smiled. "I would love to see what another teller might do with it."

The very next week Christina came to a club meeting with the story memorized. As she told it, I could see her mentally turning the pages as she called up Mikolaycak's drawings and Bunting's words. I instantly recognized the problem: memorizing instead of stepping into the tale and just telling it. Like Christina, I too had tried to walk through the story via the artist's pictures and the writer's words. Christina had mastered the phrasing—she still had the child's ability to memorize easily—but she wasn't telling a story. Instead she moved clumsily from one chunk of the text to another, like someone crossing a river by jumping from rock by rock, pausing each time to look for the next one.

Later that afternoon, I asked her to sit and talk to me about the story in her own words. Did she picture the boy in her mind differently from how Mikolaycak had drawn him? What scene did she like the most? Did parts of the tale trouble her? Did she still feel a little afraid of it? Once we began talking about the story, seeing the people and events as they existed in her mind's eye and in mine, we began to unlock the hold the words seemed to have on us both. A teller moving away from memorizing often does so reluctantly. Asking questions about the story's images or the feelings they inspire helps. "Tell me about the story" can also nudge the teller to create the story images in her mind's eye and realize that they are not set in stone.

One day the storytelling club members and I visited two local elementary schools to tell stories to children, teachers, and librarians. In each session Christina came closer to a comfortable balance between holding fast to much of Bunting's language and making the story her own. After each telling, she proudly held up Mikolaycak's cover to invite listeners to discover the book's beauty on their own. Yet once she had set down the book, the story was hers again. I could tell she saw her own image of "the cloak of softest white" and the owls "swooping on noiseless wings." By the end of that day, Bunting's beautiful tale belonged to us both.

THIRTEEN

Critics, Coaches, and Storyteachers

f our classrooms are to be places where children's personal stories rise to the surface, where children dare to step inside the folktales, poems, songs, and other works they tell, we have to grow as storytellers and storyteachers.

Doug Lipman, a Boston storyteller, has been my story-teacher since 1991. I attend a weekend coaching workshop once a year in Boston and invite him to lead a similar gathering of tellers in the Albany area each spring. Many full-time teachers attend, as well as therapists, parents, and business people who want to bring the art of storytelling into their work. Lipman "coaches," preferring that term over "critiques" or "directs." Critique focuses on a skillful or poor presentation. Direction implies that the performance should conform to the director's vision rather than the artist's. Lipman believes *the story belongs to the teller*. She is completely in charge. The role of the coach is to help her find within herself her unique performing abilities (Lipman 1995). As Lucy Calkins has said many times, "Teach the writer, not the writing." Lipman coaches the teller and leaves her with experience she can apply to any story.

As teachers, we often believe we are developing a young writer's or storyteller's abilities when we play the role of critic or director. We see the vision of what the story could be and we nudge or push the student toward our improved version. We believe our purpose is to bring out the best of what is within the child. What I have discovered in my own storyteaching, however, is that when I find myself critiquing and directing my students, I am really trying to bring out the best of what is in *me*. In a keynote address at a Whole Language Umbrella Conference, Donald Graves said that when we start taking charge of children's work, we need to realize that we do so because our own artistry is not finding enough expression. We need to get writing or storytelling, painting or singing; we need to find some way for our own artistry to receive recognition. The more I come to understand this, the better I am as a coach, drawing from student writers and tellers what is uniquely theirs, no matter how unconventional or unpolished it seems or how unlike what I imagine it could be.

Doug Lipman's coaching has also helped me abandon the phrase "constructive criticism," an expression commonly used among teachers but one that has always troubled me. Lipman gives me suggestions on my storytelling, and I have taken suggestions about reworking this book. But they were offered after I had received lots of appreciative comments about its strength. "Constructive criticism," however, is often given with a heavy hand as soon as the critic has viewed the work. The term is really a contradiction. Inserting "constructive" is an attempt to mask what criticism actually does: tear down what Brian Cambourne calls a student's "approximation" or best effort. Criticism, regardless of how gently it is offered, means "You are not doing it right or doing it well enough." In fact, it is the teacher, parent, or person or group in power saying, "You're not doing what *I* want you to do."

There is nothing constructive in that, unless it is that the one being criticized "constructs" a defense against the pain of being torn down. He survives, perhaps to try again. But the criticism didn't help him use his own thinking to "construct" something better, although it may have forced him to try once again to approximate the critic's view of what the performance should have been.

Movie reviewers are vivid examples of the truly subjective nature of criticism. One reviewer finds a movie to be daring and true to life:

thumb up. Another doesn't see it that way. It's too out on the edge; it doesn't in the least represent common experience: thumb down. Criticism is really just the word of the more powerful against the less powerful.

Teachers and parents get sold the idea (by *their* teachers and parents) that criticizing is part of the job description. But when I look back on my own lifelong learning, I realize that criticism has never, not even once, fostered my development. When I am criticized, I retreat. I dare a little less and build up my defenses a little more. It is true that not all learners retreat. Some grow thick skins and claim to let criticism roll off. Unfortunately, thick skins and other defenses block potential learning from coming in and keep the creativity we yearn to express from flowing out.

Coaching Means Believing in the Success of the Artist

What fertilized the soil of my learning was someone else's belief in my ability, my individual artistry. A teacher's or coach's or grandmother's expectation that I was capable and smart lighted up the path ahead. When there was no one around to shine that light, I either retreated and my growth slowed or I went in search of other teachers in books and professional journals and at teacher workshops. I found those who believed without hesitation that I could grow as a teacher, a writer, and a storyteller.

When students in my class did not appear to succeed, I now realize, I had stopped believing they could. It is not always easy to believe in children. Our teachers didn't all believe in us. But I am finally learning to shine my own teacherly light, my own unfaltering belief, upon my learner self, and learning has become easier, as has teaching reluctant learners. But that doesn't mean I don't need the high expectations of my long-distance teachers, or that my students don't need my unquestioning belief that they will be successful.

Learning From a Diving Teacher

When I first heard Lipman use the expression "coach," it troubled me. The coaches I saw in the media, real or fictional, did their share of belittling players in the name of helping them improve. Then I returned to the image of my dad coaching young divers, from toddlers to teens, on Saturdays at the city pool, and I made peace with the term. Dad knew that anyone who wanted to succeed as a diver could. He also knew that the diver first had to believe in himself. So Dad spread praise on lavishly, like a coat of primer, not generic praise but pointed feedback. "Hey, you got nice height on *that* one. Think about what you did differently." "Oooh, that entry was pretty! Did you feel that? Hop right up and see if you can do it again!" In two or three sentences, he boosted the diver's belief in himself and gave him something new to think about for the next try.

Dad didn't need to encourage practice. Kids practiced naturally. All week, when he was at work, my friends and I tried dive after dive, hoping to improve by the following Saturday. Divers need to dive to get better just as young writers, readers, and storytellers need continuous opportunities to work with language and try their creations out on the world to see what response they get.

It is impossible to improve as a diver if no one watches and responds and if there are no good divers around to observe. In the same way, inexperienced storytellers need to be surrounded by the sounds and sights of other tellers and then given lots of opportunities to try telling stories themselves. Dad knew that. He didn't separate the advanced divers; they stood in line with the rest of us. Teaching became a part of everyone's job. There was always someone more skillful to look up to and someone less experienced who needed encouragement. Dad did take the most advanced divers to out-of-town meets and exhibitions on occasion, but he also borrowed movies of college practice sessions so all of us could see how a diving team went about improving.

When Dad offered specific technical help, which he did, he tried to be sure a young diver could make sense of it. He would reword it a hundred ways if necessary. He knew that when the diver was ready to integrate the idea of a new dive, she would. Dad would demonstrate as he talked. "Drive your arms into the tuck, like this. Then feel how the spin is different." Describing the forward approach and hurdle, he would jump up on the board demonstrating, "I lift my arms as if I'm taking off like a bird. See how the board comes along? Then I press down and ride it up into the dive. Now you try." There was lots of talk of the "how" of diving.

One day a fourteen-year-old named Sam, who didn't usually come to lessons, showed up. Dad matter-of-factly offered him some pointers on how to improve a certain dive. Sam's reply was, "Who asked you?" or something a little less polite. I was at home sick that day, and my siblings all told different versions of the story when they came home. I went to Dad to get the scoop on what happened because Sam was a friend of mine. Dad just laughed it off. "Oh, honey, Sam did exactly what I would've done when I was his age. He felt criticized and got a little hot-headed. Sam just needs a few good coats of praise. He's taught himself to dive by watching and trying, and he's learned a lot all on his own. You get him to come again. I'll let him know just how much he already knows and wait till he *asks* for help before I give it."

That memory has guided my "coaching" since I was twelve. As a young teacher, I ran across "hot-headed" kids who resisted my attempts to "fix" their work. Thanks to my father and many other fine teachers, I finally figured out that it wasn't my job to fix anyone's work. My remedy, applied to a child's piece of writing or a storytelling effort, was usually unwelcome, and even when it was accepted, I watched how it robbed the child of the chance to find her own way to improve. I eventually learned that giving my students a "coat of praise," what Lipman (1993) calls "appreciations," was the most important support I could give their learning. Then, asking them to state what help they needed, or to explore aloud or in writing what they were trying to accomplish in a piece of work, often led them to insights about how to improve the work themselves. It put the power to grow and change back into their hands.

The Coach Can Be of Help

Lipman's most important question to the teller after his "apprecia-tions" is, "What do you *love* about this story?" When the teller focuses on what she believes to be the essence or heart of the tale, it often becomes clear that something she is doing gets in the way of that coming across. It also gives the coach a sense of what the teller isn't doing and may not be aware of. Then the coach can offer technical suggestions. "So, you love that Goldilocks has the house all to herself. What's that feel like in your body when you have something all to yourself? Would you be willing to walk around for a minute and just feel that? Is it like a strut? Like an explorer on the moon? Like getting your sister's room after she's gone to college?" The coach offers sug-gestions in a "Does this help?" tone. The teller is free to frown and say "I'll think about that" or "No."

When I describe coaching to teachers I stress that the coach leaves control of the story in the hands of the child teller. Teachers schooled in a more directive approach look at me quizzically or bluntly ask, "Are you kidding? If students have the chance to veto my sugges-tions they'll never make any improvement." I chuckle, remembering that I said almost the same words to a student teacher once when she described what she was learning about teaching revision. Sarah, my student teacher, was a writer herself. She *enjoyed* revision because she had had teachers who put the control, the "responsibility" (Cam-bourne) for her writing in her hands. They had responded positively to strengths in her work, asked her questions about what she was getting at in places that were unclear, and wondered aloud about ideas that might support her piece, asking each time whether an idea made sense to her. Then she had taken delight in reworking the piece in order to say as clearly as possible what she wanted to say. When she first described this process to me, I didn't think middle school students were ready for such responsibility. I was wrong. Once students take control of their work, they forge ahead to places we teachers can't even imagine.

But students don't immediately take control of their work the first time we ask them to revise their writing or their storytelling. They may be used to taking orders and resist taking responsibility for their work. But establishing a climate in which the students know the teacher has an unfaltering expectation that they can take charge of the excellence of their work does reap enormous benefits in time.

Early in my evolution as a writing teacher I suggested that students could abandon a piece that was going nowhere. I knew that as a writer I had done that more times than not, so why shouldn't students be able to? I said that any abandoned piece could serve as evidence of "work" at the end of the marking period. Abandoned work is also worth reconsideration later, I told them. Once I had made this pronouncement, some children abandoned piece after piece, but they soon found the practice to be unsatisfying, and the trend died. It takes time to teach students how to be in charge of accepting or rejecting coaching, but the payoff is high if you stay with it. Lynne Burns, a middle school storyteacher from West Winfield, New York, said to me recently, "They get it, now! When I coach them, 'Do you want to try this?' they don't feel threatened by my ideas or the other kids' because they know they're in charge and we respect their work. But if a suggestion heads them in a direction that doesn't fit, they let us know. They are *good*, really good!" Yes, students are capable of taking responsibility for their own learning, but they need many chances in order to learn how.

Praise Paves the Way for Learning

Praise, practice, and technical advice spoken in a tone that says "You're in charge and I believe in you" (not "Why can't you do it right? I've told you and told you!") helps just about anyone believe in themselves and improve their skill as a teller. Lipman emphasizes the importance of keeping praise or "appreciations" separate from suggestions. In this culture, and perhaps in many others, children learn very early to expect criticism. Some figure out exactly what to do to avoid it (the route I took during my years of schooling). Others learn to live with criticism and become distrustful of praise, assuming, with good reason, that it will be followed by fault-finding: "I loved your story, *but* . . . ." Praise cannot teach students to recognize and play to their strengths until it is specific, delivered without condition, and accepted. The habit of giving conditional praise runs deep in teachers. We think our job is to push students ahead, so after a quick dose of praise we jump in with our improvements.

Jane was one of my brightest and most hard-working twelve-year-olds. Over the years she had become what I would call "addicted" to praise. Watching her avoid criticism by figuring out how to get every answer "right" was like looking at a younger version of myself. She was so smart and worked so hard, I wanted to push her to risk daring to seek a higher level of understanding. That is the job of the teacher, but Jane needed to know that I valued her effort, just as it was. At the time of the following incident, I was developing new habits as a writing teacher and most often simply praised Jane for specific strengths. When I did make suggestions, assuring her she was in charge, she was eager to "mess with a draft," as my students would say. She had come to trust me. However, one day in a whole-class setting, Jane fell into her shining star syndrome and I fell into my old "yes, but" teacher mode. She reminded me how vulnerable children are to criticism and how teacher-centered my instruction remained despite the changes I had made.

For homework, at the beginning of a poetry unit, I had asked students to look at the world through a poet's eyes (Heard 1989). I wanted them to see the myriad subjects for poetry all around them. I asked them to notice the small details that so often go unnoticed. Jane was the first to raise her hand the next day as we sat in a tight circle on the rug in the talking corner. Clearly excited, she asked, "Did you ever look at the clouds? Really look? I could write so many poems about clouds."

Out of an old habit, I slipped into my take-control-of-the-lesson mode. I sincerely believed that if I just nudged Jane to look more closely at the world (my way) she would be a better poet. Maybe the whole class could benefit from this nudge. "Clouds," I said, smiling, but with a somewhat patronizing tone in my voice. "Jane, it's *so* true, clouds *are* really magical and they *do* hold so much meaning." At this point I literally and figuratively turned my back on Jane, breaking the circle and walking over to write on the chalkboard. I pretended I was still addressing her, when I was actually teaching the class how her answer didn't quite measure up. "As a matter of fact, poets have been writing about clouds for years. You are so right. But do you know the meaning of *cliché*?" I wrote the word in big letters on the board. Jane was sitting to my left where I couldn't see her as I wrote and expounded upon the importance of avoiding worn-out subjects and looking at the world with new eyes. Finally, I sat back down to ask the students for more thoughts on possible topics for poetry. When I happened to glance toward Jane, briefly, I saw huge tears in the corners of her eyes. She was doing everything humanly possible to keep them from rolling down her face.

I knew instantly that I had replicated what I had despised about my own schooling experience. I had discounted her answer, finding it lacking in quality, and I had "fixed" it with my "superior" knowledge. Many teachers believe this is what we are supposed to do. They think a teary student needs to form a tougher skin, like they did. My guess is that the experience did toughen Jane a little more to criticism, but it probably also made her more cautious about offering her ideas and even trusting her own insights.

When I work in high schools now, I see that very few students risk saying what they really think, although perhaps it is as much a factor of peer pressure as it is fear of teacher criticism. I think the inability to speak one's truth begins very young and builds as the child learns to fear criticism and pressure from the adult world (Miller 1981, 1988). We have become people who avoid taking and giving compliments because of such fear. All of us have probably had the experience of someone brushing off a compliment we have meant sincerely: "Who me? Oh don't be ridiculous." Or such words are translated into body language, or a look that says "I don't trust you" or "What price do I have to pay for this compliment?" It is the rare person who simply lets a compliment sink in and savors the delight of it. We are also so used to the supposed validity of criticism, we assume someone should find fault with our work. We ask out of habit, "Are you sure it was okay? You *really* think I did well?" Women are especially practiced at turning compliments away: "Oh, it was nothing." or "Oh, this old thing? I've had it for years." The same is true of giving compliments. It is so much easier to take note of how others don't measure up.

Taking in Praise and Suggestions

In the last ten years I have had to learn how to hear what was powerful in my writing and storytelling. Only then could I begin to make it even better. School experiences had made me defensive against criticism but wary of praise. In some ways I had become my own worst critic, hearing the echo of past criticisms and censuring my writing before it even got on the paper. I didn't necessarily improve it by doing that. I starved for praise but distrusted it. Until I heard and accepted specific responses to the strengths of my work, I wasn't able to listen to suggestions and incorporate the ones that made sense to me. Once I began to believe in my writing, I found I could cut and redesign it without feeling defensive. I became a better teacher of writing and storytelling.

In school I had hated to revise because teachers told me what was wrong but not how to rewrite. If my teachers did write and knew that a writer has options when revising, they certainly never showed me that. As a result my adult writing was limited to entries in personal journals or personal letters. I didn't know that my writing had any particular strengths or that I could learn strategies for revision. My attitude was "I like my writing just the way it is, thank you." Sadly, I showed little of it to anyone, though I quietly yearned to have it do some good in the world.

At my first International Women's Writing Guild conference I began to see my writing through the eyes of others. I got to read my work aloud and hear what people liked about it. That experience helped dissolve my unwillingness to listen to suggestions. One day, in the parking lot, I gathered all my courage and asked one of the guild's teachers, Lynne Barrett, if she had any thoughts about a piece I had read aloud at the previous evening's reading. I had spotted her in the audience. She thought for a moment while I stood wondering if I would regret my question. "Remember that long part where you describe the two women?" she began. I flinched at the word "long" and wanted to run, but I knew this woman knew how to teach writers, so I stayed. "I liked those women," she said, "but I did long to hear them talk." She smiled. "Can you tighten the narration and let them talk, see what they reveal about themselves? Hmmm. Let's see, oh yes, and I liked your use of the phrase . . . ." She went on for about ten minutes. She had really heard my work and remembered details clearly. She responded as a listener as well as a writing teacher. Even her "but" didn't keep me from hearing "I *liked* those women." Her attentiveness, given with the sincere belief that I could improve as a writer, helped me value rather than reject her comments. She left me the work of how to, or whether to, put her suggestions in place. Like a young diver, I couldn't wait to jump back on the board.

David Dillon, once editor of *Language Arts*, used to write in his "Dear Readers" column each month about what he had valued in the many manuscripts he had seen and what had troubled him. More than once he said that he could hear teachers developing their voices but that he wanted them to speak their own hard truths even more, not just to parrot the gurus who were helping them change. That message of appreciation and challenge sent over the miles to this inexperienced writer was enough to keep me searching for the truths of my teaching by writing about my classroom. Response, even from a distance, is a powerful thing.

Fear and Conformity

Today teachers still need the challenge to be our unique selves and to teach in a way that engages children. From many directions voices call us to conform to a standard way of teaching: to use certain books (and not others), to adopt certain programs we may strongly believe do not engage children and foster their development as thinkers. We must speak and write in support of teaching in the way we believe. The voices, subtle or blatant, ask us to censor ideas, books, and practices. Storytelling colleagues have told me that they have worked in districts where the authorities have outlawed the use of imagination in the schools. Teachers are told not to ask children to close their eyes to ponder ideas. Some are forbidden to touch children, even in a kind or comforting way. It is time we teachers claim our profession back from such fear-based conformity. We have to shine the light of our belief on ourselves and coach our own uniqueness back to life.

One problem is that, in our own early education, too many of us were taught to "give the authority what he wants" or "do it *this* way or you won't get credit." Nonsense! We cannot conform to mandates that fly in the face of what we know about how children learn. We must be wary of teaching children to be such good rule-followers that they fail to think for themselves. I understand the need to teach conformity to rules established for the common good, just as any teacher does. But we need to establish environments in which children get practice *thinking* and *deciding* and *reflecting* upon the decisions they have made. "Try, try again" should be exciting not embarrassing. Our children need practice in intellectual and emotional risk-taking in safe, loving environments, if they are going to solve their own problems and those of the world.

When I taught undergraduate and graduate students in education for a few years, I saw the extent to which teaching conformity has deadened the minds of students. I was shocked to see men and women preparing to be teachers become furious that I, their professor, wouldn't tell them flat out *what* to learn. They wanted to be able to go home and learn only that (whatever "that" was) so they would be prepared to spit "it" back on a test "covering" only what I had promised the test would cover. Those students had let their ability to think and question and learn independently atrophy, or, perhaps, they no longer dared bring their independent thinking to school with them. After years of being reminded to do exactly what the teacher said, and of feeling powerless to change the situation, they had forgotten that their minds are their own. Some students rebounded when they saw that I was asking them not to learn a commodity but to read widely, to become reflective and wonder-filled, and to take charge of their own learning. Others, sadly, never came around, at least not by the end of the semester. School to them had become a matter of being told what to learn and being rewarded with a good grade for learning it. I was discouraged to think people with that attitude would become the next generation of teachers.

Yet I knew I had to believe in the best efforts of my college students, just as I had believed in my middle schoolers, if I was to help them out of their lethargy. Others hadn't believed in their ability to think, or had at least fed them the idea that the teacher holds the controls of learning. I had to do my best to feed the flame of learning now dim within them. If I criticized them I would just perpetuate the problem. They would deny their own thinking all the more. I had to shine the light of my belief on them and respond with a "coat of praise" every time they "approximated" thinking for themselves. Then I would ask, "Do you want a suggestion?" and be prepared to back off if they said "No."

I *do* give suggestions. I instruct students by providing all kinds of information they decide how to use. I am not a laissez-faire teacher. I simply guard appreciation time. Tellers need to know where they shine. When I give suggestions, I don't give them in the form of "should." If, from old habit, I say "What you should do is . . . ", students remind me by grinning and asking, "I *should?*" Teachers may see all kinds of things that would improve a telling, but only the teller's own experimentation and tinkering with the story will make it the unique masterpiece it is meant to be. Doug Lipman tells me to set the suggestions of others like gifts around my queenly throne and use only those I like. But "appreciations," he says, I'm obliged to accept. I have to let down defenses I have constructed as protection from insincere praise, backhanded compliments, and criticism long enough for the appreciations to come in and stay in. In the end I will know just how to improve my story.

Tellers Rehearsing

The tellers in my class often rehearsed just by telling. One way we rehearsed was to stand in two enormous concentric circles facing each other. Each facing pair would tell a story for five to eight minutes apiece and then give "appreciations" alone: "I love the way you . . . " or "I could really picture . . . " or "My favorite scene was . . . ." Sometimes the listener simply reflected back a phrase or image that stood out. Then we would rotate the circles a few steps and each teller would face a new listener for another rehearsal. Sometimes we did this in complete silence, telling the story through gestures and mime just to let go of the words. Believe it or not, it worked in getting students to make the story more physical and less mental.

Students learned to concentrate because they had to block out what others were doing. We sometimes stopped after two tellings and talked about the differences between the two. What things had they left out or added? What had changed in the structure of the story? Had they begun and ended the same way both times? What had they discovered about their stories that they didn't know before? This last question always brought interesting results.

"How else might your story begin/end?" as an exercise helped students see how much control over their storytellings they have. If I model three different beginnings to a story students usually know already, that also gives them ideas. In storytelling it isn't so important to have a catchy "lead." Often "Once upon a time an old man and an old woman . . . " is quite sufficient. However, experimenting with openings reinforces for the teller that he is in charge of composing the story in the moment, despite what the words in the text say.

Another exercise involved having students work with a story other than the one they were rehearsing for class. At the beginning of class we would briefly review the list of events in a commonly known story, such as the fable "The Boy Who Cried Wolf." Then in groups of three or four, students would talk for a short time about how to tell the story as a group. The children improvised, for the most part, because they didn't have a lot of time. Each telling was unique in style, tempo, and tone. In some the boy's character was lonely, in others more mischievous. Some tellings made use of four narrators and others had only one, with students playing such parts as the townspeople or the boy's family members. In some versions the wolf character came to life, while in others he was but a menacing shadow. What this showed the children was the variety that a teller can bring to a common tale. Their own individual or tandem tellings improved immeasurably after such an exercise.

I often shared with students how stories of mine had evolved and they liked hearing such process talk. It gave them ideas for their own stories and furthered their understanding of the process. I think it also made them feel grown-up to see inside a grown-up's thinking. The following process story is an example of working on a story passage in order to get more "inside" it.

I had been working on Constance Veatch Toney's "Sanyan, The Storyteller," but was having trouble telling it at the moment when the evil sorcerer orders his servants to kill Sanyan. The sorcerer is furious because Sanyan can make pictures, as if by magic, and she won't give him the secret of her power. She patiently explains how she makes pictures, that it isn't magic as he knows it, but he fails to understand. When he threatens her life, she "loses her patience," you might say, and begins to tell the sorcerer's servants how he stole *his* magic from them and their families. They turn their arrows from her toward him.

I wanted Sanyan's voice at this point to be strong and sure, perhaps angry but not from weakness. In truth, I felt more scared than angry at the thought of someone killing a storyteller just because he didn't understand the power of her work. In a coaching session, Doug Lipman suggested I play with the sound of "No!" trying to find a place where it felt strong and determined. In between each "No!" I talked about all kinds of things I was fed up with in the world from child-abuse to unreasonable rate hikes. I just kept saying "No!" after every few sentences, and before long, I started to feel the clear difference between the strong, determined "No!" of Sanyan's response and the angry feeling of a person who's run out of patience. Although I worked on a fragment of the story, I understood the storyteller's character better and was able to present her differently throughout the tale. By feeling her strength, I was able to envision the waning strength of the evil sorcerer and find a way to establish his character earlier.

If I coach even a few of my students through such "play with the possibilities" exercises, others begin to see that they can play with their own stories, and they suggest such experiments to each other. I remind them to leave the teller veto power as well as the right to suggest her own exercises. The students truly become each other's coaches. My job is to remind them of the concepts of coaching, to provide models of telling and coaching, and to create opportunities for them to talk about the process of making revisions. The workings of such rehearsals differ with every class, but some patterns do emerge. Then, as soon as we get feeling a little smug, a student's uniquely imaginative or perplexing telling stretches us in another direction.

There is no right way. Storyteachers and storytellers evolve. It may look different in seventh grade than in second, but the concept of the teller taking charge of her work under the ever-supportive light of the storyteacher remains the same. My middle schoolers would always caption photographs I took of them with what they had learned from storytelling. Here is some of what they said:

At first you're nervous, but when you start it's fun.

When you're done you want to do it again.

Storytelling's something not to be nervous about. Let it out.

Storytelling helped me speak to an audience as if speaking to a friend.

I learned that the more time I get to practice my story, the better I will do.

I was very nervous the first time I told, but after that I had the class in my hand!

I learned how to pick out the main points in a story and then add my own detail.

This experience taught me to have a lot of confidence in myself.

After storytelling, I can go in front of everybody and not be scared.

I learned that folktales tell us more about our life than anything in school.

I learned that you're usually not as scared as you think you are.

My story taught me that if you are one of the little guys you can beat the big guys if you have big brains.

When I was telling my story it was so fun! I was in my own world.

Storytelling taught me you can do anything if you put your all into it.

FOURTEEN

Relinquishing Old Beliefs in Order to Grow

toryteachers evolve. We are where we are in the evolution of our teaching. Just like our students, we arrive with unique gifts. Then we move forward. We find mentors in books or in the pages of journals, in our families, and right across the hall. We hold on to certain ideas about the nature of teaching and learning all our lives. Yet in order to make room for new ideas we discard some of the beliefs we have held for many years. Armed with new beliefs, we learn new methodologies, slowly or quickly, and keep our eyes and ears open for what enthusiastic and reluctant learners can teach us.

I spent a lot of years wishing I could be smarter or read important books earlier or come upon certain insights sooner than I did. All the negative energy I put into wishing "If only I'd known . . . " didn't make me a better teacher. It probably even retarded my development. We are the teachers we are. We can accept what we now understand, be grateful for it, and then move ahead.

I heard the author, lecturer, and drama teacher David Booth describe what he was like as a teacher at age seventeen. He gave orders in a voice like Mr. Bumble's from *Oliver Twist*. Just listening to him mimic the powerfully authoritarian tone he had used with his students back then unnerved me. Most of the audience, who knew him for the loving educator he is, laughed, but I felt the seriousness of what he was revealing. I recognized the humor in it, but at that moment felt sad. We begin our teaching careers by copying the people who have taught us. I knew that if he had been cruel as a young teacher, somewhere along the line he had had cruel teachers. He was telling us a trauma tale by returning to the image of his youthful authoritarian style, but clearly he had found the triumph in his evolution and was asking us to find the triumph in our own.

I want to touch on some assumptions that blocked my growth as a storyteacher and an artist for years. Some of these ideas were given to me with good intentions, but they only served to obstruct my development. Although I cannot cover any of them in depth here, I hope my current thinking will challenge you to look at these and other, similar messages passed on by teachers, authority figures, and friends.

Competition Is Good for You

I have finally relinquished the idea that competition is "good for you." My childhood was filled with competition: diving and swimming meets, costume contests, speech and recitation contests, and various other rivalries. Competition may have made me try harder at my diving on occasion, but I realize now I wanted to "win" more to please my parents and those who believed in me than I did to "beat" someone else. Competition, like criticism, made me feel small. I found myself applauding my opponent's mistakes, contrary to my upbringing, and that left me feeling ashamed. I also worried constantly about not measuring up, a worry that almost always made me dive worse and do worse in other kinds of competitions. When I find myself feeling competitive toward another storyteller, my work suffers every time.

My first time up for merit pay, I didn't know how to play the game because teachers were urged not to talk about merit ratings. I received a mediocre grade after my first six years of teaching even though I knew I had done a meritorious job. I asked my closest colleagues if they knew who was high on the scale and what it took to get there. An experienced teacher showed me how she kept a file for each merit category and saved everything from parent thank-you notes to lists of duties she had taken on for various committees. "*Documentation* not quality teaching, really, is the key." When I got a high merit rating during my next evaluation after submitting a large notebook of "proof," I was asked not to tell anyone because that would cause friction on the staff. I had to laugh. Such secrecy, and the realization that we were playing this game in competition with each other for higher pay, caused plenty of friction. The merit system was eventually abolished but not before it served to chip away at staff morale.

As a teacher I have also watched competition hurt far too many children (Kohn). In every essay contest, costume contest, and magazine drive there are many more losers than winners. I have seen kids have a "bad year," according to their parents, because they were put on a losing soccer team. One mother reported, "The year his team was on top of the league, he did *so* much better in school."

There is a thrill in winning that can spread to the other work we do. I also loved the camaraderie of being on a team and rooting for my friends. But putting energy into striving against opponents drained me of energy that could have gone into learning more about my diving or the other activities I pursued competitively.

Somewhere around fifth grade I asked a boy who always won the annual Halloween costume contest how he got such "neat" ideas. I don't remember exactly what he said, but I soon figured out that winning wasn't that much fun for him. It separated him from all of us. He worked on the costumes in secret with his uncle, I think, who designed them. After our conversation I appreciated the fun my brothers and sisters and I had every year going through the piles of old dress-up clothes and telling all our friends what we were going to be.

My goal is to teach children—and colleagues—how to support each other's individual quests and common goals. I no longer want to encourage the kind of striving that perpetuates loneliness or the hurt and embarrassment of losing, in school or out. I couldn't get competition off the playground or out of the magazine drives or other teachers' classrooms when I worked at a particular school, but I gently weeded it out of my own room every time it sprang up. The only kids who missed it were the ones who always managed to win, the ones addicted to winning. Once freed from the burden of constantly competing, those children eventually relaxed and let their learning stretch in new directions. They became less afraid to take risks and be not-so-great at something. Their *learning* took off. The struggle to stay on top takes time and energy away from learning. Exploration of the unknown is too scary to attempt if you have to be right all the time.

This Rule Is for Your Safety

Rules are generated by caution. Caution has its positive side, but it is basically a form of fear. When applied with a heavy hand, it can hamper children's physical, emotional, and psychological development.

Artistry, like the desire to learn, abounds in the child. Language, fantasy play, and problem-solving to make sense of the world—all of these are the gifts of the child. Undaunted, alive, without taint and without worry, the child artist thrives. Then along comes caution: physical restraint and social rules meant to tame and protect the child. But the creative artist self also gets tamed or retreats in the face of too much caution.

Some rules are important to keep children safe, but they threaten to put out the light if applied harshly or before children learn to honor the creative individuals they are. With wonderful intentions we adults, who long to *nurture* the child, make rules that curb the child's natural tendency to be sloppy, long-winded, changeable, and even metaphorical in a way that is not standard or does not conform to social acceptability. We basically ask the child not to be himself, to hide what is naturally spontaneous, creative, and unique.

The adult or societal intention may not be to put out the creative flame, only to protect children from their own brilliance. Protective, cautious adults tell themselves that the world will not accept brilliance. The injured artist in all of us knows that, at least unconsciously.

Our lights were dimmed by well-meaning adults. The child artist within us knows only too well how the world has failed to make room for, let alone honor and encourage, our unique gifts.

Even when the world honors artistry it honors the few. By putting only the "good" artists forward (and we all know how foolish and fickle popularity is), the world keeps all the rest of us in our places. The ridiculous conception that only *some* people are artists causes hard-to-repair (though not irreparable) damage to the artistry alive within us (Estés 1992). The artist too evolves: the storyteller, musician, dancer, architect, gardener, chef, flower arranger, doctor, jewelry-maker, painter, midwife, writer, actor, masseuse—whatever form of artistry burns within us or our children—longs to grow and expand. When we link our artistry with learning, we fan our own flames (Cameron).

If Your Students Like You, They Won't Look Up to You

I have wrestled with messages like "If they like you, they won't look up to you" since the beginning of my career. I understand why teachers make these pronouncements to young teachers. In my second year of teaching I had a "tough" class. After a blissful first year with terrific kids, I naively believed I could pick up in September where I had left off in June. I was too nice, people told me. It was "the great mistake." Through trial and error and asking questions and reading, however, I learned how to be both an "equal" learner with and a friend to students. I did take the role of teacher every September in order to establish the procedures that would give us order and allow us to respect each other. That is what I hadn't done the year I was "too nice." But once I became a co-learner with my students, wrestling with my own writing and storytelling, learning from *them* new meanings in texts, new rehearsal strategies, and new viewpoints on many subjects, I was able to let those old pronouncements go. I do share friendship with my students and gain more by doing so. I wish someone could have explained this difference to me as a young teacher and not simply told me to stop smiling in September.

You Will Know How to Teach (Right) After a Few Years

It is time we abandon the truism, "You will know how to teach after a few years," because it chips away at our sense of self. I heard Donald Murray say once in a talk at the University of New Hampshire, "As soon as you begin feeling certain, watch out." Yet for years I had the misconception that some end point would come. I would finally "get" how to teach, and it would stop being hard. It didn't. Yes, moments came along when teaching felt easier. Wonderful moments. I *had* found ways to make the learning more natural in my classroom, and I could be proud of that and relax, for a while. But to borrow Patrick Shannon's (1990) apt book title, the struggle continues.

There is always more to understand. Each of the pictures that comes clear, each "Ah-ha!" is part of a greater picture, an enormous "Ah-ha!" We cannot become complacent. Complacency is the death of good teaching. The expectation that teacher development is on-going must guide us like a beacon in the darkness. Learning, the kind we make our own, will light the path.

Close Your Door and Figure It Out

There is some truth to "Close your door and figure it out." Teaching in a new way is a lot like drafting a new piece of writing. To some extent you have to do it alone. But you can "talk" a draft of your teaching to a like-minded friend just as you can draft a piece of writing, plan your garden, or fantasize about building your new house. You can see how your ideas sound to someone else. (Hint: choose someone who will genuinely respond and gently ask you to clarify, not only enthusiastically reply, "Ah, yes.")

Find a friend who will observe you with encouraging eyes or listen and not judge as you talk through the hard parts of bringing about change. Lucy Calkins used to use the metaphor of the classroom teacher as the circus performer keeping all the plates spinning. She later admitted that the image didn't work for her anymore, but I think it is a good one to remind us of what happens when we try to learn or teach or tell stories all alone. Trying to do it all alone almost killed me (Gillard 1995). Keeping the plates spinning exhausts even the best performer, the most self-motivated learner.

I see instead an image of teachers standing in a circle on soft grass. We toss each other a beanbag. We call each other by name to signal that we are looking for a receiver. We laugh a lot, even when somebody flubs up, because "it's no big deal." We go on playing and after a while we collapse and laugh and talk about all the things in our hearts.

Teachers Have to Forego Expensive Conferences

When my cousins used to get new clothes every year I asked my dad why we didn't. All he said was, "You spend your money on what's important to you." Eventually I figured out that my family spent our money on food. Even with ten people we always had plenty to eat, and on special occasions even "good cuts" and treats.

It wasn't until I attended the International Women's Writing Guild Conference (at my own expense) in the summer of 1979, and left my husband and five-month-old alone to fend for themselves for a week, that I knew what I had been missing. I went at the invitation of Dorothy Meyer, one of those wonderful across-the-hall mentors.

At a lengthy conference (even a few days will suffice), your learning deepens. It resonates with your past experience and moves you in the direction of your future. You get the time to understand all that is coming in, and that meaning stays and grows with you. Previously, I had attended only inexpensive local workshops, which my district had paid for, but having to return to school the next day or the following Monday didn't give me the time to think and write about, or even talk about, what I had heard or experienced. Sometimes I never made much sense of what I took in until I heard something similar at another conference, perhaps years later.

I began to spend my own money on conferences because the professional friendships I made, the "experts" I got to see as real learners (just like me), and the speakers I got to hear whom I might never have heard otherwise, have had a tremendous impact on my teaching and on my life. I understand that teachers, especially women, have many responsibilities. I understand that money is in short supply these days. But I think many teachers don't invest in their own development as professionals because we have been taught to resent the financial support other professions give to employee development. Our resentment gets in the way of our saying, "Hey, I need this. If you won't give it to me I'm going to take it." Instead we whine, "Why should I pay for it?" As a result we cut ourselves off from the life-giving force of learning that extended conference time provides.

I am not advocating martyrdom. I am suggesting that if we want to advance our understanding of learning and teaching—and everywhere I travel I hear that teachers desperately hunger for more contact with the profession at large—we either need to make enough noise about the importance of this enrichment so we get more funding into our contracts and budgets, or we need to buy it for ourselves.

That means that before we purchase new clothes or cars or jewelry or trips or books or whatever else our "spending money" goes to, we need to think about putting money and time aside for our learning. Teachers complain to me that they can't go to conferences because their districts are out of money. Then we switch to talk of kitchen renovations, new Saabs, trips to Cancun, and the joy of shopping. I don't stand in judgment of how anyone spends their own hard-earned money. I just believe we can take more control of our professional joy. Next to my family, the ongoing professional friendships and new ideas I have brought home from conferences have given me more pleasure and deeper satisfaction than anything else in my life.

"Just" Talking with Students Is a Waste of Class Time

Most teachers agree that reading aloud in class is important. Encouraged by the speeches and writings of Shelley Harwayne, Charlotte Huck, Bill Martin Jr., Bee Cullinan, Jim Trelease, and many others, we have finally reclaimed our right to use class time for reading good literature to children. We see its many benefits to literacy and will no longer accept being told that it isn't teaching. Now it is time to reclaim our students' right to talk.

Help is at hand on this issue as well. *Primary Voices*, a relatively new quarterly published by the National Council of Teachers of English, invites teachers to write about the blending of theory and methodology. Recent issues (January and April 1995) have dealt with the importance of talk in approaching everything from racism to responding to literature. The November 1994 issue of *Language Arts* also focuses on the theme of discussion. In all three journal issues, teachers write about their methods and share their children's words, arguing for the importance of orality in literacy and offering extensive bibliographies for further reading.

We are slowly emerging from the days when people believed a good classroom is a quiet classroom, yet we still complain when children "ramble on." We must begin to respect children's talk if we hope to teach them ways to control it. My impression as I visit many schools is that children want desperately to talk, not just as a way to get out of work—the excuse we give for not allowing more talk—but because talk is a way they make sense of their world.

If the purpose of school is to make sense, it follows that school should be a place that encourages talk. While it is true that we need new ways to approach children's talk so it doesn't seem to eat up the day, first we must commit ourselves to the belief that talk is valuable.

One way my middle schoolers learned to talk with more purpose was by keeping logs and writing reflectively. We used logs during our storytelling and poetry units. Every quarter we also took one or more class periods to reflect in writing on our work for the marking period. Students responded to my questions about the value of activities we had tried, about time allotment, about how they had changed in ten weeks. Reflective writing turned them into more reflective talkers. I have always believed that both talk and writing have a place in a classroom, but I was surprised to learn how much each influenced the other. As students talked more they wrote better. Practicing reflective-ness in their logs, they became more articulate during discussions.

No One Above the Age of Seven Wants to Hear a Story Again

Storytellers have a bad habit of apologizing to each other when they are about to tell a story they know the other teller has already heard. I have done it myself. The world bombards us with the idea that new is better. New is fine, and new is often a delightful surprise, but one of the most significant gifts storytelling has given me as a language arts teacher—and as a human being for that matter—is respect for the old. Ancient stories are imprinted with important psychological truths because people have told them over a very long time (Estés 1992; Meade 1993). For teller and listener stories deepen in the *returning*. I love hearing stories over and over now, partly because I have stopped thinking, "I've already heard this!" Such thinking shuts learning down.

I think differently about this issue because retelling my stories, hundreds of times in some cases, has taught me the pleasure of return-ing to the world of the tale. It is like returning to the wonderful familiarity, as well as the newness, of playing or hearing a favorite piece of music. In storytelling, as in music, both the artist and the listener bring a new self to the experience each time.

Once I recognized how much I enjoyed returning to tales, I began to listen in a different way when another teller told a tale I had already heard. Listening for newness I saw how the teller had evolved and how her new insights about the tale revealed themselves in this telling. I also brought to the experience whatever ways I had grown since I had first heard the story. Now I have developed an uncanny ability to forget the endings of stories I have already heard. That could be an unconscious desire to enjoy the experience more or just growing forgetfulness, but either way I don't mind. Retelling and rereading stories is important at every age.

"When I Retire I'll Have Time for Myself"

Our dad's death when my five siblings and I were young undoubtedly had an enormous effect on the way each of us has viewed and lived life. We have made some unconventional choices. But even more than the loss of my dad, my mother's death, just a few years after her retirement from teaching elementary school, has made me want to shout to the world *"Live your life now!"*

I know teachers feel that "there is so little time." Some of us also feel the pinch of not having much money. But how much time and money we actually have to spend on ourselves depends on the choices we make. Human beings devised the way we think about time and money. Once, neither existed as we now perceive them. True, we can't unmake the world's view of time or money, but we can begin to think about both differently and make choices that reflect our beliefs. Myths, folktales, and children have taught me this. The old stories and the young people know that life is so much simpler than we make it.

Once I figured out I could save money for learning, I began to apportion time for developing my artist self. At first, I took an evening a week until I wrote my first article. Then I wrote or told stories during vacations, but that robbed me of the "let go" time I needed. Then, feeling courageous and a little crazy, I took a leave, came back and taught a few more years, and took another. When my sister said, "You'll still be a teacher, even if you resign and call yourself a story-teller," I left teaching.

Even when I had my own classroom, I came to look upon it as a place where I could express my artistry as well as teach. I really had to change my thinking to begin to see my classroom as a garden I could relax in, a place where everything was growing at its own pace, including me. A change in perspective makes a big difference.

I also chose my before and after school activities more carefully, saying a polite but firm "No" to tasks that brought me little satisfaction or disproportionately drained my energy. Good friends and mentors encouraged me to consider what gave me pleasure, increased my energy, and furthered my artistry. If I walked before school (some teachers walk at lunch or take a dance class after school), I slept better and had more pep throughout the day. If I ate raw vegetables and drank water instead of soothing my mental fatigue with caffeine, sugar, and alcohol (some people use other substances), I thought more clearly. I am not saying it was easy, but it was simple.

My mother had a full life, I don't deny that. She raised six children on her own after age forty-two, taught one grade or another for nearly forty years, and took post-graduate courses in elementary counseling. She taught me about the healthy side of caution and more than I can say about love. She always wore a dress that twirled, and at the family parties she orchestrated, everyone from great-grandparents to the diapered set had fun. Sometimes, late at night, her piano playing traveled up to my bedroom through the heating system of our house. It spoke of her wishes and dreams.

She started a journal after she retired—this former editor-in-chief of her high school paper who told me many times that she had longed to study journalism (but didn't). She was the oldest of five children, and her father told her to go to the local teacher's college because it was free. The year was 1939. Her postretirement journal contains five entries, all from a week in March 1985 just before and including her sixty-third birthday. She lived for two years more but she never wrote in it again.

I can only guess why she stopped writing. I have started and abandoned my share of journals over the years. I got "lazy" or distracted or discouraged or too busy. Beginning a new journal always reminded me that I keep secrets in my head and heart. My mother was brought up to guard her secret self and perhaps she feared that in a journal she would reveal more than she wanted to. Or perhaps she got busy or distracted or discouraged.

Maybe she started the journal as a way of encouraging herself, now that she was retired, to write again. She wrote a speech for her retirement party that was as funny and touching as any keynote address I have ever heard. In it I encountered her first, one-room school, her view of superintendents, and her impressions of key people, colleagues and kids, who supported her over the years. I think my mother needed an audience for her writing. It is clear that she hadn't forgotten how to write. A journal just didn't suffice.

We teachers must claim our artistry and not let the principal's demands, children's needs, parents' outcries, and our own families' clamors for attention drain us of the energy to create and take our creations out into the world. That teaching itself is an art is true, and we claim that truth when we seek mentors and grow as teacher-artists. But a creative being, separate from the teacher, dwells in each of us too. It may be a storyteller or painter, bread baker or gardener, potter or quilter or tree-house designer, but it is there. If we wait till we retire to nurture that artist, time or money or the fear that it is too late may still stop the flow.

Losing my parents has helped me to claim my artistry and to break the chains of caution and competitiveness. I didn't know I thought all I have written here until I bought myself the time and space to write this book. My hope is that in some way, through our artistry, through our teaching, we will touch the children in our care as well as the too-long silent child in ourselves.

Resources for Storyteachers

Those who want to put storytelling consciously into their lives must find a personal path into this ancient art. Not every book and tape on the list below will encourage the nervous new teller nor satisfy the experienced storyteacher. This list is far from comprehensive. Yet, by sharing my mentors and friends—which these resources have become—I only hope to offer you assistance as you walk *your* path into storytelling.

Books About Storytelling, Literacy, and Creativity

Allen, J. and J. Mason, eds. 1989. *Risk makers, risk takers, risk breakers: Reducing the risks for young literacy learners.* Portsmouth, NH: Heinemann.

Baker, A. and E. Greene. 1987. *Storytelling: Art and technique.* 2d ed. New York: Bowker.

Barton, B. 1986. *Tell me another: Storytelling and reading aloud at home, at school, and in the community.* Portsmouth, NH: Heinemann.

Bauman, R. 1975. "Verbal art as performance." *American Anthropologist* 77: 290–311.

Bausch, W. 1984. *Storytelling: Imagination and faith.* Mystic, CT: Twenty-Third Publications.

Bissex, Glenda and R. Bullock, eds. 1987. *Seeing for ourselves: Case-study research by teachers of writing.* Portsmouth, NH: Heinemann.

Borysenko, J. 1990. *Guilt is the teacher, love is the lesson.* New York: Warner Books.

Bosma, B. 1992. *Fairy tales, fables, legends, and myths: Using folk literature in your classroom.* 2d ed. New York: Teachers College Press.

Bradbury, R. 1990. *Zen in the art of writing.* Santa Barbara, CA: Capra Press.

Britton, J. "Breaking the threads." *Teachers Networking.* 11(4):1–5. Katonah, NY: Richard C. Owen.

Bruchac, J. 1987. "Storytelling and the sacred: On the uses of Native American stories." *The National Storytelling Journal.* Spring:14–18.

Bruner, J. 1986. *Actual minds, possible worlds.* Cambridge, MA: Harvard University Press.

———. 1990. *Acts of meaning.* Cambridge, MA: Harvard University Press.

Bunce: M. 1991. "In the classroom or on the stage. . .What to do when the telling jitters take over." *Yarnspinner.* 15(8):3–5.

Cameron, J. 1992. *The artist's way.* New York: Jeremy P. Tarcher/Putnam.

Campbell, J. [1949] 1968. *The hero with a thousand faces.* Princeton, NJ: Princeton University Press.

Coles, R. 1990. *The spiritual life of children.* Boston: Houghton Mifflin.

Cooper, P. 1993. *When stories come to school: Telling, writing & performing stories in the early childhood classroom.* New York: Teachers & Writers Collaborative.

Cordeiro, P. 1992. *Whole learning: Whole language and content in the upper elementary grades.* Katonah, NY: Richard C. Owen.

———. 1993. "Becoming a learner who teaches." *Teachers Networking.* 12(1):1–5. Katonah, NY: Richard C. Owen.

Drummond, M. J. 1994. *Learning to see: Assessment through observation.* York, ME: Stenhouse.

Dyson, A. 1989. *Multiple worlds of child writers: Friends learning to write.* New York: Teachers College Press.

———. 1993. *Social worlds of children learning to write in an urban primary school.* New York: Teachers College Press.

Edwards, S. and R. Maloy. 1992. *Kids have all the write stuff: Inspiring your children to put pencil (or crayon or felt-tip marker or computer) to paper.* New York: Penguin.

Egan, K. 1989. *Teaching as storytelling: An alternative approach to teaching and curriculum in the elementary school.* Chicago: University of Chicago Press.

Engel, S. 1995. *The stories children tell: Making sense of the narratives of childhood.* New York: W. H. Freeman.

Fawcett, G. 1992. "Moving the big desk." *Language Arts.* 69(3):183–185.

Five, C. 1992. *Special voices.* Portsmouth, NH: Heinemann.

Fletcher, R. 1991. *Walking trees: Teaching teachers in the New York City schools.* Portsmouth, NH: Heineman.

———. 1994. *What a writer needs.* Portsmouth, NH: Heinemann.

Gallas, K. 1992. "When the children take the chair: A study of sharing time in a primary classroom." *Language Arts.* 69(3):172–182.

———. 1994. *The languages of learning: How children talk, write, dance, draw, and sing their understanding of the world.* New York: Teachers College Press.

Galt, M. 1992. *The story in history: Writing your way into the American experience.* New York: Teachers and Writers Collaborative.

Goldberg, N. 1986. *Writing down the bones.* Boston: Shambhala.

Grant, J. M. 1995. *Shake, rattle and learn: Classroom-tested ideas that use movement for active learning.* York, ME: Stenhouse.

Hamilton, M. and M. Weiss. *Children Tell Stories.* Katonah, NY: Richard C. Owen.

Harwayne, S. 1992. *Lasting impressions: Weaving literature into the writing workshop.* Portsmouth, NH: Heinemann.

Heinig, R. 1992. *Improvisation with favorite tales: Integrating drama into the reading/writing classroom.* Portsmouth, NH: Heinemann.

Hubbard, R. 1989. *Authors of pictures, draftsmen of words.* Portsmouth, NH: Heinemann.

Kitagawa, M. and C. Kitagawa. 1987. *Making connections with writing: An expressive writing model in Japanese schools.* Portsmouth, NH: Heinemann.

Kohl, H. 1984. *Growing minds: On becoming a teacher.* New York: Harper & Row.

Lamott, A. 1994. *Bird by bird: Some instructions on writing and life.* New York: Pantheon.

Livo, N. and S. Rietz. 1986. *Storytelling process and practice.* Littleton, CO: Libraries Unlimited.

Maguire, J. 1985. *Creative storytelling: Choosing, inventing and sharing tales for children.* Cambridge, MA: Yellow Moon Press.

Mallan, K. 1991. *Children as storytellers.* Portsmouth, NH: Heinemann.

Manuel, D. 1991. "Once upon a time, storytelling was revived." *The Boston Sunday Globe.* March 17.

Mellon, N. 1992. *Storytelling & the art of imagination.* Rockport, MA: Element.

O'Keefe, V. 1995. *Speaking to think/thinking to speak: The importance of talk in the learning process.* Portsmouth, NH: Boynton-Cook/Heinemann.

Pierce, K. M. and C. Gilles. 1993. *Cycles of meaning: Exploring the potential of talk in learning communities.* Portsmouth, NH: Heinemann.

Portalupi, J. 1995. "Autobiographical understanding: Writing the past into the future." *Language Arts.* 72(4):272–275.

Rief, L. 1992. *Seeking diversity: Language arts with adolescents.* Portsmouth, NH: Heinemann.

Romano, T. 1987. *Clearing the way: working with teenage writers.* Portsmouth, NH: Heinemann.

Rosen, H. 1986. "The importance of story." *Language Arts.* 63(3):226–37.

———. 1992. "The power of story." *Teachers Networking.* 11(1):1–6. Katonah, NY: Richard C. Owen.

Smith, H. 1995. "An interview with Augusta Baker." *Horn Book.* 71(3):292–296.

Spear, K. 1988. *Sharing writing: Peer response groups in English classes.* Portsmouth, NH: Boynton/Cook-Heinemann.

Stewig, J. and C. Buege. 1994. *Dramatizing literature in whole language class-rooms*. New York: Teachers College Press.

Stillman, P. 1989. *Families Writing*. Cincinnati, OH: Writers Digest Books.

Stone, E. 1988. *Black sheep and kissing cousins: How our family stories shape us*. New York: Penguin.

Swartz, L. 1988. *Dramathemes: A practical guide for teaching drama*. Markham, Ontario: Pembroke Publishers Ltd.

Teaching storytelling. A position statement from the committee on storytelling of the National Council of Teachers of English. Urbana, IL.

Watson, D., C. Burke, and J. Harste. 1989. *Whole language: Inquiring voices*. New York: Scholastic.

Witherell, C. and N. Noddings. 1991. *Stories lives tell: Narrative and dialogue in teacher education*. New York: Teachers College Press.

Yolen, J. 1981. *Touch magic: Fantasy, faerie and folklore in the literature of childhood*. New York: Philomel.

Story Collections and Historical Works of Fiction and Fact

Bresnick-Perry, R. 1992. *Leaving for America*. Illus. M. Reisberg. San Francisco: Children's Book Press.
A simple and true tale about a girl's fear and excitement upon leaving the comfort and love of a shtetl for an unknown land.

Brody, E. et al., eds. 1991. *Spinning tales, weaving hope: Stories, storytelling, and activities for peace, justice and the environment*. Illus. B. Lanki. Philadelphia: New Society Publishers.
Selections of traditional and original tales on important themes written by storytellers for teachers. Includes lesson plans, background on the stories, and more.

Bruchac, J. 1993. *Dawn land*. Golden, CO: Fulcrum Publishing.
A fascinating saga about an ancient Abenaki Indian boy's heroic journey, set in the area around Lake Champlain. Bruchac, a respected anthologist and storyteller, told me that much of it came to him in dreams.

Chinen, A. 1992. *Once upon a midlife: Classic stories and mythic tales to illuminate the middle years*. New York: Jeremy P. Tarcher/Putnam.
A psychiatrist talks about stories and therapy. Great for teachers on the subject of what stories say about our place in the world.

Choi, S. 1991. *Year of impossible goodbyes*. Boston: Houghton Mifflin.
Heartbreaking yet hopeful young adult novel about a child living in North Korea during the Second World War.

Davis, D. 1990. *Listening for the crack of dawn*. Little Rock, AR: August House.
This is the first of Donald Davis's many written collections of tales about growing up in the South. Every one is compellingly honest and side-splittingly funny. (See Davis tapes also.)

Davis, O. 1992. *Just like Martin*. New York: Simon & Schuster.
Actor Ossie Davis's first novel for children about a boy who wants to attend the March on Washington, 1963.

Douglass, F. 1968. *Narrative of the life of Frederick Douglass, An American slave*. New York: Dutton.
Beyond all I have read in history books or fiction about slavery, this still touches me most.

Finney, J. 1970. *Time and again*. New York: Simon & Schuster.
A novel that helped me believe in time travel, mental or other.

Geras, A. 1990. *My grandmother's stories: A collection of Jewish folk tales*. Illus. J. Jordan. New York: Knopf.
Ten traditional narratives told as a grandmother would.

Kipling, R. 1956. *Kipling: A collection of his stories and poems*. Garden City, NJ: Doubleday.
My father's signature as well as my first view of India inside the cover of this book make it precious to me.

Lanker, B. 1989. *I dream a world: Portraits of black women who changed America.* New York: Stewart, Tabori & Chang.
This remarkable collection of personal narratives and black-and-white photographs never stops taking my breath away.

Lester, J. 1968. *To be a slave*. Illus. T. Feeling. New York: Dial.
Slave narratives collected originally by abolitionists and by the Federal Writers' Project.

———. 1987. *The tales of Uncle Remus: The adventures of Brer Rabbit*. New York: Dial.
This is one of four collections. Lester explains why these tales became popular, went out of favor, and must be kept alive. The introduction itself is good literature.

Lindbergh, A. 1974. *Hour of gold, hour of lead*. New York: Harcourt Brace Jovanovich.
The diary entries and letters of Anne Morrow Lindbergh, which reveal the spirit of a woman in love and in pain.

MacDonald, M. 1986. *Twenty tellable tales*. New York: H. W. Wilson.
Margaret Read MacDonald is one of the backbones of storytelling in this country. This is but one of her important contributions.

Mayer, M. 1981. *Pinocchio*. Trans. and adapt. by author. Illus. G. McDermott. New York: Four Winds.

Reading this translation of the original Carlo Collodi tale showed me how much I had to learn about stories. Talking with Mayer for an hour about her love of folk literature inspired me to get reading.

Millender, D. 1986. *Martin Luther King, Jr.: Young man with a dream*. Illus. A. Fiorentino. New York: Macmillan.

I loved how this biography showed young Martin's admiration of the works of Langston Hughes and Martin's thrill at meeting the poet who visited his school as a teacher-artist.

Miller, T. and A. Pellowski. 1988. *Joining in: An anthology of audience participation stories and how to tell them*. Ed. N. Livo. Intro. L. Simms. Cambridge, MA: Yellow Moon Press.

The title says it all. A great book for those who want the "how."

Paulsen, G. 1985. *Dogsong*. New York: Macmillan.

A young man sees the importance of story and the old ways in this mystical novel for young adults.

———. 1986. *Sentries*. New York: Macmillan.

Paulsen weaves together remarkable stories of four young people for adolescents and adults in love with writing and living.

Parks, R. with J. Haskins. 1992. *Rosa Parks: Mother to a movement*. New York: Dial.

Working on Martin Luther King Jr.'s story made me want to know more about Rosa Parks. This book is full of surprises.

Porter, A. P. 1992. *Jump at de sun: The story of Zora Neale Hurston*. Minneapolis, MN: Carolrhoda Books.

A young adult book that introduces readers to Hurston, a contemporary of Langston Hughes, and to her writings, which were almost lost to history.

Riley, P., ed. 1993. *Growing up Native American, an anthology*. New York: Morrow.

Twenty-two writers of fiction and essay tell of their childhoods.

Rosen, B. 1988. *And none of it was nonsense: The power of storytelling in school*. Portsmouth, NH: Heinemann.

This amazing inner-city London teacher's book about storytelling is a must for all storyteachers. My hope is to meet Betty Rosen and have a long talk.

Schimmel, N. 1982. *Just enough to make a story: A sourcebook for storytelling*. 2d ed. Berkely, CA: Sisters' Choice Press.

Good theory and practice in one book.

Schram, P. and S. Rosman. *Eight tales for eight nights: Stories for Chanukah*. Northvale, NJ: Jason Aronson Inc.

All the joy and sadness of this holiday—its many meanings for each generation—are reflected in this book by tellers Peninnah Schram and Steven Rosman.

Sierra, J. 1992. *The Oryx multicultural folktale series: Cinderella*. Phoenix, AZ: Oryx Press.

Twenty-five versions of the Cinderella motif—some with a male character. Oryx has also published collections of the beauty/beast and "knock at the door" motifs as well as one on small characters such as Thumbelina and Tom Thumb.

Steinbeck. E. and R. Wallsten, eds. 1975. *Steinbeck: A life in letters*. New York: Viking.

Steinbeck's writing life and love life are here to be marveled at.

Strickland, D., ed. 1986. *Listen children: An anthology of black literature*. New York: Bantam.

A treasury of poetry and poems easily accessible to children.

Uchida, Y. 1991. *The invisible thread*. New York: Simon & Schuster.

The memoir of a Japanese American girl before and during her internment in Topaz during World War II.

Yolen, J. ed. 1986. *Favorite folktales from around the world*. New York: Pantheon.

I return again and again to this rich collection.

―――. 1990. *The devil's arithmetic*. New York: Puffin.

My middle school students couldn't get enough of time-traveling with Hanna to glimpse what it was like for a Jewish girl in a Nazi concentration camp.

Poetry Collections and Books About Teaching a Love of Poem Telling

Adoff, A. 1982. *All the colors of the race*. Illus. J. Steptoe. New York: Morrow.

Bagert, B. 1984. *If only I could fly: Poems for kids to read out loud*. New Orleans, LA: Juliahouse Publishers.

Baron, L. 1981. *Rhythm and dues*. Hempstead, NY: Harlin Jacque.

―――. 1982. *The sun is on*, rev. ed. Intro. R. Dee. Illus. K. Elam. Hempstead, NY: Harlin Jacque.

Berry, J. 1991. *When I dance*. Ed. B. V. Ingber. Illus. K. Barbour. San Diego: Harcourt Brace Jovanovich.

Bober, N. 1991. *A restless spirit: The story of Robert Frost*. Illustrated. New York: Holt.

Booth, D. and B. Moore. 1988. *Poems please!* Markham, Ontario: Pembroke.

Brooks, G. 1967. *Bronzeville boys and girls.* Illus. R. Solbert. New York: HarperCollins.

Bruchac, J. *Near the mountains.* Fredonia, NY: White Wine Press.

Colin, B. 1994. "The train in the chimney: Teaching poetry writing and art." *Teachers & Writers.* 25(5):1–5. New York: Teachers & Writers Collaborative.

Collom, J. and S. Noethe. 1994. "Poetry everywhere." *Teachers & Writers.* 25(3):1–11. New York: Teachers & Writers Collaborative.

Copeland, J. 1993. *Speaking of poets: Interviews with poets who write for children and young adults.* Urbana, IL: National Council of Teachers of English.

Cullinan, B., M. Scala, and V. Schroder. 1995. *Three voices: An invitation to poetry across the curriculum.* York, ME: Stenhouse.

cummings, e. e. 1963. *Collected poems.* New York: Harcourt, Brace & World.

Denman, G. A. 1988. *When you've made it your own: Teaching poetry to young people.* Portsmouth, NH: Heinemann.

Duke, C. and S. Jacobsen, eds. 1992. *Poets' perspectives: Reading, writing and teaching poetry.* Portsmouth, NH: Boynton/Cook-Heinemann.

Dunn, S. with L. Pamenter. 1990. *Crackers and crumbs: Chants for whole language.* Portsmouth, NH: Heinemann.

Dunning, S., E. Lueders, and H. Smith, eds. 1966. *Reflections on a gift of watermelon pickle . . . and other modern verse.* New York: Scott, Foresman & Co.

Fleischman, P. 1988. *Joyful noise: Poems for two voices.* New York: Harper & Row.

Fletcher, R. 1994. *I am wings: Poems about love.* New York: Bradbury.

Gendler, J. R. 1988. *The book of qualities.* New York: Harper & Row.

Glenn, M. 1986. *Class dismissed II: More high school poems.* Photos M. J. Bernstein. Boston: Houghton Mifflin.

Greenfield, E. 1986. *Honey I love and other love poems.* Illus. D. Dillon and L. Dillon. New York: HarperCollins.

Gregory, C. 1990. *Childmade: Awakening children to creative writing.* Barrytown, NY: Station Hill Press.

Grossman, F. 1991. *Listening to the bells: Learning to read poetry by writing poetry.* Portsmouth, NH: Boynton/Cook-Heinemann.

Halpern, D. ed. 1994. *Holy fire: Nine visionary poets and the quest for enlightenment.* New York: HarperCollins.

Heard, G. 1989. *For the good of the earth and sun: Teaching poetry.* Portsmouth, NH: Heinemann.

———. 1992. *Creatures of earth, sea and sky.* Honesdale, PA: Wordsong/Boyds Mills Press.

Hermsen, T. "The poem in the painting." *Teachers & Writers.* 25(5):6–15.

Hopkins, L. [1972] 1987. *Pass the poetry, please!* rev. ed. New York: HarperCollins.

Hughes, L. [1959] 1987. *Selected poems of Langston Hughes*. New York: Random.

Kennedy, X. J. and D. M. 1985. *Knock at a star: A child's introduction to poetry*. Illus. K. A. Weinhaus. Boston: Little, Brown.

Larrick, N. *Let's do a poem!: Introducing poetry to children through listening, singing, chanting, impromptu choral reading, body movement, dance and dramatization*. New York: Delacorte.

Little, J. 1989. *Hey world, here I am!* Illus. S. Truesdell. New York: Harper-Collins.

McKim, E. and J. Steinbergh. 1983. *Beyond words: Writing poems with children*. Green Harbor, MA: Wampeter Press.

Meltzer, M. 1988. *Langston Hughes: A biography*. New York: HarperCollins.

Merriam, E. 1984. *Jamboree: Rhymes for all times*. New York: Dell.

———. 1986. *A sky full of poems*. Illus. W. Gaffney-Kessell. New York: Dell.

Rosen, M. 1986. *When did you last wash your feet?* London, UK: André Deutsch Ltd.

———. 1989. *Did I hear you write?* New York: Scholastic.

Rosen, M. and J. Nichols. 1994. *Count to five and say "I'm alive!": Two poetry workshops*. Video. York, ME: Stenhouse.

Slier, D., E. Turner, and D. Patrick, eds. 1991. *Make a joyful sound: Poems for children by African-American poets*. New York: Checkerboard Press.

Soto, G. 1991. *A fire in my hands: A book of poems*. New York: Scholastic.

Strickland, D. and M., eds. 1994. *Families: Poems celebrating the African American experience*. Honesdale, PA: Boyds Mills Press.

Viorst, J. 1984. *If I were in charge of the world and other worries: Poems for children and their parents*. Illustrated. New York: Macmillan.

Wood, N. 1992. *Many winters*. Illus. F. Howell. New York: Doubleday.

———. 1993. *Spirit walker: Poems*. Illus. F. Howell. New York: Doubleday.

Worth, V. 1987. *All the small poems*. Illus. N. Babbitt. New York: Farrar, Straus and Giroux.

Tapes

I include here records and tapes I've purchased during the last ten years when I needed encouragement to tell the stories I already knew from childhood, wanted to learn more stories, or longed to hear the voices of new friends I'd made in the storytelling world. I learned from each. Have fun finding my favorites and yours.

Beekman, J. 1989. *One Texan's tales*. Houston, TX: Spellweaver Productions. Jeannine Pasini Beekman is a female teller with the strength of Paul Bunyan and the wit of Mark Twain.

Black, J. 1988. *Waiting for Elijah*. Marblehead, MA: Judith Black.
Judith is the bravest and funniest teller I know. While this collection of tales for Passover (or anytime) is funny, it will also make you cry. My son and I will never forget a certain ride home from Boston to Albany because of it.

Bruchac, J. 1988. *Iroquois stories*. Greenfield Center: New York: Good Mind Records.
Bruchac, now known for *Keepers of the Earth* and other texts has been telling Native American tales locally for years. To see Joe tell tales live is to begin to feel that peace among all people *will* come someday.

Bryan, A. 1985. *The dancing granny and other African stories*. New York: Caedmon.
Ashley Bryan roars like a real African lion. His stylized vocalizing always raises my consciousness about the *power* of language.

Burrows, D. 1990. *Once upon a time: Stories from the Bahamas*. Cambridge, MA: Yellow Moon Press.
Derek Burrows transports you to his native land and makes its Caribbean/Afro-American stories not so different from your own growing-up tales.

Cabral, L. *Ananzi Stories and others by Len Cabral*. Cranston, RI: Story Sound Productions.
Len Cabral flavors "The Three Pigs," "The Gunny Wolf," and of course, Ananzi, in own African-American way.

Davis, D. *Listening for the crack of dawn*. Little Rock, AR: August House.
———. *LS/MFT*. Little Rock: AR: August House.
Don't ever turn down the chance to see Donald Davis tell the stories of his North Carolina boyhood. He is the living Jack of Beanstalk fame. Just two of his many wonderful recordings.

deBeer, S. 1991. *Seven stories: Tales of deep-rooted magic and of women wise and wonderous*. New Haven, CT: Sara deBeer.
Sara's haunting style takes listeners deep into a tale and into themselves. She has been an inspiration to me.

Doyle, D. 1993. *Tales of transformation*. Video. Mesa, AZ: Don Doyle.
I feel the healing power of the beauty of the Southwest when I see this videotape of a fine storyteacher.

Forest, H. 1985. *Tales of womenfolk*. Weston, CT: Weston Woods.
Heather Forest's storysong versions of folktales about women including Three Strong Women (Japan), The Squire's Bride and others are no less than the work of a pioneer in women's storytelling. This is only one of her many recordings.

Harley, B. 1987. *Cool in school: Tales from 6th grade*. Seekonk, MA: Round River Productions.
If you haven't experienced Bill Harley, you get a flavor of his craziness and truth-telling on this one of his many tapes. My 6th graders fought over it.

Joy, F., ed. *Choices of voices*. Johnson City, TN: Storytelling World.
This tape accompanied the Winter/Spring 1995 issue of *Storytelling World*. Its nine versions of the fable "Crow and the Pitcher" make clear how each teller tells in his or her own way.

Johnson, L. and E. Wynne. "Key of see storytellers." *Running scared and flying high*. Minneapolis, MN: Larry Johnson and Elaine Wynne.
This educator husband and psychologist wife team share true life tales. I have learned so much about storytelling from knowing these two human beings.

Lane, Marcia 1985. *Tales on the wind*. Albany, NY: A Gentle Wind. Mostly traditional tales from many lands told with a spirit of love.

Leavitt, T. 1990. *Whispers of light: Stories of transformation*. Pleasant Valley, NY: Visions Story Center.
Adaptations of folktales and "Wishland," an original tale about honesty and courage in facing the darkness.

Lee, D. 1995. *The gentle giant and other stories*. Selkirk, NY: Dee Ellen Lee.
Any child would have sweet dreams after falling asleep to this tape of original and retold folktales.

Lipke, B. 1995. *Tales from the Vineyard*. Newton Centre, MA: Barbara Lipke.
By one of my favorite storyteachers, this tape includes tales of *real* ghosts in an old house and along the rocky coast of Martha's Vineyard and heart-warming stories as well. A treat.

Lipman, D. 1983. *Folktales of strong women*. Cambridge, MA, Yellow Moon Press.
———. 1990. *One little candle: Participation stories and songs for Hanukkah*. West Somerville, MA: Enchanters Press.
———. 1991. *The amazing teddy bear: Stories with songs for parent and child*. West Somerville, MA: Enchanters Press.
These are my favorites of Doug Lipman's many tapes. A combination of carefully researched folk versions and original tales that touch the heart. The wisdom for parents and teachers in the Teddy Bear collection is truly "amazing."

———. 1992. *Now we are free: Stories and songs of freedom for Passover and anytime*.West Somerville, MA: Enchanters Press.

MacGregor, G./The Ivy Vine Players. 1993. *MacGregor's Garden*. Lake Hill, NY: Turnip the Volume Productions.
Grian MacGregor's puppets will make you laugh as they tell and sing of fears, fantasies, and "real" growing up.

McQuillan, S. and J. 1991. *Tales from the first world*. Guilford, CT: American Melody.
Synia sings and tells accompanied by Jeff's instrumentation and vocal assistance. Traditional African-American, Haitian and other tales are given new life.

O'Callahan, J. 1983. *Raspberries*. Marshfield, MA: Artana Records.
This is my second favorite of Jay's stories, about a man's good fortune and bad. *The Pill Hill Stories*, fictional versions of Jay's own boybood, mentioned in the references, just about tie with it. I especially delight in these because I have seen them performed live. You'll never be the same after a Jay O'Callahan telling.

———. 1983. *The herring shed*. Marshfield, MA: Artana Productions.
This touching tale of a girl and her neighbors at home in Canada during wartime will stay with you. The tape contains other original tales as well.

———. 1982. *The little dragon and other stories*. Weston, CT: Weston Woods.
Jay's voices and his fantasies first delighted his own children at bedtime.

Stallings, F. 1992. *Crane's gratitude*. Bartlesville, OK: Prairieflower Productions.
Cat lovers will howl all night at the first tape and enjoy the variety of animal tales from all over the world.

———. 1994. *Cat o'nine tales: songs and stories about cats*. Bartlesville, OK: Prairie-Fire.

Stansfield, J. 1989. *Song of the mountains, song of the plains: Stories, ballads and poetry of the American West*. Monument, CO: John Stansfield.

Sweetland Storytellers. 1989. *Sweetland Storytellers keep Christmas Eve*. Saratoga Springs, NY: Jeannine Laverty.
These four women, my teachers, originally recorded for WGY Radio in Schenectady an evening of stories about courage, love, loneliness, and holiday wintertime memories.

———. 1991. *The thing without a name and other strange tales of the Ozark Hills*. Saratoga Springs, NY: Jeannine Laverty.
These are Ida Chittum stories adapted with her permission for telling, great for a Halloween program or just for around the campfire.

Weiss, M. and M. Hamilton. 1985. *Beauty and the beast storytellers: Tales of magic, mystery and humor from around the world*. Ithaca, NY: Beauty & the Beast Storytellers.

Supporting Organizations and Folk Literature Publishers

The National Storytelling Association, PO Box 309, Jonesborough, TN 37659, 800-525-4514 or 615-753-2171, Fax: 615-753-9331, publishes an annual directory of names and descriptions of tellers, resources, educational opportunities, advice about bringing a teller to your school or community, tips for planning a storytelling festival and more. Members receive a journal, regular organization updates, a catalog of resources and discounted registration at the annual festival (every October in Jonesborough, TN) and conference (which relocates each year and will be held in July 1996 in Philadelphia). An archive of resources about storytelling is housed in Jonesborough and open to the public.

LANES, the League for the Advancement of New England Storytelling, c/o Mike Myers, PO Box 323, Wrentham, MA 02093, 508-384-3195. This organization of storytellers produces a regional directory of tellers and learning opportunities, offers a conference each March in Boston, gives member discounts at local book establishments, and publishes *The Museletter* including excellent articles and a calendar of storytelling events.

Storytelling World, c/o Dr. Flora Joy, Eastern Tennessee State University, Box 70647, Johnson City, TN 37614-0647. This user-friendly journal, published twice a year, contains information from storytellers nationwide, stories for retelling, and general encouragement for the beginner or experienced teller.

Yellow Moon Press, PO Box 1316, Cambridge, MA 02238. Ordering: 800-497-8385 or 617-776-2230. Fax: 617-776-8246. This catalog business brings you the oral tradition in books and tapes of storytelling, music and poetry. Sales representatives will bring a variety of materials for whole language/literature/folklore conferences.

August House, PO Box 3223, Little Rock, AR 72203, 501-372-5459 or 800-284-8784, carries a large number of texts and tapes related to folklore and storytelling.

Libraries Unlimited, PO Box 6633, Englewood, CO 80155-6633, 303-770-1220 or 800-237-6124. Books and instructional materials about storytelling.

Oryx Press, 4041 North Central at Indian School Road, Phoenix, AZ 85012-3397. Collections of stories and teaching materials.

H. W. Wilson, 950 University Ave., Bronx, NY 10452, 212-588-8400 or 800-367-6770. Published the American Storytelling Video Library and has books on storytelling too.

Weston Woods, 13 Francis J. Clark Circle, Bethel, CT 06801, 203-226-3355 or 800-243-5020. Specializes in films and sound filmstrip adaptations of children's books as well as audiotapes.

High Windy Audio, PO Box 553, Fairview, NC 28730, 704-628-1728 or 800-63STORY. Carries audiotapes, including the Time for a Tale storytelling series.

The International Women's Writing Guild, c/o Hannelore Hahn, Executive Director and Founder, PO Box 810, Gracie Station, New York, NY 10028-0082, Voice: 212-737-7536, Fax: 212-737-9469. This organization supports the writing of women at any age or experience level. Membership newsletter details members' successes and offers publishing tips and opportunities. Twice yearly week-long conferences, one in Saratoga Springs, NY and one in California as well as shorter writer workshops and retreats. More than any other organization this group encouraged me not only to keep writing but to think about an audience for my work.

The National Council of Teachers of English, 111 W. Kenyon Road, Urbana, IL 61801-1096, 217-328-3870, publishes *Primary Voices K-6, Voices in the Middle, Language Arts*, and *English Journal* for teachers at the elementary and secondary levels. If also offers free to teachers "Teaching Storytelling," a position paper produced by the NCTE Storytelling Committee.

Works Cited

Barton, B. and D. B. 1990. *Stories in the classroom: Storytelling, reading aloud and roleplaying with children*. Portsmouth, NH: Heinemann.

Blair, B. G. 1991. "Tips for telling from history." *Yarnspinner*. 15(8):1–2.

Bunce, M. 1991. "In the classroom or on the stage . . . What to do when the telling jitters take over." *Yarnspinner*. 15(8):3–5.

Calkins, L. M. with S. Harwayne. 1991. *Living between the lines*. Portsmouth, NH: Heinemann.

Cambourne, B. 1988. *The whole story: Natural learning and the acquisition of literacy in the classroom*. Auckland, New Zealand: Ashton Scholastic.

Cameron, J. 1992. *The artist's way*. New York: Putnam.

Coles, R. 1989. *The call of stories: Teaching and the moral imagination*. Boston: Houghton Mifflin.

Denman, G. A. 1988. *When you've made it your own: Teaching poetry to young people*. Portsmouth, NH: Heinemann.

Estés, C. P. 1992. *Women who run with the wolves: Myths and stories of the wild woman archetype*. New York: Ballantine.

Freire, P. 1987. "The importance of the act of reading." *Literacy in process*. Ed. B. M. Powers and R. S. Hubbard. Portsmouth, NH: Heinemann.

Gallagher, T. 1986. *A concert of tenses*. Ann Arbor, MI: University of Michigan Press.

Gillard, M. 1995. "Conquering depression through storytelling and writing." *Teacher Research*. 3(1): in press.

Goldberg, N. 1990. *Wild mind: Living the writer's life*. New York: Bantam.

Gould, J. 1989. *The writer in all of us: Improving your writing through childhood memories*. New York: Dutton.

Graves. D. "Rediscover the world, rediscover ourselves." Keynote address presented at the Whole Language Umbrella Conference, San Diego, CA, July 1994.

Hamilton, M. and M. Weiss. 1988. *Children tell stories*. Katonah, NY: Richard C. Owen.

Harste, J., K. Short, and C. Burke. 1988. *Creating classrooms for authors: The reading-writing connection*. Portsmouth, NH: Heinemann.

Heard, G. 1989. *For the good of the earth and sun: Teaching poetry*. Portsmouth, NH: Heinemann.

Kohn, A. [1986] 1992. *No contest: The case against competition*. Boston: Houghton Mifflin.

Kübler-Ross, E. 1993. *On death and dying*. New York: Macmillan.

Huck, C. and S. Helper. 1987. *Children's literature in the elementary school*, 4th ed. New York: Holt, Rinehart, and Winston.

Lieberman, S. 1990. "Breathing life into history." *Storytelling*. 2(2):8–11.

Lipke, B. 1993. "Bring history to life through storytelling." *Yarnspinner*. 17(4):1–3.

———. 1994. Telling tales from school. *Give a listen: Stories of storytelling in school*. Ed. A. Trousdale, S. Woestehoff, and M. Schwartz. Urbana, IL: National Council of Teachers of English.

Lipman, D. 1991 "Friendly persuasion." *Storytelling*. 3(1):15–18.

———. 1992 "Discovering the one and only you." *Storytelling*. 4(1):12–15.

———. 1993. *Coaching storytellers: A demonstration workshop for all who use oral communication*. Video. West Somerville, MA: Enchanters Press.

———. 1994. "Finding the most important thing." *Storytelling*. 6(2):16–18.

———. 1995. *Coaching storytellers*. Little Rock, AK: August House.

Meade, M. J. 1993. *Men and the water of life: Initiation and the tempering of men*. San Francisco: Harper.

Miller, A. 1981. *The drama of the gifted child: The search for the true self*. New York: HarperCollins.

———. 1988. *Banished knowledge: Facing childhood injuries*. New York: Doubleday.

Moore, T. 1992. *Care of the soul: A guide for cultivating depth and sacredness in everyday life*. New York: HarperCollins.

Murray, D. M. 1982. *Learning by teaching*. Portsmouth, NH: Boynton/Cook-Heinemann.

———. 1984. *Write to learn*. New York: Holt, Rinehart & Winston.

———. 1985. *A writer teaches writing*. 2d ed. Boston: Houghton Mifflin.

Newkirk, T. and P. McClure. 1992. *Listening in: Children talk about books (and other things)*. Portsmouth, NH: Heinemann.

Paley, V. G. 1990. *The boy who would be a helicopter*. Cambridge, MA: Harvard University Press.

———. 1992. *You can't say you can't play*. Cambridge, MA: Harvard University Press.

Portalupi, J. 1995. "Autobiographical understanding: Writing the past into the future." *Language Arts*. 72(4):272–275.

Rosen, B. 1988. *And none of it was nonsense: The power of storytelling in school.* Portsmouth, NH: Heinemann.

Schwartz, M. 1985a. "Finding myself in my stories." *Language Arts.* 62(7): 725–729.

———. 1985b. "Storytelling: A way to challenge stereotypes." *English Journal.* 74(3):91–92.

———. 1987. "Connecting to language through story." *Language Arts.* 64(6): 603–610.

———. 1989. "Alive alive oh." *Language Arts.* 66(7):733–735.

———. 1990. "The silences between the leaves." *Workshop 2.* Ed. N. Atwell. Portsmouth, NH: Heinemann.

———. 1994a. "Holding Martin's hand: Connecting to history through storytelling." *If this is social studies, why isn't it boring?* Ed. S. Steffey and W. Hood. York, ME: Stenhouse.

———. 1994b. "The journey of one young storyteller." *Give a listen: Stories of storytelling in school.* Ed. A. Trousdale, S. Woestehoff and M. Schwartz. Urbana, IL: National Council of Teachers of English.

Shannon, P. 1990. *The struggle to continue: Progressive reading instruction in the United States.* Portsmouth, NH: Heinemann.

Shaw, K. 1994. "Recalling forgotten lives." *Storytelling.* 5(4):14–18.

Smith, F. 1982. *Understanding Reading.* 3d ed. New York: Holt, Rinehart and Winston.

Spring, A. W. 1949. "A bloomergirl on Pikes Peak 1858." Denver, CO: Denver Public Library. O.P.

Stansfield, J. 1994. "Reclaiming the past: Storytelling and education." *Storytelling.* 6(3):16–18.

———. In press. "Pioneering Spirit." *Many voices: True tales from America's past.* Jonesborough, TN: National Storytelling Press.

Sundberg, E. and G. Sundberg. 1991. "Documenting true life dramas." *Yarnspinner.* 15(4):1–3.

Wason-Ellam, L. 1993. "Talk: Making connections between cultural discourse and classroom demands." *English Quarterly.* 26(1):39–42.

Yashinsky, D. 1993. "Tellingware: A headful of stories." *Storytelling.* 5(3): 10–14.

Literary Works and Songs

Aesop. 1992. *Wind and the sun.* Illus. B. Watts. New York: North-South Books.

Andersen, H. C. 1989. *The snowqueen.* Illus. Susan Jeffers. New York: Dial.

———. 1992a. *The little match girl.* Illus. E. Augenstine. Kansas City, MO: Andrews & McMeel.

———. 1992b. *The nightingale*. Illus. C. Huerta. Kansas City, MO: Andrews & McMeel.

Arkhurst, J. C. 1964. *The adventures of Spiderman*. Boston: Little, Brown. O.P.

Barrett, J. 1985. *Cloudy with a chance of meatballs*. Illus. R. Barrett. New York: Macmillan.

Barrie, J. M. 1992. *Peter Pan*. Mahweh, NJ: Troll Associates.

Bemelmans, L. 1977. *Madeline*. Illus. by author. New York: Puffin.

Benét, S. V. 1942. "The mountain whippoorwill." *Selected works of Stephen Vincent Benét*. New York: Holt, Rinehart & Winston. O.P.

Bishop, C. H. [1938] 1983. *Pecos Bill: The greatest cowboy of all time*. New York: Coward-McCann. O.P.

Blood-Patterson, P. ed. 1988. "Cockles and mussels." *Rise up singing: The group-singing song book*. Bethlehem, PA: Sing Out. O.P.

———. 1988. "When Irish eyes are smiling." *Rise up singing: The group-singing song book*. Bethlehem, PA: Sing Out. O.P

Bright, W. 1993. *A coyote reader*. Berkeley, CA: University of California Press.

Brown, J. [1964] 1989. *Flat Stanley*. Illus. T. Ungerer. New York: Harper-Collins.

Brown, M. W. [1947] 1992. *Goodnight moon*. Illus. C. Hurd. New York: HarperCollins.

Bruchac, J. 1990. *Gluscabe stories*. Recording. Cambridge, MA: Yellow Moon Press.

Brunhoff, J. de. [1938] 1966. *Babar and his children*. Trans. Merle Haas. New York: Random.

Buck, P. 1931. *The good earth*. New York: Harper & Row. O.P.

Bueler, G. 1981. *Colorado's colorful characters*. Denver, CO: Pruett.

Bunting, E. 1983. *St. Patrick's Day in the morning*. Illus. J. Brett. Boston: Houghton Mifflin.

———. 1984. *The man who could call down owls*. Illus. C. Mikolaycak. New York: Macmillan.

Burton, V. L. [1942] 1978. *The little house*. Illustrated. Boston: Houghton Mifflin.

Cauley, L. B. 1983. *Jack and the beanstalk*. New York: Putnam.

Chase, R. 1943. *Jack tales*. Boston: Houghton Mifflin.

Cohen, B. 1983. *Molly's pilgrim*. Illus. M. J. Deraney. New York: Lothrop.

Cole, J. 1989. *Anna Banana: One hundred one jump-rope rhymes*. Illus. A. Tiegreen. New York: Morrow.

Cole, J. and S. Calmenson. 1990. *Miss Mary Mack: And other children's street rhymes*. Illus. A. Tiegreen. New York: Morrow.

Collodi, C. 1981. *Pinocchio*. Trans. M. Mayer. Illus. G. McDermott. New York: Four Winds.

Dewey, Ariane. 1983. *Pecos Bill*. New York: Greenwillow.

Dickens, C. 1991. *A tale of two cities*. Chicago: Dearborn Trade.

———. 1994. *Oliver Twist*. New York: Books of Wonder.

Dillard, A. 1987. *An American childhood*. New York: Harper & Row.

Dryden, J. 1950. "A song for St. Cecilia's day." *The poetical works*. Boston: Houghton Mifflin. O.P.

Evslin, B. 1986. *Jason and the Argonauts*. Illus. B. Dodson. New York: Morrow.

Fox, C. and N. Gimbel. [1972] 1982. "Killing me softly with his song." Recording by R. Flack. Beverly Hills, CA: Fox-Gimbel Productions.

Frost, R. 1971. *New enlarged anthology of Robert Frost's poems*. New York: Washington Square Press.

Gackenbach, D. 1984. *Harry and the terrible Whatzit*. Illus. by author. Boston: Houghton Mifflin.

Galdone, P. 1979. *The magic porridge pot*. Illus. P. Galdone. Boston: Houghton Mifflin.

———. 1988. *The three little kittens*. Illus. by author. Boston: Houghton Mifflin.

Gallaz, C. 1986. *Rose Blanche: Based on the original idea of Roberto Innocenti*. Ed. E. Delessert and A. Redpath. Trans. M. Coventry. Mankato, MN: Creative Ed.

Gibson, W. 1984. *The miracle worker*. New York: Bantam.

Gillard, M. 1992. *Snapshots*. Recording. Rochester, NY: Local Folkel Records.

———. 1994. *Maria Gillard*. Recording. Rochester, NY: Gilbane Publishing.

Gleeson, B. 1992. *Anansi*. Illus. S. Guarnaccia. Saxonville, MA: Picture Book Studio.

Goodchild, P. 1991. *The Raven tales*. Chicago: Chicago Review Press.

Grimm, J. and W. K. Grimm. 1991. *Snow White*. Retold by Jennifer Greenway. Illus. E. Augestine. Kansas City, MO: Andrews & McMeel.

———. 1992. *Little Red Riding Hood*. Illustrated. Kansas City, MO: Andrews & McMeel.

Haley, G. E. 1986. *Jack and the bean tree*. Retold and Illus. by author. New York: Crown.

Hart, L. 1978. *Steinmetz in Schenectady: A picture story of three memorable decades*. Scotia, NY: Old Dorp Books.

Hawkinds, C. and J. Hawkins. 1992. *Humpty Dumpty*. Illustrated. Cambridge, MA: Candlewick Press.

Hillert, M. 1963. *The Three Bears*. Illustrated. Cleveland, OH: Modern Curriculum Press.

Hìtakonanu'laxk. 1994. "Rainbow Crow." *The grandfathers speak: Native American folk tales of the Lenapé people*. New York: Interlink Books.

Hoban, R. 1976. *Bedtime for Frances*. Illus. G. Williams. New York: Harper-Collins.

Hutton, W. 1989. *Theseus and the Minotaur*. Illus. by author. New York: Macmillan.

———. 1993. *Perseus*. Ed. M. McElderry. Illus. by author. New York: Macmillan.

Janeczko, P. B. 1990. *The place my words are looking for: What poets say about and through their work*. New York: Macmillan.

Kasza, K. 1989. *The wolf's chicken stew.* Illus. by author. New York: Putnam.

Keillor, G. 1987. *Leaving home.* New York: Viking.

Kellogg, S. 1984. *Paul Bunyan.* Adapted and illus. by author. New York: Morrow.

Kipling, R. [1892] 1992. *Rikki-Tikki-Tavi.* San Diego: Harcourt Brace.

Kraus, R. 1986. *Whose mouse are you?* Illus. J. Aruego. New York: Macmillan.

Lennon J. and P. McCartney. 1968. "Rocky Raccoon." *The Beatles* (White Album). Recording. EMI Records Ltd.

Lester, J. 1987. *The tales of Uncle Remus: The adventures of Brer Rabbit.* Illus. J. Pinckney. New York: Dial.

Lieberman, S. 1989. *The Johnstown flood of 1889.* Recording. Self-published. Available from National Storytelling Association, Jonesborough, TN.

Lipman, D. 1993. *Grass roots and mountain peaks—taking charge of our future: Visions for the storytelling movement.* West Somerville, MA: Enchanters Press

Lobel, A. 1983. "The hen in the apple tree." *Fables.* Illus. by author. New York: HarperCollins.

———. 1985. *Frog and Toad are friends.* Illus. by author. New York: Harper-Collins.

Loewe, F. "I remember it well." *Gigi.* Recording. New York: Columbia.

Lowell, A. 1955. "Patterns." *The complete poetical works.* Boston: Houghton Mifflin.

Martin, R. 1989. *Will's mammoth.* New York: Putnam.

Mayer, M. 1982. *The unicorn and the lake.* Illus. M. Hague. New York: Dial.

———. 1987. *Beauty and the Beast.* Illus. by author. New York: Macmillan.

———. 1989. *Twelve dancing princesses.* Illus. K. Y. Craft. New York: Morrow.

McCutcheon, J. 1991. "Calling all the children home." *Live at Wolf Trap.* Recording. Cambridge, MA: Rounder.

McDermott, G. 1978. *The stonecutter.* Illustrated. New York: Penguin.

McGovern, A. 1986. *Stone soup.* Illus. W. P. Pels. New York: Scholastic.

———. 1991. *Wanted dead or alive: The true story of Harriet Tubman.* New York: Scholastic.

———. 1992. *Too much noise.* Illus. T. Simms. Boston: Houghton Mifflin.

Merriam, E. 1984. *Jamboree: Rhymes for all times.* New York: Dell.

Miller, F. 1962. *The man who tamed lightning.* New York: Scholastic.

Milne, A. A. [1926] 1992. *Winnie-the-Pooh.* Illus. E. H. Shepard. New York: Puffin.

Montgomery, L. M. [1920] 1985. *Rilla of Ingleside.* New York: Bantam.

———. [1908] 1989. *Anne of Green Gables.* New York: Scholastic.

Mosel, A. 1992. *Tikki Tikki Tembo.* Illus. B. Lent. New York: H. Holt.

Munsch, R. 1985. *Thomas' snowsuit.* Illus. M. Martchenko. Buffalo, NY: Firefly.

———. 1986. *Love you forever.* Illus. S. Mcgraw. Buffalo, NY: Firefly.

Noyse, A. 1990. *The highwayman*. Illus. N. Waldman. San Diego: Harcourt Brace.

O'Callahan, J. 1990. *Pill Hill stories: Coming home to someplace new*. Recording. Marshfield, MA: Artana Productions.

Perrault, C. 1990. *Puss in boots*. Trans. M. Arthur. Illus. F. Marcellino. New York: Farrar, Straus & Giroux.

Piper, W., ed. [1932] 1952. "Boots and his brothers." *The road in storyland*. New York: Platt & Munk. O.P.
"How little bunny rabbit caught the sun."
"King Midas."
"The cap that mother made."
"The country mouse and the city mouse."
"The little turtle who could not stop talking."
"The old woman who wanted all the cakes."
"The pine tree and its needles."
"The shoemaker and the elves."
"The star dipper."
"The stone in the road."

———. [1925] 1955a. "The little red hen and the grain of wheat." *Nursery tales children love*. New York: Platt & Munk. O.P.
"The Three Little Pigs."

Poe, E. A. 1946. "The tell-tale heart." *The complete poems and stories*. New York: Knopf.

Pouliot, S. Unpublished. *Grandma Moses*. Booked by Big League Theatre. Produced by S. Adler, New York.

Reiss, J. 1972. *The upstairs room*. New York: HarperCollins.

Rey, H. A. 1973. *Curious George*. Illus. by author. Boston: Houghton Mifflin.

Richards, L. E. [1932] 1983. Eletelephony. *The Random House Book of poetry for children*. Ed. J. Prelutsky. Illus. A. Lobel. New York: Random.

Rodgers, R. 1973. *The sound of music*. Recording. New York: Columbia.

Rogasky, B. 1986. *The water of life: A tale from the Brothers Grimm*. Retold by author. Illus. T. S. Hyman. New York: Holiday.

Rölvaag, O. E. 1929. *Giants in the earth*. New York: Harper & Row. O.P.

Salten, F. 1992. *Bambi*. Illus. M. J. Woods. New York: Simon & Schuster.

Sendak, M. [1962] 1991. *Chicken soup with rice: A book of months*. Illus. by author. New York: Scholastic.

Seuss, Dr. 1973. *Did I ever tell you how lucky you are?* Illus. by author. New York: Random.

———. [1958] 1986. *Yertle the Turtle and other stories*. Illus. by author. New York: Random.

———. [1957] 1987. *The cat in the hat*. Illus. by author. Boston: Random.

Shakespeare, W. 1993. *Much ado about nothing*. Video. Burbank, CA: The Samuel Goldwyn Co.

Sharp, M. 1959. *The Rescuers*. New York: Dell.

Sierra, J. 1992. *Oryx Multi-cultural folk series: Cinderella*. Phoenix, AZ: Oryx Press.

Slobodkina, E. [1947] 1987. *Caps for sale*. Illus. by author. New York: HarperCollins.

Stailey, J. 1990. "Sawhorse stallions." *Sittin' together, talkin' to each other, sometimes singin'*. Recording. Clear Lake Shores, TX: Self-Published. (Available from 723 E. Shore Dr., Clear Lake Shores, TX 77565.)

Stansfield, J. 1990. *Song of the mountain, song of the plains*. Recording. Monument, CO: Self-Published. (Available from Box 588, Monument, CO 80132)

Stevenson, R. L. [1905] 1992. *A child's garden of verses*. Illus. C. Robinson. New York: Knopf.

Stone, I. 1965. *Those who love: A biographical novel of Abigail and John Adams*. New York: Doubleday. O.P.

Stone, J. 1977. *The monster at the end of this book*. Racine, WI: Western Publishing Company.

Strauss, S. 1991. *Coyote stories for children: Tales of Native America*. Ed. H. Norman. Illus. G. Lund. Hillsboro, OR: Beyond Words Publishing.

Switzer, E. and C. 1988. *Greek myths: Gods, heroes, and monsters—their sources, their stories, and their meanings*. Illustrated. New York: Macmillan.

Tarcov E. H. 1973. *Rumpelstiltskin*. Retold by author. Illus. E. Gorey. New York: Scholastic.

Thayer, E. L. 1992. *Casey at the bat*. Illus. P. Polacco. New York: Putnam.

Thayer, J. 1962. *Gus was a friendly ghost*. New York: Morrow.

Tolkien, J. R. R. 1989. *The Hobbit*. Illus. M. Hague. Boston: Houghton Mifflin.

Toney, C. V. 1993. "Sanyan, the storyteller." *Cricket*. 21(4):44–49.

Twain, M. 1992. *The adventures of Tom Sawyer*. Majweh, NJ: Troll Associates.

Ungerer, T. 1990. *Heidi: The classic novel by Johanna Spyri*. New York: Delacourt.

Van Laan, N. 1991. *Rainbow Crow*. Illus. B. Vidal. New York: Knopf.

Waldherr, K. 1993. *Persephone and the pomegranate: A myth from Greece*. New York: Dial.

Weakley, T. 1992. Tommy. *Harry and the Texaco boys*. Recording. Arlington, VT: Highland Publications.

———. 1994. *White mules and hoop snakes*. Recording. Arlinton, VT: Highland Publications.

Williams, M. 1992. *The velveteen rabbit*. Illus. W. Nicholson. New York: Dell.

Yashima, T. 1976. *Crow boy*. Illustrated. New York: Puffin.

Yates, E. 1989. *Amos Fortune, free man*. Illus. N. S. Unwin. New York: Puffin.

Yolen, J. 1987. *Owl moon*. Illus. J. Schoenherr. New York: Putnam.